New Casebooks

A MIDSUMMER
NIGHT'S DREAM

W

New Casebooks

New Casebooks

A MIDSUMMER NIGHT'S DREAM

EDITED BY RICHARD DUTTON

First published 1996 by
MACMILLAN PRESS LTD
Houndmills, Basingstoke, Hampshire RG21 6XS
and London
Companies and representatives
throughout the world

ISBN 0–333-60196–3 hardcover
ISBN 0–333-60197–1

A catalogue record for this book is available
from the British Library.

10   9   8   7   6   5   4   3   2   1
05   04   03   02   01   00   99   98   97   96

Printed in Malaysia

Contents

v

Acknowledgements

The editor and the publishers wish to thank the following for permission to use copyright material:

David Bevington, for '"But We Are Spirits of Another Sort": The Dark Side of Love and Magic in *A Midsummer Night's Dream*', from *Medieval and Renaissance Studies*, 7, 80–92, ed. Siegfried Wenzel. Copyright © 1975 by The University of North Carolina Press, by permission of The University of North Carolina Press; Shirley Nelson Garner, for '*A Midsummer Night's Dream*: "Jack shall have Jill/Nought shall go ill"', *Women's Studies*, 9 (1981), 47–63, by permission of Gordon and Breach Science Publishers; Terence Hawkes, for 'Or', from *Meaning by Shakespeare* (1993) revised and shortened by the author, by permission of Routledge; Barbara Hodgdon, for 'Gaining a Father: The Role of Egeus in the Quarto and the Folio', *Review of English Studies*, 37 (1986), 534–42, by permission of Oxford University Press; Norman N. Holland, for 'Hermia's Dream', from *The Annual of Psychoanalysis*, 7 (1979), 369–89, by permission of International Universities Press, Inc.; Elliot Krieger, for '*A Midsummer Night's Dream*' from *A Marxist Study of Shakespeare's Comedies* (1979), pp. 37–61, by permission of Macmillan Publishers Ltd; Philip C. McGuire, for 'Hippolyta's Silence and the Poet's Pen', from *Speechless Dialect: Shakespeare's Open Silences* (1985), pp. 1–18, University of California Press, by permission of the author; Louis Adrian Montrose, for '"Shaping Fantasies": Figurations of Gender and Power in Elizabethan Culture', *Representations*, 1, 2 (1983), 61–94. Copyright © 1983 by the Regents of the University of California, by permission of the University of California Press; Annabel Patterson, for 'Bottom's Up: Festive Theory' from *Shakespeare and the Popular Voice* (1989), pp. 52–70, by permission of Blackwell Publishers;

Richard Wilson, for 'The Kindly Ones: The Death of the Author in Shakespearean Athens', *Essays and Studies*, 46 (1993), 1–24, by permission of The English Association.

General Editors' Preface

The purpose of this series of New Casebooks is to reveal some of the ways in which contemporary criticism has changed our understanding of commonly studied texts and writers and, indeed, of the nature of criticism itself. Central to the series is a concern with modern critical theory and its effect on current approaches to the study of literature. Each New Casebook editor has been asked to select a sequence of essays which will introduce the reader to the new critical approaches to the text or texts being discussed in the volume and also illuminate the rich interchange between critical theory and critical practice that characterises so much current writing about literature.

In this focus on modern critical thinking and practice New Casebooks aim not only to inform but also to stimulate, with volumes seeking to reflect both the controversy and the excitement of current criticism. Because much of this criticism is difficult and often employs an unfamiliar critical language, editors have been asked to give the reader as much help as they feel is appropriate, but without simplifying the essays or the issues they raise. Again, editors have been asked to supply a list of further reading which will enable readers to follow up issues raised by the essays in the volume.

The project of New Casebooks, then, is to bring together in an illuminating way those critics who best illustrate the ways in which contemporary criticism has established new methods of analysing texts and who have reinvigorated the important debate about how we 'read' literature. The hope is, of course, that New Casebooks will not only open up to this debate to a wider audience, but will also encourage students to extend their own ideas, and think afresh about their responses to the texts they are studying.

John Peck and Martin Coyle
University of Wales, Cardiff

Introduction

RICHARD DUTTON

A Midsummer Night's Dream has been peculiarly central to the
critical concerns of the last twenty years. A play in which dream is
the dominant metaphor, licensing all kinds of Ovidian transformations and unspeakable thoughts, is inevitably of interest to psychoanalytic criticism. One in which the dramatic action hangs on a
father's refusal to allow his daughter to choose her own husband,
and more generally (like many of Shakespeare's comedies) on the
transition from daughterhood to wifehood, has naturally been of
interest to feminists. The fact that these processes are linked with
the seasonal rites of Maying and Midsummer locates the play
broadly in the influential tradition of festive comedy first explored
by C. L. Barber (1959); that whole approach was given a new, and
politically-charged edge when Mikhail Bakhtin's theories of carnival first became known in the west in the late 1960s, and a debate
about the status of popular art in the processes of social subversion
and containment has rumbled on ever since.[1]

But the very question of whether *A Midsummer Night's Dream*
is in any real sense 'popular art' – from the people, for the people –
has also exercised many critics. The possibility that the play may
have been written for an aristocratic wedding raises very pointed
questions about the status of the actors, and the men who wrote
for them, in late Elizabethan England. For much of this century it
was virtually an article of faith that Shakespeare was a free spirit
who inclusively addressed a remarkable cross-section of society,
from the highest to the lowest in the land. Latterly this has been
challenged from both extremes: on the one hand, there are those
who argue that audiences were preponderately composed of the
privileged classes (including the court itself, whose patronage was
crucial to the survival of the theatres), and that dramatists consequently catered for their tastes and interests; on the other, those
who emphasise the marginal status of the actors, scarcely separable
from vagabonds and masterless men in Elizabethan legislation,
their theatres deliberately excluded from the city itself and located
in the anomalous liberties, alongside brothels and lunatic asylums,

1

and peddling dangerous wares. The status of this play – either specifically commissioned by aristocrats, or written for the general repertoire of the popular theatre – is thus of particular importance.[2]

In a play where so much of the laughter is generated by the incompetence of Peter Quince as a playwright, and the inadequacies of his fellow mechanicals as actors – failings which all revolve around the fact that they are not at home with the tacit contractual understandings which usually surround the performance of a play – questions of imagination and representation cannot but be issues. Theseus and Hippolyta famously debate the reports of the lovers about what went on in the woods. He commonsensically dismisses them as the products of 'seething brains ... that apprehend / More than cool reason ever comprehends' (V.i.4–6), arguing that lovers, poets and lunatics are all prone to fantasise. Hippolyta, however, insists that the consistency of their stories makes them add up to 'something of great constancy ... strange and admirable' (ll.26–7). These differences are not resolved within the play, nor in the structuralist and poststructuralist debates that have flowed from this dimension of the text. Bottom, released from his 'translation', seeks for words to express it, for a real relationship between words and experience: 'The eye of man hath not heard, the ear of man hath not seen, man's hand is not able to taste, his tongue to conceive, nor his heart to report what my dream was' (IV.i.208–11). If the processes of signification and representation are themselves problematic, how much more so is a play which explicitly dramatises the fact – indeed, has entered the cultural currency as a key battleground of the debate.

Moreover, in the sophisticated Marxism of Louis Althusser and the post-Marxism of Michel Foucault, which both lie behind the new Historicisms so central to Renaissance studies for the last fifteen years, questions of linguistic representation are inseparable from those of political ideology, of personal subjectivity and of the manipulation of power.[3] For Althusser, the domination of one class over another is primarily effected 'in words' rather than by brute force or economic necessity (the classic Marxist arguments). So Shakespeare's comedies, which commonly revolve around challenges to law and the social order it protects – challenges, however, that are effaced before the end of the play – may be seen as agents in the preservation of established order. Cultural materialists, however, argue that they are liable to deconstruction on those very grounds, that they lay bare the processes of repression they ostensibly endorse, authority being revealed as a product of cultural illusions. Yet for Foucault power is much more diffuse and insidious than this, endlessly identifying, classifying and regenerating challenges to itself – criminals, madmen, unruly women, aliens, things contrary to 'nature' (and so the hallmarks by which we construct our own 'normality') – and then repressing them to demonstrate and enforce its own necessity: a cycle which art represents but cannot challenge.[4] A Midsummer Night's Dream, for all its comic lightness, is a play that speaks to all these concerns: the various 'powers' of Oberon, Theseus and Egeus are all in different ways challenged, the status and identities of their subjects all called into question. In such ways the play remains as politically charged in the 1990s as it was in the 1590s.

David Bevington (essay 1) enters the critical debate at a point of some turbulence, in the wake of two landmark 'revisionings' of the play: Jan Kott's essay in his Shakespeare Our Contemporary (1964) and Peter Brook's iconoclastic 1970 production of it, largely inspired by Kott (described in the Context Note at the end of Bevington's essay). Kott, a Pole, focused exclusively on those elements and dimensions of Shakespearean drama which, he argued, spoke directly to post-Second World War concerns: existential angst and its associated violence, the Freudian rawness of human behaviour and its motivations, all of which challenged the aesthetic distancing and sentimentality of traditional approaches to the plays (represented forcefully, in the case of A Midsummer Night's Dream, by Mendelssohn's incidental music and its famous wedding march). So for Kott the Dream enacts a struggle between the repressive tendencies of the conscious mind, the civilising super-ego embodied in a strong, patriarchal social structure, and the anarchic, libidinous forces of animal instinct and sexual desire. Such a reading inevitably voiced a number of uncomfortable questions, which used discreetly not to be asked: why is Oberon so determined to have the 'little changeling boy' (II.iii.120) whom Titania has adopted? What exactly goes on between Titania and the ass-turned Bottom? For Kott, the boy is wanted as a minion to feed Oberon's imperious bisexual lust; and Titania and Bottom are consumed by quasi-bestial carnal desires in which it is all too significant that 'the ass was credited with the strongest sexual potency and among all the quadrupeds was supposed to have the longest and hardest phallus'.[5]

Bevington does not deny that there is an element of truth in what Kott had said, but insists that it had been exaggerated (under the influence of the 1960s sexual revolution) in a way that distorted the balance of the play: 'Jan Kott has shown to us most forcefully this dark side of love; indeed, he has done so too forcefully, and with an often exaggerated effect upon contemporary productions of this and other plays. Still, his insight has something to commend it.'[6] In essence, the argument with which Bevington counters Kott – or rather, attempts to put him in perspective – is a New Critical one, insisting that the text itself determines how it should be read, and the limits of its own meaning. Thus, for example, when he talks of 'the play's delicately understated portrayal of Eros', the 'ambivalence' of the forest and the moon, or 'a false note of sexual perversity and compulsion,'[7] Bevington is suggesting that the text sets its own tone, creates its own checks and balances of nuance, and that the text as a whole defines the terms within which all its constituent parts may be interpreted.

So, for Bevington, Oberon and Titania's behaviour towards each other is shown at the level of text to be 'mysterious', 'puzzling', 'deliberately ambiguous', 'ultimately unknowable and incomprehensible' – for Kott to reduce this to a Freudian formula of the perverse and the unspeakable is unsupportable in terms of what the text actually says and shows. Similarly, to suggest that the lovers in the forest actually do indulge their sexual instincts runs against the evidence of constant interruptions, confusions and their plain protestations that they have not done so. The only court of appeal to which Bevington resorts, except that of the text itself, is the averagely educated reader, the embodiment of judicious common sense – not the specialist psychoanalyst, who reads everything through the distorting lenses of his own preconceptions. Such a reader will readily recognise that 'The motif on which the action of the play is based, that of escape into a forest on the eve of Mayday (Walpurgisnacht) or on Midsummer Eve, is traditionally erotic' or that 'the coupling of Titania and Bottom has long been regarded as a comic version of Beauty and the Beast.'[8] In other words, that Kott has been getting hot under the collar about matters all sensible people knew about all along (though perhaps they needed reminding of them), and in doing so distorting their real significance within the text, where they are treated with far more discretion, playfulness and comic distance than he ever allows for.

Bevington's mode of argument is relevant to the other essays in this collection, because it implicitly challenges most of them (though, of course, they were all written after it) as much as it does Kott. And it speaks for a large constituency of traditional readers, whose voice has often been drowned out in successive waves of critical theory over the last twenty years, but whose influence is still institutionalised in, for example, the British university-qualifying examinations (A-levels) for students intending to read English. All critical theory – formalist, structuralist, Marxist, psychoanalytic, deconstructionist, and all their various subspecies – is ultimately a re-examination of the reading process itself, a questioning of how we construe the marks on a page into words and sounds, how we ascribe to those words and sounds meaning and value, and how finally we locate those words and sounds within all the other signifying practices with which we are familiar.

By its very nature, then, critical theory challenges the consensual reading to which Bevington implicitly appeals. It variously acknowledges that meaning is arbitrary, or multiple, or culture-specific; that it is not defined by either the author or the text; that silence, implication and inference are as important as statement; that every reading is different – not necessarily better or worse, stronger or weaker, more or less accurate, but different. Such formulations, not exactly coincidentally, allow a voice to many constituencies who feel that the 'consensual' voice never actually represented them – feminist women, black people, homosexuals, political radicals and others, who felt that New Criticism was actually the voice of predominantly male, privileged, heterosexual Anglo-Saxon academics masquerading as a consensus. By the same token, such formulations inevitably interrogate traditional assumptions about which texts deserve particular attention – the so-called canon of literature – and why; and challenge the concept of 'literature' itself, as a separate and privileged form of high art, different in kind from other forms of communication. And Shakespeare is inevitably at the centre of all such debates, as traditionally the most privileged author, the most studied corpus of texts, in the English literary canon. Bevington's voice in all this is liberal, sane, humane and balanced; but in some vocabularies that is the same thing as reactionary.

One of those vocabularies is that of Marxist critics, who have consistently rejected the implicit elitism of New Criticism and its concentration on texts as self-contained aesthetic objects (verbal icons or well-wrought urns, to invoke two of its most influential expositions)[9] at the expense of considering their wider functions. Marxist criticism, in the words of Edmund Wilson, has always been 'about the historical interpretation of literature – that is, about the interpretation of literature in its social, economic, and political aspects'.[10] This is the clear focus of Elliot Krieger's chapter (essay 2), which rigorously explores the social, economic and political aspects of *A Midsummer Night's Dream*. The nub of his argument is encapsulated in a throw-away line: 'from Theseus's point of view – the point of view that the play enforces – ... '. Every feature of the play, in his analysis, is subsumed within an exploration of the authority of Theseus, and of the strategies by which that authority is maintained. The key to this is 'the law of Athens' which 'subordinates human qualities and subjective judgements to the abstract systems of hierarchy and possession within both family and state'.[11] That is, the system of order itself, of which Theseus projects himself as the disinterested upholder, is one which reduces all lesser beings to the status of servants, less than fully human, at least in part reified (made into inanimate things).

This is despite the rebellion against that order made by the Athenian lovers, who refuse to accept the pairings proposed for them by Hermia's father, Egeus, and endorsed by Theseus. Krieger argues that the rebellion is more apparent than real, since the lovers carry off with them an internalised sense of what he calls 'primary-world order' and of their socio-economic places within it. The forest is not, thus, an escape from the Athenian court, but an extension of it by other means, and replicated in the hierarchy of the fairies. (In this he dissociates himself from C. L. Barber's notion of festive comedy, which he regards as insufficiently historicised, not alert to the ways in which 'holiday' release underpins specific strategies of social control.) As Krieger puts it: 'It is important to realise that the flight to the forest, in some ways, satisfies Duke Theseus's needs and helps solidify his position as a figure of social authority.' This is largely because the 'nature' which the lovers confront there, the nature of Oberon, Titania and Puck, is not in fact an alternative or 'second-world', but a further projection of Theseus's authority. Here Bottom, Quince and co. lose the potential dignity and independence of their crafts and 'function as a coarsened version of a class of servants'; note Krieger's rejection of Puck's label, 'rude mechanicals', often used unthinkingly by critics as shorthand but here identified as a form of social condescension typical of the play as a whole. So 'the craftsmen and the fairies, like the protagonists themselves, function as further extension and development of the primary-world, authoritarian consciousness.'[12]

Krieger's approach, I have argued, is implicitly at odds with that of David Bevington. But it is more explicitly opposed to earlier, non-Marxist forms of historicism, and particularly that of E. M. W. Tillyard in his highly influential *The Elizabethan World Picture* (1943). Tillyard has been much derided in recent years, not because the pattern of corresponding cosmic, natural and social hierarchies which he explicated bore no relation to Elizabethan thinking, but because it did not bear the relationship that he claimed it did. What he said he intended to do was 'to extract and expound the most ordinary beliefs about the constitution of the world as pictured in the Elizabethan age', 'some of the notions about the world and man which were quite taken for granted by the ordinary educated Elizabethan', 'essential commonplaces'.[13] In so doing he depicted a society comfortably at ease with its own assumptions, an organic structure modelled on a God-given natural world, in which everybody knew his or her place; and he implied that authors like Shakespeare reflected and endorsed it almost without thinking. Krieger is typical of the modern response to Tillyard in insisting that these notions of organic order were not 'commonplaces', but were in fact arguments advanced by the Elizabethan aristocracy to justify their own rule – in effect propaganda, attempts to wrap their less-than-self-evident authority in a spurious mystique of legitimacy. But where some have argued that Shakespeare was a willing stooge of this propaganda, Krieger credits him with a sophisticated 'understanding of the strategies used by the ruling class to justify its power and its retention of centralised authority through hypothetical analogy with the forces of nature',[14] arguing that *A Midsummer Night's Dream* is essentially an analysis of aristocratic power, not a celebration of it.

Norman N. Holland's psychoanalytic approach (essay 3) is far removed from the Marxist concentration on class and power, though it has something to say about the processes of growth and psychic identity by which one of the women characters – Hermia – prepares for subjection of a kind, as a lover and wife. Following a brief exposition, the first section of his essay offers a reading of Hermia's dream in the woods, closely keyed to what we see of her character elsewhere in the play and related to a broadly Freudian template of psychological development and its phases – oedipal, phallic, anal and oral. This is the classic mode of psychoanalytic criticism, the kind with which readers are perhaps still most familiar. As Holland points out, such readings could be deployed to one

of two ends: to demonstrate how Shakespeare had intuitively anticipated modern advances in psychological theory (as Freud acknowledged that great artists had always done), or to show by reference
to modern clinical formulae just how complex and sophisticated
Shakespeare's portrayal of character could be: 'In effect, the
Shakespearean critic got a boost from psychoanalysis, and the psychoanalyst got a lift from Shakespeare.'[15]

But Holland has come to see these as inadequate critical goals,
for reasons which parallel other critical dissatisfactions with the assumption that there is only one true or definitive meaning to a text.
Earlier psychoanalytic criticism took it as axiomatic that characters
and situations were straightforwardly realistic, even when a play
was a highly stylised fantasy like a romantic comedy and had its
characters speaking blank verse. One response to the palpable limitations of such an approach is to transfer the insights gained from
studying a character closely to a generalised observation of the play
as a whole – in effect subjecting the *text* to a form of psychoanalysis. So Holland's account of the different facets of one adolescent
character expands to see them as 'variations on the comedy's theme
of ambivalence, separations that are both loving and cruel'.[16] This
approach is analogous to, but different in aim and emphasis from,
that of Jacques Lacan, which is not represented here but discussed
in the Context Note at the end of Holland's essay.

Arguing that the detached or abstract analysis of either a character or a text in some respects belies the interactive relationship
between subject and analyst which is part of clinical psychoanalysis,
Holland advocates a highly subjective form of reader-response criticism, what he calls 'transactive criticism'. So he articulates what for
him is uncomfortable about the psychology of *A Midsummer
Night's Dream*, what it does not articulate, what it leaves unsaid.
As he puts it: 'I want these couples married at the end, but I don't
see – I don't trust, really – the way the comedy gets them together.'
That is, he recognises in himself a longing for the traditional reassurance offered by romantic comedy, that lovers will find
harmony and fulfilment in marriage. But he is not convinced that he
finds it there in the play: Hermia awakes while her dream is still a
nightmare, and both she and Helena fall silent as soon as they are
paired with their 'proper' partners. The play goes through the
motions, 'Shakespeare's lovers proceeded in their own day to a sure
and socially structured Renaissance conclusion',[17] but not convinc-
ingly for him.

Holland acknowledges that in this he is projecting his own anxieties, products of the post-1960s sexual revolution, on to social expectations and customs of the 1590s – but sees in this an essential truthfulness. Shakespeare's play only really lives in as much as it continues to engage modern readers, and this implies an object–subject relation analogous to that in identity theory itself: 'Just as self and object constitute each other in human development, so in the literary transaction the reader constitutes text so that text may constitute its reader.'[18] This celebrates a subjectivity, or even solipsism, of the reading experience to which few schools of criticism (even most reader-response criticism) will admit – though Holland challengingly implies that most critics actually read this way, but try to hide it under quasi-objective methodologies. Interestingly, the doubts and contradictions which Holland voices about his own reading of the play mirror the ambivalences about much historicist criticism. Holland takes it rather for granted that marriage was 'a sure and socially structured Renaissance conclusion' which the play presents unambiguously, while all doubts and contradictions arise from his modern consciousness. But was it? Feminists in particular have their doubts (as Shirley Nelson Garner's article demonstrates). Is it not equally possible that Holland is responding to cultural tensions of the 1590s embedded in the text, whether or not Shakespeare articulated them consciously? One of the key debates around revisionist historicist practices is the extent to which they impose twentieth-century sensibility on the writing of earlier eras, or conversely allow those earlier eras to speak more fully than other modern reading practices have tended to allow. Holland's frankness sharply outlines the issue.

Shirley Nelson Garner (essay 4) sidesteps these historicist issues by universalising her argument about gender in *A Midsummer Night's Dream*. Her starting point is C. L. Barber's idea of festive comedy, which invariably 'concludes with high celebration, ritual blessing, and the promise of regeneration'. She has no quarrel with this formula but insists (as Barber does not) that this is a celebration in which all the partners are not equal, one in which men define the terms, asserting a pattern of order which effectively silences women and all forms of sexuality which are taken to threaten male dominance: 'the renewal at the end of the play affirms patriarchal order and hierarchy, insisting that the power of women must be circumscribed, and ... recognises the tenuousness of heterosexuality as well.'[19] None of this is related to the specific conditions of sexuality or gender in sixteenth-century England. The argument is conducted, rather, in Freudian terms which presuppose universal conditions of gender-identity and of relationships between the sexes (as emerges very clearly in the notes). Many feminists have challenged the Freudian models precisely because they ignore the extent to which gender may be culturally determined; others because they believe these models implicitly underpin patriarchal values themselves in the extent to which they prioritise male perspectives. Garner nevertheless deploys them to illuminate the position of the women in *A Midsummer Night's Dream*, in ways that traditional criticism often simply ignored.

She focuses, in particular, on the tacit sexual weaknesses and ambivalences of the male characters in the play: Oberon's need for the 'changeling boy', which she takes to be self-evidently an erotic impulse, though one which reveals the tensions in his relations with Titania (whom he 'humiliates' and 'torments' in order to reduce her to compliance) rather than undisputed power; Egeus's insistence that Hermia marry Demetrius, which is seen not merely as an act of arbitrary will, but as an attempt to perpetuate his control over his daugther and her sexuality, while at the same time gratifying unspoken homoerotic impulses of his own; Theseus's marriage to the 'androgynous' Hippolyta, which is seen as a necessary psycho-sexual solution to the deep insecurities of a man notorious for repeatedly deserting women (in which he 'acts similarly to men Freud describes as evincing a dissociated erotic life').[20] Precisely what pre-knowledge and view of Theseus the Elizabethans might have brought to the play has become something of a moot point: where once he was seen unequivocally as the embodiment of ducal dignity and military prowess, there has recently been much more emphasis on his chequered career as a lover (some of which is glanced at in the play) and on the dark associations of his triumph over the minotaur.[21] For Garner, 'Whatever other associations Theseus had for Shakespeare's audience, he was notorious as the first seducer of Helen [of Troy].' A play built around the wedding of such a figure is inevitably a celebration of a most problematic kind. In it, heterosexual marriage can be seen not as an instinctive and joyous rite, but as a defence mechanism in which 'Shakespeare's male characters act out of a fear of women's bonding with each other and a feeling of sexual powerlessness',[22] denying women the threatening possibility of coming together to build an alternative society (the

Amazons) and at the same time repressing sexual instincts of their own which might otherwise undermine their authority.

Louis Adrian Montrose's article (essay 5) is perhaps the most influential writing on *A Midsummer Night's Dream* in recent years. Although, like Garner, it is centrally concerned with 'the Elizabethan sex–gender system', its methods and conclusions are very different, precisely because Montrose is determined to historicise the material, to locate the patterns of thought in the play within wider patterns of cultural circulation in Elizabethan England (which had to include ways of accommodating a female at the top of what were designed to be patriarchal systems of politics, society and religion). Hence the characteristically New Historicist structure of the essay, in which the analysis of the play emerges from and blends with a string of anecdotes, discussions of social history, and observations on the history of ideas: Simon Forman's dream (and other intimate accounts of Elizabeth's presence), Amazon lore, sixteenth-century thinking about sexual reproduction and the respective roles of the two partners, Elizabeth's own strategies of self-presentation as a warrior Virgin-Queen. These are advanced, not exactly as influences on the Shakespeare text, but as analogues to it, instances of the mind-set which generated this particular fiction – a fiction which did not emerge as a discrete event, in a separate realm of aesthetic experience, but as part of a continuous process in which symbolic forms underpinned the power structures of the day. Hence Montrose's insistence on the dynamic interplay between literature and society (in which the former does not merely *reflect* the latter, as a conventional Marxist might argue, but takes part in its construction). So he talks of 'the dialectical character of cultural representation: the fantasies by which the text of *A Midsummer Night's Dream* has been shaped are also those to which it gives shape', arguing that 'symbolic forms may do more than *represent* power: they may actually help to *generate* the power they represent'.[23]

Such an approach challenges many conventional assumptions about the relationship between a text and the time in which it was written. In the particular context of *A Midsummer Night's Dream* it prompts a reconsideration of an assumption often paraded as fact: that the play was written as an aristocratic wedding entertainment, and specifically one at which the Queen herself was present.[24] That assumption largely derives from references within the text to 'a fair vestal, throned in the West', also described as an 'imperial votress' (II.i.159, 164). But Montrose's argument undermines the assumption that such 'compliments' need imply the physical presence of the Queen: 'Shakespeare's play is neither focused upon the Queen nor structurally dependent upon her presence or her intervention in the action. On the contrary, it might be said to depend on her absence, her exclusion.' A system of symbolic representation which carried power even without her literal presence would be inherently and insidiously more authoritative and wide-ranging than anything that depended on the physical person of the monarch. On the other hand, that authority would be partly shared by the dramatist who helped give it currency, so that the '"metadrama" of *A Midsummer Night's Dream* – its calling of attention to its own artifice, its own artistry – analogises the powers of parents, princes, and playwrights; the fashioning of children, subjects, and plays'.[25] Yet this subtle, sophisticated and penetrating analysis of power and its operations offers no obviously transferable insights to the present day, because what it explores is so inextricably tied in with the culture in which it was formulated.

The early modern period is of particular interest to those concerned with the nature of government because (it has been argued) that is when the state as we know it, and the instruments of power as we experience them, took shape: in the literature of the period we can observe that process with unblinking clarity, before bourgeois apologists and Enlightenment philosophers obscured the underlying reality. Yet, for Montrose, that past is inalienably a foreign country: they do things differently there (a fundamental lesson of the immersion in Elizabethan lore, which can never be too thorough). Even though we may appreciate that it led to the world as we now know it, the particularities of power are specific to their own time. This is a point of difference between a New Historicist like Montrose and cultural materialists (such as Alan Sinfield, Jonathan Dollimore, Catherine Belsey and Steven Mullaney) for whom a recognition that power is in some respects always a cultural construction is an important first step towards its deconstruction.

Philip McGuire's 'Hippolyta's Silence and the Poet's Pen' (essay 6) is far removed in methodology from the arguments of Holland, Garner and Montrose, and yet it overlaps with all of them in the crucial question of what Shakespeare's text means to a modern audience – how its voices (and, just as crucially, its silences) communicate to them. His entire argument grows out of the virtual silence of

Hippolyta throughout the first scene of *A Midsummer Night's Dream*. She does, indeed, speak four and a half lines early on, but they – as he shows – establish nothing with any certainty about the relationship that then exists between her and Theseus. They voice different attitudes to the passage of time (he thinks it 'slow', she insists it moves 'quickly'), but this may be the difference either of antagonism or of complementarity. In themselves they tell us nothing of how she feels about the man who 'wooed [her] with my sword, / And won thy love doing thee injuries' and now promises to wed her 'With pomp, with triumph, and with revelling' (I.i.16–17,19). That being so, her silence from this point on means we are given no textual indication of how she is likely to respond to the whole situation of Egeus's complaint against Hermia and of how Theseus handles it. 'Hippolyta's silence is textually indeterminate'[26] – for whatever reason, Shakespeare has failed to assign it a particular significance. So it only acquires such a significance in performance, where the actors cannot ignore it, but must make it comprehensible. As McGuire demonstrates, reviewing five well-documented productions, there are at least five ways of doing that, none of which can be accused of straining or distorting the words Shakespeare actually wrote (or did not write).

The consequences of this are complex and wide-ranging. For one thing, it means that the actors 'must enact intentions that are theirs, not Shakespeare's'; for another, it means that the play has a kind of openness which allows it to be adapted ('translated') from era to era, without any artificial distortion. So, for example, it 'can better and more revealingly accommodate and be adapted to the values and concerns brought to the fore by the feminist movement precisely because Hippolyta's silence allows for the possibility that she, like Hermia, does not submit to male authority.'[27] So McGuire implicitly reaches a conclusion adjacent to that of Holland, though he reaches it by an entirely different route. *A Midsummer Night's Dream* is a play of indeterminacies, which are only to be resolved by the imaginative engagement of its readers – in this case taking the actors, whose professional livelihood depends on such engagement, as particularly attentive readers. By the same token he implicitly challenges Bevington's assumption that all matters of interpretation may be resolved by an appeal to the text itself or to a consensus within the readership.

If McGuire's argument is that indeterminacy is an integral feature of what Shakespeare actually wrote, Barbara Hodgdon carries the issue into a further dimension by reminding us (in essay 7) that what he wrote is itself far from being a settled quantity. The transcription into print of what was meant for performance always carries with it any number of imponderables, not least when the author himself is not responsible for it; but when two or more versions of a play have survived – as is the case with *A Midsummer Night's Dream* – the question of textual authority becomes especially fraught. Most readers are shielded from a realisation of this because, in buying a modern edition, we lose lose sight of them, deferring the responsibility to another species of professionally attentive readers, the editors. Responsible editors, of course, provide a textual apparatus, explaining how they have reduced the competing information available from the early versions to a seamless modern text. But few readers consult it, and even fewer think to challenge the principles on which specific decisions are based.

Yet the world of editing confronts (only latterly all too often then to conceal) some issues crucial to an informed reading of Shakespeare. Some of his plays have only survived in the version edited seven years after his death by his acting colleagues, John Heminge and Henry Condell, the Shakespeare First Folio (1623), an expensive and elaborate volume. Others were also printed earlier in much cheaper, individual quarto texts: some (e.g. *Hamlet*) in more than one version, some (e.g. *The Merry Wives of Windsor*) in what most people would agree were palpably unsatisfactory versions, but also some (e.g. *I Henry IV*) in versions fuller than and at least as good as those preserved by Heminge and Condell. In each case the relationship between the text and what Shakespeare wrote is a moot point, as is the relationship between what he wrote and what was performed, since it is apparent in at least some cases that the two were not conterminous. So, in producing a single, and apparently authoritative modern text, editors have to mediate on our behalf among a variety of conflicting claims. And they do so with views on matters about which our knowledge is far from complete: how and why the actors allowed some of their plays to be printed, and not others; what the precise contractual arrangements were between Shakespeare and his acting company; what view Shakespeare might have had of his own role and social standing as a writer of plays (and whether this might have changed in the course of his career); whether he might have revised plays after their first performance, and if so whether this was purely for practical reasons – such as the need to accommodate fewer actors in a touring production – or out of what we might call artistic considerations.

Barbara Hodgdon's brief but closely argued essay evokes all of these issues in challenging the almost universal preference of modern editors of *A Midsummer Night's Dream* for the 1600 quarto as their copy-text, over the 1623 folio. In particular, she concentrates on the consequences of this preference for the small but important role of Egeus. In the quarto, and so in most modern editions, Egeus disappears in Act IV, still calling for 'the law, the law', but overruled by Theseus; there is no indication that he is so much as on stage in the final act. In the folio, however, he is explicitly called for by Theseus and presents him with 'a brief of how many sports are ripe' for the wedding entertainment, usurping most of the role which in the quarto goes to Philostrate, Theseus's 'usual manager of mirth' or Master of the Revels. So the quarto comfortably forgets Egeus's unrelenting opposition to the marriage of Hermia and Lysander in the 'tragical mirth' of *Pyramus and Thisbe*. But the folio keeps it in front of our eyes. What exactly it may be said to make of it is as open a point as Philip McGuire shows Hippolyta's early silence to be: his very involvement may reflect acquiescence, bowing to Theseus's will and the communal spirit of celebration. On the other hand, if the actor makes it clear that Egeus is acting under protest, the play might end with an unresolved friction. In any event, as Hodgdon points out, his mere presence leaves directors with a problem they face in many other Shakespearean comedies: a solitary male character, who somehow has to be got off stage by the end. Either his isolation will be in marked contrast to the couplings which are the centre of attention, or he must be seen to be reconciled, perhaps to Theseus, perhaps also to Hermia and Lysander. At first sight these are minor textual differences. On reflection, they embody substantially different emphases, resonances and rhythms, which may in fact reflect Shakespeare's own rethinking. Their implications for, in particular, feminist readings of the play, where the father–daughter–husband triangle is of marked significance, have yet to be fully thought through.

Annabel Patterson's 'Bottom's Up: Festive Theory' (essay 8) starts by reflecting on how the performance history of the play has tended to universalise it as an 'airy nothing', downplaying the role of Bottom, Quince and their fellows, and ignoring its social and political specificities (except to the extent that its supposed endorsement of Theseus as a model of sound government can always be adduced as an act of conservative piety). The text itself, however, seems to insist on elements of its own historic location, with references to Elizabeth and to economic and climatic distress; these have long fuelled the supposition that the play was written for an aristocratic wedding attended by the queen (Patterson very properly questions the way this supposition has been installed as fact in some editions) and located it in 1595/96, when repeated wet summers caused poor harvests, bringing in their wake economic distress and social unrest. Even so criticism has been slow to see anything radical in this, assuming that the references to the queen must by definition be deferential, that the allusions to social disorder resonate no further than to demonstrate how it comes to nothing in a well-governed state, and that the voices of the working men who elect to celebrate their duke's wedding with a play are inherently insubstantial and not to be taken seriously.

The main substance of the essay is then taken up with a discussion of festive theory in its various forms, as explorations of the possibility that the play might actually be more radical – more sympathetic to the subversive voices to which it alludes – than it has usually been given credit for being. Patterson identifies three ways in which the play might be described as 'festive', acknowledging that they cut across and even possibly contradict each other. One relates to the 'occasionalist' suggestion that the play was written to celebrate an actual marriage, and that the 'revels' and 'merriment' evoked within the play to celebrate the Theseus–Hippolyta wedding mirror that event; while remaining agnostic on whether such an occasion actually occurred, Patterson associates even the possibility with the Elizabethan absorption of all popular drama under court control, suggesting that the amateur dramatics within *A Midsummer Night's Dream* offer 'a parodic version of that discontinuous patronage relation' and so voice 'uneasiness' and 'self-consciousness' about it.[28]

Another branch of festive theory (that most commonly identified in Shakespeare criticism with C. L. Barber) is anthropology-based, and concerns popular rather than courtly rituals – the popular rites of 'Easter, May, Whitsun, Midsummer, or Christmas holidays, or the harvest home'. The very title of the play (like that of *Twelfth Night*) encourages such associations, though references to Maying make its precise location in the festive calendar less clear-cut than it might be. Barber saw the plays of Shakespeare and his contemporaries absorbing such traditional and quasi-instinctive social actions into the commercial (and urbanised) sphere of professional play-acting, but his 'strongest message', in Patterson's view, 'was that both the archaic festivals and their Elizabethan echoes functioned to reaffirm, through reconciliatory symbolic action, the hierarchical structure of society'. The later work in this field of Victor Turner seems to offer the possibility of a more radical critique of social structures through ritualised suspensions of normal relations, especially 'in the space Turner called *liminality*, in which social distinctions are temporarily suspended. In liminal situations, the lower social strata become privileged, and bodily parts and biological referents, conceived as the source of regenerative energy, are revalued.' Although in theory such radical topsy-turveydom might be subversive in its implications Patterson concludes that, for Turner, 'the purpose of festive rituals is, in the last analysis, reconciliation, getting the social rhythms running smoothly once more' – not changing them.[29]

One branch of festive theory has been consistently more radical than these other two in seeing a clear class-based subversive potential in popular rituals, especially those of carnival. The originating voice here is Mikhail Bakhtin, in his study of Rabelais, though the most influential spokesman in Shakespeare studies is Robert Weimann in a series of articles collected as *Shakespeare and the Popular Tradition in the Theater*.[30] Yet even here, and despite in both cases a commitment to a Marxist reading of history, Patterson finds something akin to a failure of nerve in their final theoretical positions, Weimann talking of 'playfully rebellious gestures' in the echoes of popular misrule in Shakespeare, rather than outright dissent, and Bakhtin finding no 'critical and clearly defined opposition' in the traditions of carnival. In the face, then, of a consistent failure by all branches of festive theory to find in 'misrule' or carnivalesque elements of the Shakespearean text a truly radical popular voice, one explicitly opposed to the status quo, and prepared to contemplate its overthrow, she resolves to cut the Gordian knot, 'to create a gargantuan mingle-mangle of the strongest and boldest suggestions that these different festive theories proffer, while pushing them beyond their own aesthetic or precedural inhibitions'.[31] In effect she opts to take this 'voice', as it speaks in *A Midsummer Night's Dream*, at face value, not as distanced or contextualised by other elements in the text, nor as artificially constrained by the anthropology of pre-scribal festive practice, nor even as circumscribed by Shakespeare's cultural positioning as a writer. The proposition is essentially that the play allows us to take its working-class characters seriously, without condescension, even if their aristocratic masters (and their masters' counterparts in the Elizabethan audience) do and did not.

Although Richard Wilson's concerns (essay 9) are in a way very similar, his methodology and conclusions could hardly be further removed from those of Patterson. He follows Marx in seeing *A Midsummer Night's Dream* as emblematic of the curiously deferential power relations in Britain, in which rulers and ruled carefully avoid each other's gaze, an accommodation which leads to her famously non-revolutionary politics. His densely argued reading of the play is keyed with great historical specificity to power relations in the 1590s, inflected as they were by the childless queen's advancing age, disastrous harvests, the threat and actuality of urban unrest, all of which are obliquely mirrored in the play. It is also centrally concerned with the status of the theatre, and of the poets who wrote for it, at that early modern political moment delicately poised between older systems where the threat of violent physical repression was ever-present for those who spoke without the voice of authority and a more modern patronage system where 'literary criticism is superseding torture as the more subtle means of cultural control'. In that context, he argues, 'Like *Julius Caesar*, *A Midsummer Night's Dream* is a play about poetry and power, and how they read each other'.[32]

This was, in the view of Michel Foucault, the moment of the birth of the individuated modern author, and so at the very heart of Wilson's argument lies the question of Shakespeare's own identity or self-definition as an artist at this critical time. The play circles around this in a variety of ways, notably in its depiction of the 'playwright' Peter Quince, and all his efforts and those of his fellow actors not to offend the Duke and the ladies, but also in the repeated evocation of the play's own sources, antecedents and analogues, replete with tales of death, violence and dismemberment (notably Ovid's *Metamorphoses* and the tale of the archetypal poet-singer, Orpheus, torn to pieces by the frenzied followers of Bacchus). In none of this does Shakespeare stand four-square before us but he is self-effacingly represented, Wilson argues, in the manner of a Baroque painting, such as that of Velazquez, where the scene is multiply mirrored, visually playing with subjects, objects, patrons and their artists. In this rather nervous stand-off,

Shakespeare emerges as 'a comparativist in anthropology, and what he compares are ancient and modern rites to propitiate the powers that be'[33] – rather than, as Patterson argues, rites through which popular radicalism speaks defiantly.

The 'dream' of Shakespeare's theatre is thus one of deferral, obliqueness, self-effacement, entertainment mirroring the real world without confronting it, just as – through Bottom – it represents the dangerous, prickly fairy world as harmless, child-like fantasy. So 'by collapsing his own meaning into the diminutiveness of an inaccessible aesthetic domain, the poet tamed the Furies into Fairies where Orpheus and Ovid had failed, and ensured his troupe became "but shadows" of reality ... not shades.'[34] But if this can be seen as Shakespeare's pragmatic policy for self-preservation in the instability of 1590s England, it can also be seen as an explanation for his emergence as the national poet in the generations after his death, which was only consolidated after the failure of the Commonwealth. In Wilson's post-Marxist critique the aesthetic self-effacement, rather than death, of the author allows for a representation of power relations which perfectly – and, at least until very recently, uncontentiously – mirrored the stand-off of the non-revolutionary political culture of Britain for the last 350 years.

Terence Hawkes (essay 10) stands back from the historicism of Krieger, Montrose, Patterson and Wilson – which, in their various ways, all seek to define the play's meaning in the circumstances of the culture which created it – and explores, with McGuire and Hodgdon, the indeterminacies of the text. Yet he does so in a spirit which is closer to much of the historicist criticism than to that of most performance-orientated or editorially charged writing, in the sense that his ultimate concern is the role and status of the text in relation to the community to which it (now) belongs. The first section of the book from which it is abstracted has some reflections on comments by the present Prince of Wales on the place of Shakespeare in the English curriculum, and so by implication in our culture's definition of itself. In such moments his concerns are clearly parallel to those of Wilson, though his methodology is very different.

Hawkes's approach might be described as deconstructionist or poststructuralist, though in a witty, humane and accessible mode not always characteristic of these schools. It takes the arcane theory which underpins their thinking for granted, and concentrates on the implications of the slipperiness of language which they take to be axiomatic. Note, for example, the claim that Peter Quince's use of the word 'disfigure' 'casually disgorges its subtext'.[35] All words have subtexts – senses not immediately apparent – which it is the function of the critic to elucidate. And verbal structures as complex as *A Midsummer Night's Dream* have myriad such subtexts, as Hawkes demonstrates in spot-lighting one of the least observed and memorable of details, the fact that Helena has a parent (never seen) called Nedar. In as much as anyone *has* noticed this shadowy character's existence, it is to assume a parallel with Hermia's father, Egeus, who (as both Shirley Nelson Garner and Barbara Hodgdon remind us) is very forcefully a character in the play, however small his speaking role. Hawkes, however, proposes that Nedar is a woman, Helena's mother, and even finds sanction in Greek mythology and etymology for this proposition. One wonders at this point about the relative dispositions of tongues and cheeks – though the central question is a perfectly serious one. Why not a woman? After all, as he goes on to demonstrate, the play is surrounded by shadowy elder women, most notably Queen Elizabeth.

In this one instance, therefore, he opens up a whole alternative reading of the play, against the grain of received assumptions, opinions and expectations which inevitably accompany a cultural force as potent as Shakespeare. But – and this is equally important – well within the parameters of what the text 'says' or 'means'. Or might say, or might mean, given the free-play of sense which operates when the play is subjected to the lottery of readership. In this, Hawkes is at the furthest remove of any in this collection from Bevington's New Critical assumptions about the determinacy of the text and the limited, consensual role of the reader in confirming (rather than establishing) meaning. McGuire's argument assumes that it is the actors, or at least their performance, which fixes the meaning of the indeterminate text; Wilson denies indeterminacy in ascribing ambiguities and evasions in the text to historical and cultural specificities. But Hawkes implies – indeed, goes on openly to argue – that the role of the critic is to resist such closure, to open up endless alternative meanings.

This is the nub of his central argument about the difference between 'or' and 'and': '"and" could be said to be the opposite of "or". "And" certainly proposes repetition, more of the same. But "or" has a more disturbing function. It introduces alternatives, realignments, different possibilities, unconsidered consequences, surprising subsequence; it signals a worrying, revisionary and subversive current'[36] – very much at odds with conservative pressures in the play, largely associated with Theseus, and equally at odds with most traditional forms of criticism (even those driven by radical ideology). This is because most criticism takes the form of a reading which in some sense replicates or substitutes for 'the text' and its 'meaning': in that sense it extends and perpetuates closure, the idea (fundamentally challenged by deconstruction) that texts have a final, determinable meaning. What Hawkes both demonstrates and argues for in this piece is a criticism which does not allow itself to be trapped by illusions of completion and definition.

This is the point of what may seem a diversion, the discussion of Harley Granville-Barker's 1914 'golden' production of *A Midsummer Night's Dream*, which for once brought 'Nedar' on stage – as a man. Hawkes quickly sketches in a whole range of contexts: the First World War, threats of mutiny and rebellion in Ireland, the troubled marriage of the director and Lillah McCarthy (who played Helena), and above all the agitation of the Suffragette movement. Any or all of these *could* have informed that famous production, giving it a more radical edge and taking the smile off Prime Minister Asquith as the representative patriarch, or Theseus, of his day. But they did not, and Hawkes registers this as a kind of failure, which critics must not replicate. Just as *A Midsummer Night's Dream* has ending after (apparent) ending, and shrewd entrepreneurs have whittled away with outrageous productivity at the mullberry-tree legacy of Shakespeare's works, the critic's role is the endlessly open one of saying 'or'.

NOTES

1 For Barber and Bakhtin, see Further Reading.

2. On discussions of the place of this stage, see Further Reading.

3. For discussion of the question of power in Shakespeare, see Further Reading.

4. For an illuminating example of the use of Foucault, see Stephen Greenblatt's essay 'Invisible Bullets: Renaissance Authority and its Subversion, *Henry IV and Henry V*', in *Political Shakespeare*, ed. Jonathan Dollimore and Alan Sinfield (Manchester, 1985).

5. Jan Kott, *Shakespeare our Contemporary* (London, 1964), pp. 227.

6. See p. 25 below.

7. See p. 25, 29, 34 below.

8. See pp. 30, 33 below.

9. The allusion is, of course, to W. K. Winsatt's *The Verbal Icon* (Lexington, MA, 1967), and Cleanth Brooks' *The Well Wrought Urn* (London, 1949).

10. Edmund Wilson, 'The Historical Interpretation of Literature' (1940), in his *Triple Thinkers* (Harmondsworth, 1962), p. 288.

11. See pp. 48, 39 below.

12. See pp. 47, 51 below.

13. E. M. W. Tillyard, *The Elizabethan World Picture* (London, 1943), pp. 7–8.

14. See p. 55 below.

15. See p. 71 below.

16. See p. 74 below.

17. See pp. 76, 80 below.

18. See p. 81 below.

19. See p. 84 below

20. See p. 99 below.

21. See Further Reading, 'Background, Sources, Context', for studies of Theseus in the Renaissance.

22. See pp. 89, 96 below.

23. See pp. 101–2, 129 below.

24. See 'Further Reading', under 'Background, Context, History'.

25. See pp. 126, 132 below.

26. See p. 142 below.

27. See p. 156 below.

28. See p. 179 below.

29. See pp. 181, 182 below.

30. See Further Reading, under 'Festive Comedy' and 'Historical Readings', respectively.

31. See p. 184 below.

32. See pp. 203, 204–5 below.

33. See p. 215 below.

34. See p. 215 below.
35. See p. 225 below.
36. See p. 231 below.

1

'But We Are Spirits of Another Sort': The Dark Side of Love and Magic in *A Midsummer Night's Dream*

DAVID BEVINGTON

When Oberon instructs Puck in Act III, scene ii of *A Midsummer Night's Dream*, to overcast the night with 'drooping fog as black as Acheron', and to lead the 'testy rivals' Demetrius and Lysander astray so that they will not actually harm one another in their rivalry, while Oberon for his part undertakes to obtain the changeling boy from Titania whom he will then release from her infatuated love of Bottom, Puck replies that the two of them will have to work fast. Such fairy doings need to be accomplished by night, insists Puck. With the approaching break of day, and the shining of Aurora's harbinger or morning star, ghosts and damned spirits will have to trip home to churchyards and their 'wormy beds' beneath the ground. Puck's implication seems clear: he and Oberon, being spirits of the dark, are bound by its rules to avoid the light of day.

Just as clearly, however, Oberon protests that Puck is wrong in making such an assumption. 'But we are spirits of another sort', Oberon insists.

I with the Morning's love have oft made sport,
And, like a forester, the groves may tread
Even till the eastern gate, all fiery red,
Opening on Neptune, with fair blessèd beams
Turns into yellow gold his salt green streams.
(III.ii.388–93)[1]

Oberon may frolic until late in the dawn, though by implication even he may not stay abroad all day. The association of Oberon with sunlight and dawn is thus more symbolic than practical; it disassociates him from spirits of the dark, even though he must finish up this night's work before night is entirely past. He concedes to Puck the need for hurry: 'But notwithstanding, haste; make no delay. / We may affect this business yet ere day.' The concession implies that Oberon has made his point about sporting with the dawn not to refute Puck's call for swiftness, but to refute Puck's association of the fairies with ghosts and damned spirits.[2]

This debate between Oberon and Puck reflects a fundamental tension in the play between comic reassurance and the suggestion of something dark and threatening. Although the fairies act benignly, Puck continually hints at a good deal more than simple mischief. The forest itself is potentially a place of violent death and rape, even if the lovers experience nothing more than fatigue, anxiety, and being torn by briars. In the forest, moreover, the experience of love invites all lovers to consider, however briefly, the opportunity for sexual revelling freed from the restraints of social custom. Of late, Jan Kott has shown to us most forcefully this dark side of love; indeed, he has done so too forcefully, and with an often exaggerated effect upon contemporary productions of this and other plays.[3] Still, his insight has something to commend it. If his overstated emphasis on the dark side of love can perhaps be seen as a manifestation of the new sexual freedom of the 1960s, the sometimes overheated reactions against Kott can perhaps be related to the reluctance of most of us to give up the romanticised and sentimentalised nineteenth-century reading of the play (epitomised in Mendelssohn's incident music) to which Kott is addressing his attack. Even today, we find it distasteful to speak openly of sexual longing in this comedy, for fear of dealing grossly with the play's delicately understated portrayal of Eros. My purpose, however, is to suggest that in its proper context the dark side of love is seldom very far away in this play.

Let us return to the debate between Oberon and Puck, and to Shakespeare's dramatic purpose in presenting to us both the king of fairies and his mischievous attendant. This purpose is not restricted to the fairies' function in the plot, in which Puck comically misapplies Oberon's ambiguous instructions about the love juice or extemporaneously creates a monster with whom Titania is to fall in love. Puck constantly brings before our eyes a more threatening vision of fairydom than is apparent in Oberon's more regal pronouncements. In part, of course, he is the practical joker making Oberon laugh at his ability to mimic a filly foal, or a three-foot stool, or Demetrius and Lysander. Puck is infinitely versatile in changing shapes, just as he can also put a girdle round the earth in forty minutes. On the other hand, Puck also loves to frighten people. He gladly confesses to being the elf who 'frights the maidens of the villagery' (II.i.35). It is he who conjures up, for the delectation of the audience, a morbid image of the night-time as fearful, and as associated with gaping graves in churchyards, ghosts and damned spirits, screeching owls, and howling wolves:

> Now the hungry lion roars,
> And the wolf behowls the moon;
> Whilst the heavy ploughman snores,
> All with the weary task fordone.
> Now the wasted brands do glow,
> Whilst the screech owl, screeching loud,
> Puts the wretch that lies in woe
> In remembrance of a shroud.
> Now it is the time of night
> That the graves, all gaping wide,
> Every one lets forth his sprite,
> In the churchyard paths to glide.
> (V.i.360–71)

Although, as he says, the fairies are now 'frolic', their usual custom is to run 'By the triple Hecate's team / From the presence of the sun'. Earlier, too, as we have seen, Puck associates his own nocturnal activities with 'night's swift dragons' and with ghosts 'wand'ring here and there', 'damnèd spirits all, / That in crossways and floods have burial', hastening home to their 'wormy beds' before the break of day, lest the daylight should 'look their shames upon' (III.ii.379–85).

Even in the action of the play, Puck does in fact frighten many of the persons he meets – virtually all of them, in fact, except Bottom.

As he chases Quince, Snout, and the rest from their rehearsal spot in a forest clearing, he makes the incantation:

> I'll follow you; I'll lead you about a round,
> Through bog, through bush, through brake, through brier.
> Sometime a horse I'll be, sometime a hound,
> A hog, a headless bear, sometime a fire;
> And neigh, and bark, and grunt, and roar, and burn,
> Like horse, hound, hog, bear, fire, at every turn.
>
> (III.i.96–101)

And he later reports to his master, with glee, the startling effect upon the rude mechanicals created by Bottom's re-emergence from his hawthorne tiring house with an ass's head on his shoulders:

> When they him spy,
> As wild geese that the creeping fowler eye,
> Or russet-pated choughs, many in sort,
> Rising and cawing at the gun's report,
> Sever themselves and madly sweep the sky;
> So at his sight away his fellows fly,
> And at our stamp here o'er and o'er one falls;
> He murder cries and help from Athens calls.
> Their sense thus weak, lost with their fears thus strong,
> Made senseless things begin to do them wrong,
> For briers and thorns at their apparel snatch:
> Some, sleeves – some, hats; from yielders all things catch.
>
> (III.ii.19–30)

Our own laughter at this comic chase should not obscure the fact that Puck creates truly frightening illusions in the forest. Similarly, our sense of assurance that Demetrius and Lysander will come to no harm must not cause us to forget that Puck's game with them is to lead them astray, like those night-wanderers whom he is known to mislead, 'laughing at their harm' (II.i.39).

In the relationship of Puck and Oberon, it is Puck who tends to stress the irrational and frightening while Oberon's position is that of a ruler insisting on the establishment of proper obedience to his authority.[4] When Puck mistakenly applies the love-juice intended for Demetrius to Lysander's eyes, thereby inducing Lysander to desert his true love for Helena, Oberon's first reaction is one of dismay:

> What hast thou done? Thou hast mistaken quite
> And laid the love-juice on some true-love's sight.

Of thy misprison must perforce ensue
Some true-love turned, and not a false turned true.

(III.ii.88–91)

Whereupon the fairy king immediately orders Puck to find Helena
and return with her, so that Demetrius (who now lies asleep at their
feet) can be induced to love her. Oberon seeks always to right
unhappy love. His insistence that he and his followers are fairies of
'another sort' is thus an appropriate and consistent stance for him,
even if what he says does not always square with Puck's role as the
hobgoblin who skims milk of its cream, prevents milk from turning
into butter, or deprives ale of its 'barm' or head. Oberon's very
presence at the wedding is intended to assure that such things won't
happen to Theseus, Hippolyta, and the rest of the happy young
people about to marry; Oberon guarantees that their issue 'Ever
shall be fortunate', free of 'mole, harelip; nor scar', or any other
'blots of Nature's hand' (V.i.395–400).[5]

Together, Oberon and Puck represent contrasting forces within
the fairy kingdom. Perhaps their functions can best be reconciled by
reflecting that their chief power to do good lies in withholding the
mischief of which they are capable. Like Apollo in book 1 of the
Iliad, whom the Greek warriors venerate as the god of health
because he is also terrifyingly capable of sending plagues, Oberon is
to be feared because he has the authority both to prevent birth
defects and other marks 'prodigious, such as are / Despisèd in nativ-
ity' (V.i.401–2), and to inflict them. Only when placated by men
and called by such names as Hobgoblin or 'sweet Puck' will these
spirits work for men and bring them good luck.

The forest shares many of these same ambivalent qualities as do
the fairies. It is in part a refuge for young lovers fleeing the sharp
Athenian law, a convenient and secluded spot for clandestine play
rehearsals, and a fragrant bower for the fairy queen decked out
'With sweet musk-roses, and with eglantine' (II.i.252). For the
young lovers, however, as their quest for amorous bliss grows more
and more vexed, the forest becomes increasingly a place of darkness, estrangement, and potential violence. Demetrius warns
Helena, in an attempt to be rid of her,

You do impeach your modesty too much
To leave the city and commit yourself
Into the hands of one that loves you not,
To trust the opportunity of night

> And the ill counsel on a desert place
> With the rich worth of your virginity.
> (II.i.214–19)

Demetrius recognises the opportunity for a loveless rape and briefly recognises his own potential for such sexual violence, though he is also virtuous enough to reject the temptation. The alternative he offers Helena is scarcely more kind: he will run from her and leave her 'to the mercy of wild beasts' (l.228).

The ever-present moon shares this same ambivalence. Although it is at times the beneficent moon shining at its full on the palace wood to facilitate a rehearsal (I.ii) or through a casement window of the great chamber where the final performance of 'Pyramus and Thisbe' is to take place (III.i), it is contrastingly an old waning moon, associated with age and inhibition of pleasures, lingering the desires of would-be lovers 'Like to a stepdame or a dowager, / Long withering out a young man's revenue' (I.i.6–7). More ominously, the moon is 'the governess of floods', who 'Pale in her anger, washes all the air, / That rheumatic diseases do abound' (II.i.103–5), whenever the fairy king and queen are at enmity. Even if the 'chaste beams of the wat'ry moon' call up associations of that 'fair vestal', Queen Elizabeth (II.i.158–64), and seem to offer assurances of the kind of divine protection afforded the young lady in Milton's *Comus*, the moon is not permitted to shine continually throughout the night-time misadventures of this play. Oberon orders Puck, as we have seen, to overcast the night. 'The starry welkin cover thou anon / With drooping fog as black as Acheron' (III.ii.355–7). In the ensuing darkness, the lovers stress repeatedly their sense of bewilderment and discouragement. 'O weary night, O long and tedious night', complains Helena, 'Abate thy hours' (III.ii.431–2). The word 'weary' sounds a choric note of repetition in Hermia's entrance, immediately following the speech just quoted: 'Never so weary, never so in woe, / Bedabbled with the dew, and torn with briers, / I can no further crawl' (ll.442–4). Lysander, having fallen as he says 'in dark uneven way', has already given up pursuit of Demetrius, who all unawares joins his archrival 'on this cold bed' (ll.417, 429). Although the lovers are together, and although their tribulations are now at an end, the night-time experience has been one of separation, humiliation, and defeat. As Puck observes earlier, they have been reduced to sleeping 'On the dank and dirty ground' (II.ii.75).

Night-time in the forest repeatedly conveys the sense of estrangement and misunderstanding with which the lovers are afflicted.
When Puck creates a pitchy darkness into which he can lead
Lysander and Demetrius, he is not manufacturing mischief out of
nothing but is giving expression to their rivalry in love. As a stage
manager of his own little play, he allows the men to parody their
own tendencies toward petty vengefulness. The fact that the two
young men are rather much alike, that their contention can be resolved by a simple solution (since Demetrius did in fact pay court to
Helena before the play began, and need only return to his original
attachment to her), adds to the sense of comedy by heightening the
comic discrepancy between their anger and its lack of objective
cause. Puck's manipulation serves the benign effect of showing (to
the lovers themselves, in retrospect) the ridiculousness of exaggerated contentiousness. In a similar way Puck uses night and darkness
as an emblem to expose the catty jealousies of the two young
women and their tendency toward morbid self-pity. The effect of
such cleansing exposure is a comic purgation. Puck is a creature of
the night, but he uses darkness to produce ultimate illumination.
He mocks pretensions, even in himself, even in the play to which he
belongs: 'If we shadows have offended, / Think but this, and all is
mended – / That you have but slumb'red here / While these visions
did appear' (V.i.412–15).

Darkness and the forest, then, offer the lovers a glimpse of their
inner selves. Often, this glimpse suggests much about human nature
that is not merely perverse and jealous, but libidinous. Here again
Jan Kott offers helpful insights, though he has surely gone too far.
The motif on which the action of the play is based, that of escape
into a forest on the eve of Mayday (*Walpurgisnacht)* or on
Midsummer's Eve, is traditionally erotic.[6] The four lovers are discovered the next morning asleep on the ground, in a compromising
position certainly, though not in flagrante delicto. 'Begin these
woodbirds but to couple now?' asks Theseus humorously and continues to remain sceptical toward the lovers' story of their night – a
scepticism prompted in part, one imagines, by their insistence that
they have slept apart from one another. We know, in fact, that their
night has been a continuous series of proposed matings without any
actual consummations. 'One turf shall serve as pillow for us both',
Lysander suggests to Hermia as night comes on. 'One heart, one
bed, two bosoms, and one troth' (II.ii.41–2). She finds his rhetoric
pretty but insists on a propriety that is not mere primness. 'Such

separation as may well be said / Becomes a virtuous bachelor and a maid, / So far be distant', she instructs him (ll.58–60). She wants her lover to move away just a little, but not too much. Hermia knows, because of the person she is, that freedom to escape the harsh Athenian law does not mean the licence to try anything and that she can justify her elopement only by voluntary obedience to a code she holds to be absolutely good and that she never questions. The serpent of which she dreams, crawling on her breast to eat her heart away while Lysander watches smilingly (ll.146–50), is not an image of her own licentiousness but of an infidelity in which she is the innocent victim. Demetrius too would never presume to take advantage of Helena's unprotected condition, however much he may perceive an opportunity for rape. Kott seriously distorts the context of the love imagery in this play when he discovers sodomistic overtones in Helena's likening herself to a spaniel;[7] her meaning, as she clearly explains, is that she is like a patient, fawning animal whose master responds to affection with blows and neglect.

Repeatedly in this play, a presumption of man's licentiousness is evoked, only to be answered by the conduct of the lovers themselves. This representation of desire almost but not quite satisfied is to be sure a titillating one, but it looks forward as do the lovers themselves to legitimate consummation in marriage and procreation. At the very end, the lovers do all go to bed while Oberon speaks of the issue that will surely spring from their virtuous coupling. Earlier, Theseus has proposed to await the marriage day for his consummation, even though he captured his wife through military force; why else should he complain of the aged moon that 'lingers' his desires 'Like to a stepdame or a dowager'? (Hippolyta, with a maiden's traditional reluctance, seems more content with the four-day delay than does her amorous bridegroom.) The tradesmen's play serves as one last comic barrier to the achievement of desire, although it is mercifully brief and can be performed without epilogue in the interest of further brevity. Such waiting only makes the moment of final surrender more pleasurable and meaningful.

The conflict between sexual desire and rational restraint is, then, an essential tension throughout the play reflected in the images of dark and light. This same tension exists in the nature of the fairies and of the forest. The ideal course seems to be a middle one, between the sharp Athenian law on the one hand with its threat of death or perpetual chastity, and a licentiousness on the other hand that the forest (and man's inner self) proposes with alacrity, but from which the lovers are saved chiefly by the steadfastness of the women. They, after all, remain constant; it is the men who change affections under the effect of Oberon's love potion. (In the fairy plot, to be sure, we find a reverse symmetry that is surely intentional: the woman is inconstant, since it is Titania, the fairy queen, who takes a new lover. With a similar reversal the obstacle to love in the fairy plot is internal, since the king and queen are divided by their own quarrel for mastery in love, whereas in the plot of the four lovers the original obstacle is the external one of parental opposition.)[8]

This tension between licentiousness and self-mastery is closely related also to the way in which the play itself constantly flirts with genuine disaster but controls that threat through comic reassurance. Hermia is threatened with death in Act I, or with something almost worse than death – perpetual maidenhood, and yet we know already from the emphasis on love and marriage that all such threats to happiness are ultimately to prove illusory. Lysander and Hermia speak of 'War, death, or sickness' and of other external threats to love, but are resolved on a plan of escape that will avoid all these. Repeatedly in the forest the lovers fear catastrophe only to discover that their senses have been deceiving them. 'But who is here?' asks Helena as she comes across a sleeping man, Lysander, on the ground: 'Dead, or asleep?' (II.ii.100–1). When, shortly afterwards, Hermia awakes to find herself deserted, she sets off after her strangely absent lover: 'Either death, or you, I'll find immediately' (l.156). The choice seems dire, but the comic sense of discrepancy assures us that the need for such a choice is only a chimera. Later, again, when Helena concludes that all her erstwhile friends have turned against her for some inexplicable reason, she determines to leave them: ''Tis partly my own fault, / Which death or absence soon shall remedy' (III.ii.243–4). Only in the story of Pyramus and Thisbe, with its hilarious presentation of the very tragedy of misunderstanding that did not occur in A Midsummer Night's Dream, does comic reassurance fail. Instead of Helena's 'Dead, or asleep?' the order is reversed. 'Asleep, my love?' asks Thisbe as she finds Pyramus on the ground. 'What, dead, my dove?' (V.i.316–17).[9]

What, finally, of love and sex among the fairies? When we come to the sexual escapades of Oberon and Titania, especially the latter, we come to what is for Kott the central image of the dark side of love. Bottom's ass's head, insists Kott, is grossly animal, especially since 'from antiquity up to the Renaissance the ass was credited with the strongest sexual potency and among all quadrupeds was supposed to have the longest and hardest phallus'. Because Titania herself is presumably delicate and fair, the violent image of her coupling with Bottom calls to Kott's mind those 'white Scandinavian girls I used to see on the *rue de la Harpe* or *rue de la Huchette,* walking and clinging tightly to Negroes with faces grey or so black that they were almost undistinguishable from the night'.[10]

This reading has proved too strong for most critics and indeed it exaggerates distastefully and needlessly. I say needlessly because the coupling of Titania and Bottom has long been regarded as a comic version of Beauty and the Beast.[11] As in that fairy story, or as in Ovid's narratives of transformation in love, such pairing of opposites is plainly suggestive of the yoking of the ethereal and the carnal in human nature.

The fairies of *A Midsummer Night's Dream* do not govern themselves by the conventional sexual mores of the humans.[12] As we have already seen, many things are inverted in the mirror-image world of fairydom: it is the woman rather than the man who is inconstant, the obstacles to love are internal rather than external, and so on. Similarly, the quarrel of Oberon and Titania reflects the recently completed struggle for mastery between Theseus and Hippolyta, and yet is conducted according to the peculiar customs of the fairy kingdom. Titania's love for Theseus is apparently the occasion of her current visit to Athens, in order that she may be at Theseus's wedding; yet her love for the Athenian king has taken strange forms. According to Oberon, Titania's love for Theseus prompts her to 'lead him through the glimmering night / From Perigenia, whom he ravishèd, / And make him with fair Aegles break his faith, / With Ariadne, and Antiopa' (II.i.77–80). Titania to be sure denies the charge. The point is, however, that Oberon considers his queen perfectly capable of expressing her love for Theseus by encouraging him to ravish and then reject in turn a series of human mistresses. This is the sort of mysterious affection that only a god could practise or understand. Oberon's behaviour in love is no less puzzling from a human vantage: he punishes Titania for denying him the changeling boy by forcing her to take a gross and foolish lover. These gods make a sport of inconstancy.

The rivalry about the changeling boy is equally bizarre if measured in human terms. Conceivably, as Kott suggests, Oberon desires the boy as his own minion, although (like so much of what Kott claims) the boy's erotic status cannot be proved from a reading of the text. We are told only that he is a 'lovely boy' whom 'jealous Oberon' desires as a 'Knight of his train' to be his 'henchman' (II.i.22–5, 121). When Oberon has succeeded in winning the boy from her, he has the youth sent to his 'bower in fairyland' (IV.i.60). This slender evidence seems deliberately ambiguous. Any attempts to depict Oberon as bisexual surely miss the point that the fairies' ideas concerning love are ultimately unknowable and incomprehensible. We mortals can laugh at our own libidinous tendencies when we see them mirrored in the behaviour of the immortals, but we can never fathom how distant those immortals are from the ordinary pangs of human affection. Oberon is not so busy teaching Titania a lesson that he fails to enjoy Puck's 'fond pageant' on the theme of human passion: 'Lord, what fools these mortals be.'

Titania does of course undergo an experience of misdirected love that is analogous to human inconstancy in love and that is prompted by the same love-juice applied to the eyes of Demetrius and Lysander. To confound her with a mortal is, however, to follow Kott's erroneous lead of imagining her as a white-skinned Scandinavian in Paris coupling with a dark-skinned man. That anachronistic image may well convey to us an aura of the exotic and bizarre, but in doing so it introduces a false note of sexual perversity and compulsion. Titania abundantly demonstrates that she is motivated by no such human drive. Her hours spent with Bottom are touchingly innocent and tender. Like the royal creature that she is, she forbids Bottom to leave her presence. Even if he is her slave, however, imprisoned in an animal form, she is no Circean enchantress teaching him enslavement to sensual appetite. Instead, her mission is to 'purge thy mortal grossness so / That thou shalt like an airy spirit go' (III.i.145–6). It is because she is prompted by such ethereal considerations that she feeds him with apricots and dewberries, fans the moonbeams from his sleeping eyes, and the like. As Oberon reports later to Puck, having kept close watch over Titania, she graces the hairy temples of Bottom's ass's head 'With coronet of fresh and fragrant flowers' (IV.i.51). Rather than descending into the realm of human passion and perversity, she has attempted to raise Bottom into her own. Bottom, for his part, speaking the part of the wise fool, has noted the irrationality of love but has submitted himself to deliciously innocent pleasures that are, for him, mainly gastronomic. Titania, and Shakespeare too, have indeed purged his mortal grossness, not by making him any less funny, but by showing how the tensions in this play between the dark and the affirmative side of love are reconciled in the image of Titania and the ass's head.

From *Medieval and Renaissance Studies*, 13 (1975), 80–92.

NOTES

[Bevington's essay is a measured response to the excitement generated by Jan Kott's reading of the play in *Shakespeare Our Contemporary*, as outlined in the Introduction. Bevington was already among the most distinguished Renaissance scholars and editors of his generation when he wrote it, and seeking to discriminate between what was essentially valid in Kott's reading and what might be ascribed to local fashions and preoccupations (post-nuclear angst, the sexual revolution of the 1960s). Kott had largely been greeted with horror in Anglo-American academic circles when his work was first translated (1964), but given considerable currency in the influence he had on many productions of Shakespeare's plays, most notably two directed by Peter Brook at Stratford: his austere 1962 *King Lear* with Paul Schofield, stripped of faith, hope and charity in a world approximating to that of Beckett's *Endgame*, and his 1970 *A Midsummer Night's Dream*, described here by Stanley Wells: 'It was set ... in a white box. Costumes were timeless: loose satin garments in bright colours. Oberon and Theseus, like Titania and Hippolyta, were played by the same actor. Oberon and Puck swung on trapezes, and Titania descended, sitting on a great scarlet feather. There was rampant sexuality in Bottom's encounter with Titania ... The production was self-consciously iconoclastic, theatrically powerful, and, in its closing moments, homiletic. It did little to realise the grace, charm, and humour of Shakespeare's play, but its self-confident assertion of its own values made it a great happening in its own right. It toured the world' (Stanley Wells, 'Shakespeare on the English Stage', in *William Shakespeare: his World, his Work, his Influence*, ed. John F. Andrews, 3 vols [New York, 1985], III, p. 626). Wells's tone is cool, acknowledging a major theatrical event, but essentially questioning its status as a performance of the play Shakespeare wrote. Bevington's essay stands in broadly the same relationship to what Kott had written and to the influence he had had. Ed.]

1. Quotations are from *A Midsummer Night's Dream*, The Pelican Shakespeare, edited by Madeleine Doran (Baltimore, 1959). My title for this essay somewhat resembles that of Marjorie B. Gaber in her chapter, 'Spirits of another sort', from *Dream in Shakespeare* (New Haven, CT, 1974), but our critical purposes are essentially different.

2. Roger Lancelyn Green, 'Shakespeare and the Fairies', *Folklore*, 73 (1962), 89–103, stresses his belief that the fairies of this play are not evil or malicious, like many spirits of folklore. So does K. M. Briggs (*The Anatomy of Puck* [London, 1959]). M. W. Latham (*The Elizabethan Fairies* [New York, 1930]) contends also that the fairies in A *Midsummer Night's Dream* are unthreatening, though he concedes that Shakespeare demonstrates in other plays a power among the fairies for troublemaking. David Young (*Something of Great Constancy* [New Haven, CT, 1966]), on the other hand, ably shows what is threatening about Puck; see, for example, p. 28. See also W. Moelwyn Merchant, '*A Midsummer Night's Dream*: a Visual Re-cre-ation' in *Early Shakespeare*, ed. John Russell Brown and Bernard Harris, Stratford-upon-Avon Studies, 3 (London, 1961), pp. 165–85; G. K. Hunter, *William Shakespeare: The Late Comedies* (London, 1962), p. 16; and Michael Taylor, 'The Darker Purpose of A *Midsummer Night's Dream*', *Studies in English Literature*, 9 (1969), 257–73.

3. Jan Kott, *Shakespeare Our Contemporary*, trans. Boleslaw Taborski (New York, 1964).

4. Howard Nemerov, 'The Marriage of Theseus and Hippolyta', *Kenyon Review*, 18 (1956), 633–41, contrasts the rationality of Oberon with the magical, fabulous and dramatic character of Hippolyta.

5. On the relation of fairy magic to birth marks, see K. M. Briggs, *Pale Hecate's Team* (London, 1962).

6. On customs associated with Midsummer Night, see Sir James Frazer, *The Golden Bough*, abridged edn (London, 1933), ch. 10, p. 133, quoted in Peter F. Fisher, 'The Argument of A *Midsummer Night's Dream*', *Shakespeare Quarterly*, 8 (1957), 307–19; also Lou Agnes Reynolds and Paul Sawyer, 'Folk Medicine and the Four Fairies of A *Midsummer Night's Dream*', *Shakespeare Quarterly*, 10 (1959), 513–21; and C. L. Barber, *Shakespeare's Festive Comedy* (Princeton, NJ, 1959). Ernest Schanzer ('The Central Theme of A *Midsummer Night's Dream*', *University of Toronto Quarterly*, 20 [1951], 233–8) observes that the central events of the play seem really to have taken place on the eve of May Day. Young (*Something of Great Constancy*, p. 24) discusses the associations of the action with both Midsummer Eve and May Day.

7. Kott, *Shakespeare Our Contemporary*, p. 225.

8. Young (*Something of Great Constancy*) discusses 'mirroring' of this sort on pp. 95ff.

9. On 'Pyramus and Thisbe' as 'a foil to the entire play of which it is a part', see R. W. Dent, 'Imagination in A *Midsummer Night's Dream*', *Shakespeare Quarterly*, 15 (1964), 115–29.

10. Kott, *Shakespeare Our Contemporary*, p. 227.

11. See, for example, Young, *Something of Great Constancy*, p. 15.

12. As Alfred Harbage observes in *As They Liked It* (New York, 1947), 'For the most part we must look for our moral defect among quarrelsome fairies' (p. 140). To Harbage, the fairy scenes in *A Midsummer Night's Dream* are unique in Shakespeare in their lack of appeal to standards of moral conduct and to choice between right and wrong (p. 6). See also E. C. Pettet, *Shakespeare and the Romance Tradition* (London, 1949), p. 112, on the thematic relationship between the Oberon–Titania quarrel and that of the human lovers.

2

A Midsummer Night's Dream

ELLIOT KRIEGER

'SUCH SEPARATION AS MAY WELL BE SAID'
The Athenian Lovers

In *A Midsummer Night's Dream* the romantic protagonists, confronted with obstacles, retreat from the primary world. Two of the Athenian lovers, Hermia and Lysander, find themselves confronted by, and they wilfully oppose, three distinct kinds of obstacles: the law, the state, and the family. Hermia and Lysander wish to marry against the will of Hermia's father Egeus, against the advice of Duke Theseus, and in defiance of the abstract 'law of Athens', which, theoretically, transcends human desire, will, and judgement, which, Theseus says, 'by no means we may extenuate' (I.i.119–20). The two lovers do not try to outwit or to deceive Hermia's father, to circumvent the law of Athens, or to win each other through violence, vengeance, or heroics. They oppose these obstacles by devising a strategy of replacement, escape to somewhere beyond the reach of 'the sharp Athenian law' (l.162); they hope to find in a new location the liberating alternative to the restrictions of Athenian civilisation. The law of Athens deprives Hermia and Lysander of independence and autonomy; it considers Hermia no more than an object, a piece of property to be disposed of by Egeus:

> I beg the ancient privilege of Athens:
> As she is mine, I may dispose of her;
> Which shall be either to this gentleman,

> Or to her death, according to our law
> Immediately provided in that case;
> (I.i.41–5)

or, what may be worse, moulded by him:

> To you your father should be as a god;
> One that compos'd your beauties; yea, and one
> To whom you are but as a form in wax,
> By him imprinted, and within his power,
> To leave the figure, or disfigure it.
> (I.i.47–51)

Confronted by Egeus' will, neither Hermia's choice nor Lysander's qualities matter, for the law of Athens subordinates human qualities and subjective judgements to the abstract systems of hierarchy and possession within both family and state:

> For you, fair Hermia, look you arm yourself
> To fit your fancies to your father's will;
> Or else the law of Athens yields you up ...
> (I.i.117–19)

By escaping to the forest, the romantic protagonists attempt to replace an abstract, objective system with subjective, personal judgements, a 'father's voice' (l.54) with their own eyes.

But the play does not sustain these easy distinctions between youth and age, subjective and objective, liberation and restriction: these distinctions initiate the play but do not dominate it. The Athenian forest never becomes a second world, a version of pastoral. The initial association of the Athenian legal system with oppression and tyranny dissolves, and oppression reassembles *within* the forest, in a different, more personal, form. In the forest, subjective, internal oppositions replace and intensify the external obstacles that the protagonists had hoped to escape. Once Hermia and Lysander escape Athens and become ostensibly free to choose love with their own eyes, the vicissitudes of their subjective judgements become obstacles to romantic resolution; it is as if freedom to choose makes choice impossible. Once the lovers enter the forest, the supposed autonomy of love's judgements becomes reduced to pure mechanism; the play assigns the subjective judgements that the lovers think to be their own to an external source, the magic potion. Their own wills, that is, materialise as a specific external obstacle. By attributing the subjective judgements to an objectified, outside source, Shakespeare demonstrates a structural continuity between the forest and the court: without the fairy magic, the play would break down into worlds of objective and subjective oppression; the inclusion of an easily identifiable objective motive for the protagonists' supposedly subjective choices demonstrates that any supposedly private, subjective action (the choice of true love, for example) has objective, social contents, which escape from the codified, objective laws of everyday society does not negate. The forest allows the protagonists to escape the father's will and the law of Athens, but, as the magic potion indicates, an external authority controls the seemingly subjective choices that the lovers make in the forest – and afterwards.

This ambiguous quality of the forest in *A Midsummer Night's Dream* – as both alternative and repetition – does not appear when Lysander first proposes the escape from Athens. Lysander suggests that he and Hermia escape to the house of his 'widow aunt, a dowager,/Of great revenue' (I.i.157–8). Duke Theseus has already had his say about dowagers: in a gratuitous comparison, he has declared that the slowly waning old moon (he will not marry until 'four happy days bring in/Another moon', (ll.2–3) 'lingers my desire,/Like to a step-dame, or a dowager,/Long withering out a young man's revenue' (I.i.4–6). Shakespeare uses the word *dowager* twice in this scene; it occurs in none of his previous works, and it occurs in no other work on which he did not collaborate. But here the recurrence, with opposite connotations, of this unusual word indicates the extent to which Lysander and Theseus have opposite perceptions. The same force that metaphorically prevents Theseus's fulfilment and that deprives him of revenue to which he feels entitled appears to Lysander as a force that incorporates him into a financial, familial, and sexual community: 'And she respects me as her only son./There, gentle Hermia, may I marry thee' (ll.160–1). The perceptual opposition between the two men using *dowager* as a verbal bridge, crosses into a political opposition: Lysander proposes a liberating world, discontinuous with the laws of Theseus's dukedom; in Lysander's world one's social and familial superiors would accumulate wealth in order to bestow it, and elders would sanction rather than oppose his subjective decisions. In short, Lysander envisions a second world in which he and Hermia will be accepted by a benevolent, nurturing society.

Lysander's initial vision of the second-world alternative colours and tends to distort our perception of what he and Hermia actually accomplish by and during their retreat. Their attempt to escape to the dowager's, as we learn when we first see them in the forest, fails; Hermia is 'faint with wand'ring in the wood' because Lysander has 'forgot' their 'way' (II.ii.35–6). Shakespeare, in fact, confines their retreat to the forest, and keeps the forest within the reach of the Athenian social system. Hermia and Lysander escape to the same place where the fairies have gathered, 'come from the farthest steep of India' (II.i.69), to celebrate Theseus's wedding, the same place where the craftsmen have met to prepare for their participation in the Duke's wedding ceremony. The escape from Athenian law has led the lovers to the single place in the whole world most intensely concentrated on the confirmation and celebration of Athenian hierarchy and social custom; the forest to which the protagonists have retreated is dominated by the Athenian laws of degree and possession – the 'palace wood', 'the Duke's oak' (I.ii.101, 110).

While trying to get beyond one set of laws, the formal Athenian laws, the lovers – both couples – stay within the confines of social laws, the laws of decorum and propriety. Lysander's rival, Demetrius, suggests that now that he is outside the city, he is not bound by its laws, and that he therefore may rape the woman who pursues him, Helena:

> You do impeach your modesty too much,
> To leave the city and commit yourself
> Into the hands of one that loves you not;
> To trust the opportunity of night,
> And the ill counsel of a desert place,
> With the rich worth of your virginity.
> (II.i.214–19)

Helena replies, undaunted:

> Your virtue is my privilege.
> (l.220)

This is a telling exchange: Helena presumes that even beyond the codified legal system of the city an internalised code will govern and restrict Demetrius's behaviour; beneath her surface assumption runs the current of her own need. Despite her pursuit of Demetrius, she requires some kind of protection against physical ravishment, against violation of her internalised moral code.

Hermia and Lysander also have transported to the forest the system of Athenian moral convictions, and it is nearly their undoing. As they lie down to go to sleep in the forest, Hermia implores Lysander:

> But, gentle friend, for love and courtesy,
> Lie further off, in humane modesty;
> Such separation as may well be said
> Becomes a virtuous bachelor and a maid,
> So far be distant. . .
> (II.ii.56–60)

Lysander acquiesces. Moments later, Puck enters and misreads the empty space between the two lovers:

> Pretty soul, she durst not lie
> Near this lack-love, this kill-courtesy.
> (ll.76–7)

That is, the forest spirit can interpret the 'separation' only as one of antipathy; he has no sense of the transported city-manners that derive from an abstract moral and social convention that requires a physical separation between two lovers. Puck's failure to comprehend how real moral abstractions can be to the young Athenians, how the abstraction of social convention and the fear of moral censure can govern their sensual lives and experiences, almost destroys the romantic bond between the two.

The separation between the virtuous bachelor and the maid can be taken as a dramatic representation – an emblem – of the Athenian social code, which separates people from each other and from their senses and emotions. The separation correlates with the Athenian law and the father's will, both of which try to dictate and enforce the romantic responses of others, to replace subjective perception with external and imposed authority. The lovers flee Athens so as to win autonomy, but their actions remain systematic and codified, based on received ideas rather than on their own judgements, visions, or senses.[1] The strictest possible conventionality circumscribes the escape to the forest in *A Midsummer Night's Dream*, and thereby protects the forest, or the lovers in the forest, from sensuality. The lovers continually use language, especially the

language of pastoral and romantic convention, to protect themselves from sexual and violent physical encounters, and, by doing
so, they substitute an external system for their own perceptions.
While in the forest they reiterate, in a different form, the authoritarian social system that controls Athenian love.

In a sense, then, language and literary references function so as to
recreate, in the forest, the prohibitions expressed, at court, by the
laws of Athens: language keeps the lovers apart. This authoritarian
and restrictive function of language helps define the role of the
imagination in *A Midsummer Night's Dream*. As R. W. Dent has
argued, *A Midsummer Night's Dream,* again and again, seems to
draw our attention to 'the role of imagination in love and in art',
and to its own status as 'the product of Shakespeare's own imagination'; it does not follow, however, that the play offers us a 'disarm-
ingly unpretentious defence of poetry'.[2] Rather, as I shall try to
demonstrate, the play shows us the *use* of the imagination, the function of the imagination in society: throughout *A Midsummer
Night's Dream* the imagination has both a creative and a discrimi-
natory function. In *A Midsummer Night's Dream* the imagination,
by enforcing separation, asserts and creates a distance between the
self and the other, and thereby it protects the self and creates an implicit hierarchy: the separation between the self and the other has
an ideological as well as a protective and conventional function.
Initially, the lovers use the imagination to deny the sensual reality
of one another and thereby to incorporate the Athenian prohibitions into their own judgements; later, when the entire act of retreat
has been reincorporated into Athenian aristocratic society, the aristocracy itself uses the imagination to establish an hierarchical separation between itself and the other social classes that constitute
Athenian society. In fact, the imagination, and not the forest, functions in *A Midsummer Night's Dream* as the second world: it expresses particular interests, initially personal and later class, as if
they were universal interests and it protects those interests against
the interests of others.

Language, as it isolates the lovers from one another and perverts
their rebellious actions, works to keep the Athenian laws and conventions intact. From the outset, language forces Hermia and
Lysander to work against their own best interests and thereby to
keep their escape within the reach of Athenian convention: they
'unfold' their 'minds' to Helena, giving their private compact a
public status, making it a story, and immeasurably increasing the

likelihood of their being intercepted. Helena repeats and thereby emphasises this tendency to use language so as to ensure the failure of one's actions when she departs vowing to tell Demetrius of Hermia's plan:

> Then to the wood will he to-morrow night
> Pursue her; and for this intelligence
> If I have thanks, it is a dear expense.
> (I.i.247–9)

Helena quite obviously acts against her own best interests, in so far as her interests are identical with winning Demetrius; her real interests, however, may be more complex, may not all be conscious. In the same action with which she wilfully imposes an obstacle between herself and Demetrius, she also restores the verbal contents of her love for Demetrius. For Helena, 'love looks not with the eyes but with the mind' (l.234), and consequently she laments the loss of a verbal rather than a physical Demetrius; whereas Hermia, she thinks, has a physical relationship ('heat', 'melt') to Demetrius, Helena remembers her own relationship to Demetrius in terms of language, of 'oaths':

> For ere Demetrius look'd on Hermia's eyne,
> He hail'd down oaths that he was only mine;
> And when this hail some heat from Hermia felt,
> So he dissolv'd, and show'rs of oaths did melt.
> (I.i.242–5)

In going to 'tell him of fair Hermia's flight' (l.246), Helena restores the verbal or the narrative aspect of her dissolved love affair with Demetrius: she replaces the lost physical love with words.

Likewise, Hermia and Lysander experience love as a literary process; when they talk of love they talk not of each other but of what they have read. Lysander's lamentation, which introduces the plan to escape from Athens, derives from his consciousness not of love, but of narratives about love:

> Ay me! for aught that I could ever read,
> Could ever hear by tale or history,
> The course of true love never did run smooth . . .
> (I.i.132–4)

The lovers are so aware of language that they have no awareness of one another. Hermia and Lysander spend most of the first scene talking at cross-purposes: Lysander inverts Hermia's stoical argument ('Then let us teach our trial patience', l.152) into an invitation to run away ('A good persuasion; therefore hear me, Hermia . . . Steal forth thy father's house to-morrow night', ll.156; 164): Lysander takes Hermia's assurance 'by all the vows that ever men have broke' (l.175) as a 'promise' (l.179). Language freezes into the formulae of literary convention and thereby turns into an object; once this process begins, once the characters use language as a thing instead of as a medium, language becomes a barrier between the lovers rather than a means of communication.

The isolation imposed by language becomes more rigid and more obvious once the lovers reach the forest; there, acts of the imagination, absorption in literary style, become so predominant that the characters perceive one another as verbal beings, repositories of literary convention. When Lysander wakes up, charmed into loving Helena, he looks at her eyes and sees not physical beauty, but literature:

> Reasons becomes the marshal to my will,
> And leads me to your eyes, where I o'erlook
> Love's stories written in Love's richest book.
> (II.ii.120–2)

Demetrius awakens into a set of Petrarchan and pseudo-classical conventions:

> O Helen, goddess, nymph, perfect, divine!
> To what, my love, shall I compare thine eyne?
> Crystal is muddy. O, how ripe in show
> Thy lips, those kissing cherries, tempting grow!
> That pure congealed white, high Taurus' snow,
> Fann'd with the eastern wind, turns to a crow
> When thou hold'st up thy hand.
> (III.ii.137–43)

Hermia, similarly, perceives Lysander as only a collection of words. She makes Lysander's 'lying' pun ('Then by your side no bed-room me deny;/For lying so, Hermia, I do not lie', II.ii.51–2) into a real crux. By making him 'lie further off', Hermia forces Lysander to adopt the alternative sense of 'lying'; in forcing him to adopt the rhetorical rather than the physical sense of the verb *to lie*, she reduces his language to verbal mechanism, to pretty riddling ... .

Language continually intervenes within the couples, or the couplings; just as language replaces sex between lovers, so language replaces violence between rivals. Lysander's rivalry, from the first, is with the word *Demetrius:*

> Where is Demetrius? O, how fit a word
> Is that vile name to perish on my sword!
> (II.ii.106–7)

Language ensures that Lysander and Demetrius fight without physical violence; in their linguistic frenzy the opposition between speech and action conveniently dissolves. Speech seems to stimulate violent action:

> **Lysander** I swear by that which I will lose for thee,
>   To prove him false that says I love thee not.
> **Demetrius** I say I love thee more than he can do,
> **Lysander** If thou say so, withdraw, and prove it too.
> (III.ii.252–5)

When they go off 'cheek by jowl' to fight each other, however, language obstructs or protects them, separates them, because they follow Puck's words rather than each other's bodies.

With his disembodied voice, Puck keeps the rivals physically separated. Yet his verbal intervention constitutes more than a mechanical and comic plot device for breaking up the fight. Throughout the play, language, especially conventional literary formulation, protects each of the lovers from physical violence and from sexual aggression. When the verbal intervention fails as protection, when the lovers *think* they have come nearest to assaulting one another, the lovers in fact have directed their violence toward language itself, or toward a figuration of disembodied language: they run through the woods in pursuit of Puck's words. Their attack on language succeeds in every way: the night in the forest ends with each of the four lovers safe, separate, and in silence.

'I WILL OVERBEAR YOUR WILL' Theseus

The lovers wake up in very unusual circumstances. The leading figure of primary-world authority hovers over them, asking them to explain their actions, to explain the 'concord' ostensibly achieved during their absence from Athens. But the authority figure does not appear harsh and recriminating; he has relinquished his strict adherence to, or administration of, the abstract structure of authority, the laws of the state. Because the lovers have externalised or purged their fears and hatreds during the verbal chaos and literary excesses of the night in the forest, they seem to have achieved a new harmony, a 'gentle concord', not just as couples but among one another and within each one's psyche. This achieved concord has, apparently, a sympathetic effect, 'in the world' (IV.i.143): the will of the Duke reverses so as to certify, rather than to obstruct, the romantic resolutions that the young protagonists have achieved and had thrust upon them. Authority joins with youth to reject the irrational will of the old man:

> Fair lovers, you are fortunately met;
> Of this discourse we more will hear anon.
> Egeus I will overbear your will;
> For in the temple, by and by, with us
> These couples shall eternally be knit.
> (IV.i.177–81)

Confronted with this unusually optimistic modification of the Plautine comic model, we might ask of Shakespeare, with Theseus, 'how comes this gentle concord in the world?' To understand the process of this resolution, we must place the romance aspect of *A Midsummer Night's Dream* within the wider social and imaginative context through which it develops.The flight to the forest, which when isolated as a pattern or a structure seems to be a direct challenge of or opposition to authority, to the autonomy of the state, remains very close, metaphorically and dramatically, to the paramount ruling-class consciousness in the play, the Duke's. In this sense, the pattern of rebellion against established order, fundamental to the Plautine model, has here been turned into its opposite; youth runs away so as to confirm or reaffirm the stability of the social order. It is important to realise that the flight to the forest, in some ways, satisfies Duke Theseus's needs and helps solidify his position as a figure of social authority.

The conjunction between the flight to the forest and Duke Theseus's consciousness appears in the first few passages in the play. Anticipating his marriage four days hence to Hippolyta, Theseus commands his master of the revels, Philostrate, to:

> Stir up Athenian youth to merriments,
> Awake the pert and nimble spirit of mirth,
> Turn melancholy forth to funerals:
> The pale companion is not for our pomp.
>   (I.i.12–15)

Philostrate exits, not having said a word; four lines later, enough time to allow for a very quick doubling of parts, Egeus enters, with Hermia, Lysander, and Demetrius in tow, to present his 'complaint' to the Duke. The entire pastoral romance that Egeus' entry introduces responds, in a sense, to Theseus's call for merriment and enacts an intrinsic dramatic function subordinate to the Duke's call for pomp, triumph, and revelling (l.19). We can intensify and confirm this sense if we compare Act V with Act I: in Act V Theseus reiterates the call for revelry and entertainment to fill up the time before the consummation of his marriage:

> Come now; what masques, what dances shall we have,
> To wear away this long age of three hours
> Between [our] after-supper and bed-time?
> Where is our usual manager of mirth?
> What revels are in hand? Is there no play
> To ease the anguish of a torturing hour?
> Call Philostrate.
>   (V.i.32–8)

Theseus's psychological need and his strategic response to that need are repeated almost precisely: throughout the play Theseus uses art, acts of the imagination, to secure his own autonomy. His call for entertainment reduces the episode of the four lovers to the dramatic status of an interlude, an entertainment. In so far as the lovers have autonomy, this reduction cannot quite be justified, but Theseus's strategy partially aims to reduce and to incorporate what autonomy the lovers do have. From Theseus's point of view – the point of view that the play enforces – the pastoral retreat, like the masque of 'Pyramus and Thisbe', emphasises and secures the social status of the Athenian ruling class. The entire retreat to the forest, framed by Theseus's call for entertainment and his magnanimous transcendence of the law, functions in the first part of the play, as 'Pyramus and Thisbe' will in the second, as an aesthetic act.

Neither aesthetic act, however, exists in isolation; rather, both fulfil important functions in Duke Theseus's civic strategy, his administration of the state. Theseus declares explicitly that his wedding celebration will use aesthetics, another 'key', to gloss over the violent and destructive aspects of his history:

> Hippolyta, I woo'd thee with my sword,
> And won thy love doing thee injuries;
> But I will wed thee in another key,
> With pomp, with triumph, and with revelling.
> (I.i.16–19)

The wedding and its attendant celebrations will constitute a complete substitution, replacement of physical violence with aesthetic forms and with the organised rituals and institutions of civilised behaviour. Theseus shows the same attitude of mind in the famous scene during which he describes his hounds to Hippolyta. Theseus shows more concern for aesthetic qualities – appearance and, especially, tone – and for breeding lines than for the hunting ability, the capacity to inflict injury; the hounds are 'slow in pursuit; but match'd in mouth like bells,/Each under each' (IV.i.123–4). Theseus, it seems, has a heightened aesthetic sensibility, but Theseus's keen awareness of the power of beauty always has elements of what Howard Nemerov calls the 'administrative' attitude toward art (p. 636).[3] Theseus's aesthetics always appears as a conventional replacement of destructive human impulses, and as such forms a strategy by which he can replace disquietude with civil harmony. He facilitates the interrupted Plautine comedy as another of his opportunities to replace injury with civilisation.

Theseus's sense of beauty restates that of the four lovers, but in a broader context. The lovers use literary convention to contain their own private sexual and violent drives, to replace consciousness of another's body with an exaggerated consciousness of language. Theseus applies this strategy to society at large: he both incorporates and objectifies the process of aristocratic rebellion enacted by the lovers in that he translates the political process of rebellion against his authority into an aesthetic act, a revel. In doing so Theseus takes the potential divisions that threaten the civil peace of his society and the autonomy of his class and makes division an aspect of a larger harmony and consistency. This at once reduces the challenge to Athenian law to an act of style and gesture, an aesthetic distraction, while it also subsumes the challenge within a process that ultimately negates the need for rebellion. We could almost say, with C. L. Barber, that the rebellion against the law momentarily releases and ultimately clarifies the law, but, as usual, Barber's formulation, ignoring the class contents of the rebellion, the way in which the rebellion serves the needs of only the ruling class, misses the social context for the resolution.[4] Because the escape from Athens remains consistently within the aesthetic limitations imposed by Duke Theseus, the final clarification renews the autonomy of the Duke and confirms the 'natural' status of the Athenian social structure. The rebellion against the law, that is, stays separate from rebellion against the Duke, so that, once the law is clarified, the Duke can absorb back into the social system, without moral compromise and without relinquishing his autonomy, those aristocrats whose actions rebelled against the law. An autonomous figure of authority comprehends the turbulence, unrestraint, and whimsicality of the release/clarification movement in *A Midsummer Night's Dream*. It is therefore misleading and selective to say that *A Midsummer Night's Dream* releases society from the traditional structure of authority and degree; in fact, authority itself releases and then reabsorbs the aristocratic protagonists so as to incorporate both sides of the holiday/everyday opposition into its administration of the state.

Although I have spoken rather abstractly about 'authority', in *A Midsummer Night's Dream* authority seems almost indistinguishable from Duke Theseus: he is its agent, he bodies forth the abstract concept ... . Theseus never rests in this position of subordination: initially he established himself as a mere administrator of the law, but when he concludes the imaginative interlude and reabsorbs the aristocratic rebellion into his own consciousness – 'with us/These couples shall eternally be knit' – he also subordinates the law to his subjective will, to his autonomy. The establishment of civilised order in Athens depends on the incorporation of authority into the subjective will of a single individual: Theseus withdraws the sentence, but the law itself does not change. Concord occurs when the figure of authority replaces the objective restrictions of the civil code with the benevolence of his own subjective will. The imaginative interlude in the forest concludes by identifying the feeling of concord and liberation with a complete dependence on Duke Theseus's autonomy.

'TO TAKE WHAT THEY MISTAKE' Craftsmen and Fairies

... In *A Midsummer Night's Dream*, nature, the conditions of the forest, neither passively reflects the needs of the protagonists nor autonomously imposes its own everyday aspect on their wills. Because the retreat to nature initiated by the romantic protagonists dissolves into the will of the primary–world authority figure, the state of nature in the forest never permits true independence from the forces of authority. Pastoral romance uses retreat to explore, from within the aristocratic consciousness, the relation between subjective will and nature, but in A Midsummer Night's Dream the pastoral retreat explores the relation between authority – not autonomy – and nature. Nature, in a sense, has become an active creation of the mind of the primary-world authority figure, Duke Theseus, and the romantic protagonists assume the role of passive recipients of the action: they let nature act upon and express itself through them.

While nature acts upon them, the protagonists in A Midsummer Night's Dream remain unaware of nature: just as language intervenes to protect them from consciousness of one another's bodies and to prevent physical violence, the excessive attention to style inhibits the lovers' sensory awareness of their environment. They show such attention to the nuances of one another's words and of the alterations in their own feelings that they never emerge from the closed circuit of pursuit, rejection, and jealously that they establish in Athens and transport to the forest. Moreover, other components of the traditional pastoral vision present in the forest never take on the traditional pastoral associations in that they do not engage with the second-world aristocratic consciousness in any reciprocal way. Retreat to a second-world depends on and requires both the autonomy of one class, or group of characters, and the subordination of another class: the aristocratic leisure derives from others' labour. Within the forest itself, A Midsummer Night's Dream contains in rudimentary form both the autonomous and the subordinate groups: the fairies, as Barber has remarked, function very much like pastoral shepherds although without the labour of tending flock; the craftsmen function as a coarsened version of a class of servants, although they have no direct association with the aristocrats when within the forest. Both of these quasi-pastoral groups, however, retain explicit ties to the authoritarian structure that, according to the traditional pastoral form or formula, the protagonists would reject by retreating to the forest. In A Midsummer Night's Dream the craftsmen and the fairies, like the protagonists themselves, function as further extension and development of the primary-world, authoritarian consciousness. The pastoral components never cohere into a single autonomous pastoral structure that could work as an antithesis to the primary world. The comprehensiveness of the primary world, the ability of the laws, codes, and authority figures in Athens, to control and determine the romantic protagonists' subjective wills, prevents the lovers' use of the forest as a strategy, a separate location in time and space within which to assert their autonomy.

Because Athenian society circumscribes and controls the forest, the fairies and the craftsmen directly serve the psychological and political needs not of the romantic or pastoral protagonists but of the primary-world ruling class: they help establish the relation between man and nature in such a way as to secure the authority of Theseus and Hippolyta over the complete range of Athenian civilisation. Principally, the fairies serve the needs of the Athenian ruling class by their presupposition that nature certifies the hierarchical values, the dependence on degree and on the absolute subordination of subservients, on which the Duke's authority depends. The fairies repeat the Duke's values, his concern with authority, in an exaggerated form. Titania's court, especially, apotheosises service and obedience: the Queen of the fairies is always accompanied by at least four attendants who solely function to envelop Titania with a protective circle of song and dance. The attendant fairies demonstrate pure service; they initiate no action whatever, but speak and act only in response to Titania's (and later, Bottom's) requests for action:

> Come, now a roundel and a fairy song;
> Then, for the third part of a minute, hence, ...
> (II.ii.1–2)

or:

> Nod to him, elves, and do him courtesies.
> (III.ii.174)

In short, with their ritualistic chanting ('Ready./And I./And I./And I./Where shall we go?', III.ii.163; 'Hail, mortal!/Hail!/Hail!/Hail!/', ll.175–8) they provide the fairy queen's court with a standard of adoring, even idolatrous, service to a central authority figure.

Obviously a more complex and spontaneous character, Puck serves the King of the fairies, perhaps as a court jester of sorts (II.i.44), although he does not behave with such idolatry, with such dependence on his master's will. Puck, 'that merry wanderer of the night', (II.i.43), can act and judge independently; in fact, precisely because Oberon entrusts him with some autonomy he mistakes one Athenian for another. Puck's wanderings remain to an extent distinguished from those of the fairy whom he queries 'whither wander you?' (l.1); the fairy's wanderings directly conjoin with his (her?) service to Titania:

> I do wander every where
> Swifter than the moon's sphere;
> And I serve the Fairy Queen,
> To dew her orbs upon the green.
>   (II.i.6–9)

But Puck's relative autonomy, by indirection, reinforces the theme of servility; his service to Oberon results not from the incapacity of his own personality but from a voluntary and a 'natural' bond. Puck, enthusiastically, responds with complete subjection to each of Oberon's commands:

> I'll put a girdle round about the earth
> In forty minutes;
>   (II.i.175–6)

and:

> Fear not, my lord! your servant shall do so,
>   (II.i.268)

and:

> I go, I go, look how I go,
> Swifter than arrow from the Tartar's bow,
>   (III.ii.100–1)

and:

> Up and down, up and down,
> I will lead them up and down.
>   (III.ii.396–7)

... A Midsummer Night's Dream creates a vision of nature in which others do not or cannot resist impositions on their will: the ruling class projects its fantasies of mastery – or, more accurately, of devoted service – on to the forest spirits, who command obedience from their subordinates and who use the ecology of nature to control permanently the will of the romantic protagonists.

As their second function, also in some ways an obvious one, the fairies establish a cosmologic sympathy between the forces of nature and the actions and passions of the ruling class. On one level the turbulence in nature, which Titania describes –

> Therefore the winds, piping to us in vain,
> As in revenge, have suck'd up from the sea
> Contagious fogs; ...
>   (II.i.88–114)

– seem to derive directly from the 'forgeries of jealousy' (l.81) between Titania and Oberon:

> And this same progeny of evils comes
> From our debate, from our dissension;
> We are their parents and original.
>   (II.i.115–17)

The jealousy ostensibly concerns Titania's retention of a boy whom 'jealous Oberon would have ... / Knight of his train, to trace the forests wild', (ll.24–5); the love Oberon and Titania have for Hippolyta and Theseus also taints the jealousy:

> **Titania** Why art thou here
>   Come from the farthest steep of India?
>   But that, forsooth, the bouncing Amazon,
>   Your buskin'd mistress, and your warrior love,
>   To Theseus must be wedded, and you come
>   To give their bed joy and prosperity.
> **Oberon** How canst thou thus for shame, Titania,
>   Glance at my credit with Hippolyta,
>   Knowing I know thy love to Theseus?
>   (II.i.68–76)

The suggestion of an erotic connection between the rulers of the fairy world and the rulers of Athens transforms the fairies into spiritual manifestations of the sexual drives of Theseus and Hippolyta: Titania represents in the realm of spirit Theseus's physical desire, held in abeyance during the four-day interval before the wedding, for Hippolyta; Oberon represents Hippolyta's desire for Theseus. The destructive jealousy with which Oberon and Titania confront each other replaces, then, the injury, the actual martial opposition between their two races, with which Theseus 'woo'd' Hippolyta. The correspondence of the discord between Oberon and Titania to the disorder in nature has, by extension, flattering and imperial implications for the fairies' mortal counterparts, Theseus and Hippolyta: it implies that the conflict between their nations disrupted the entire natural world, and, further, that by introducing another 'key', by bringing harmony to their people through marriage, they can restore harmony and order to the world of nature. Here, of course, Shakespeare dramatises or expresses one of the central concepts in the 'Elizabethan World Picture'. The inclusion of the idea of correspondence here in *A Midsummer Night's Dream* does not mean, however, that Shakespeare took the picture at face value; rather, it further indicates Shakespeare's understanding of the strategies used by the ruling class to justify its power and its retention of centralised authority through hypothetical analogy with the forces of nature.

Whereas most versions of pastoral use the protagonists to separate nature from the state, to find a life in nature and independent of hierarchic authority that characterises the primary world, the presence in *A Midsummer Night's Dream* of the fairies as dominating forces within the forest completely dissolves the expected pastoral oppositions. Here, the state permeates and controls nature. The supposedly autonomous actions with which the romantic protagonists – and, in addition, Titania – express erotic desire come directly underneath control of the spiritual counterpart (Oberon) to the figure of authority in the state (Theseus). The predominant force in the play becomes not Theseus himself, but an aspect of Theseus, his spirit manifested in Oberon. The authoritarian principle, transformed into pure spirit, controls nature, uses nature to impose an order and direction on the seemingly irrational and preposterous behaviour of the youthful Athenians. *A Midsummer Night's Dream* dissolves pastoral retreat and sexual rebellion into a ritualistic acceptance of the principle of authority; those released from Oberon's magical control submit to voluntary control by deferring to authoritarian predominance. Hippolyta, after relinquishing the changeling boy, takes hands in a stylised dance with Oberon (IV.i.84–102); the Athenian lovers follow Theseus and Hippolyta 'to the temple' (ll.194–9). At the end of the play the lovers get what they wanted in the first place, but they do so in such a way as to confirm Theseus's authority and Oberon's capabilities: Theseus gets to 'extenuate' the laws of Athens and to overbear Egeus' will; Oberon overbears Demetrius's will.

The complete predominance of Oberon, his instrumental role in bringing resolution to the dramatic antagonisms and oppositions, keeps nature separate not from the state but from those who cannot or will not submit to the supposedly 'natural' forces of ruling-class authority. Nature, that is, joins with the state to transform retreat into an acquiesence to authority by imposing an order on the anarchic and apparently whimsical behaviour of all of the lovers. Like the structure of the state, the imposed order is systemic: the 'reasons' behind the erotic choices of the lovers do not appear to those who choose or are chosen, whereas to those on stage and in the audience who can see the entire system of choice – free will and enforced will – operating, the reasons for the particular choices and the motive for the imposition of such choices are evident. In isolation, the lovers' actions seem discordant: thus Puck considers 'what fools these mortals be!' (III.ii.115). As part of a system, the lovers' actions cohere into a strategy for authoritarian predominance over second-world consciousness and for transforming nature into an instrument of spirit. Through the ministrations of Puck, Oberon exercises exclusive power over nature and, consequently, over those living within nature. Because of his predominant control over nature, Oberon's (and Puck's) ritualistic language can bring about changes in the natural world, whereas the ritualistic language of others, both fairies and mortals, acts merely as rhetoric, decoration. ...

The pastoral movement in *A Midsummer Night's Dream* demonstrates, then, that taking an active and independent role in relation to authority – either retreating to nature or expressing one's own nature through erotic love – places one in a subordinate position to the spiritual forces active within nature. The characters can only achieve their subjective desires and, in that sense, transcend social and legal restrictions, by submitting their wills to the predominant authority-figure in both the primary and second worlds. This movement includes the fantasy that one can act neither upon nature nor on the social structure that the hierarchy of nature justifies. The spirits within nature act upon and change – even physically transform – the characters; the characters become the objects of nature, and cannot become subjects who will change nature. All of those in opposition to the official will of authority find that they cannot use language, retreat, or physical force to impose their independent choices on the natural world: they resist the state in order to have their subjective wills reincorporated, through the agency of nature,

into the will of the authority figure. Nature has a systemic correspondence to established human society, and as such it always
resists the active human will to change.

Their enforced passive roles as objects of natural forces reduce
the autonomy of the young aristocrats in order to reincorporate
them, without resistance of their independent wills, into the ruling
class. The passive relation to nature has the opposite effect,
however, on the craftsmen: because nature has an autonomous and
active role in regard to human society, the craftsmen are reduced in
importance and kept carefully subordinate to the ruling class. By
enacting their trades – carpenter, tailor, joiner, weaver, bellows-
mender, tinker – the craftsmen ought ordinarily to change or
control nature, or, in the Marxist sense, create nature by bringing it
within the control of human society and commerce. In *A
Midsummer Night's Dream* the craftsmen are consciously separated
from their crafts, in part because the play occurs during a proclaimed period of revelry. But in part the distinction between occu-
pation and dramatic or aesthetic function helps us understand the
significance and the use of nature in the play. The craftsmen, more
than any of the other characters in the play, become and are treated
as objects of nature: Puck refers to them, with a term unfortunately
adopted by many critics, as 'rude mechanicals', an epithet that
objectifies the men and abstracts human skill from their work.
Whereas nature manipulates the wills of the aristocrats and the
fairy queen, it transforms Bottom's body; nature uses Bottom as a
physical object, material substance for the fairy magic. Further,
nature objectifies the others so as to serve their own erotic interests,
whereas nature objectifies Bottom so as to use him in Oberon's plot
against Titania. Bottom's transformation, that is, serves no end for
Bottom himself, even though he experiences it after the fact as a
mystical vision; Bottom's change serves only to facilitate the recon-
ciliations of those with superior social status, the King and Queen
of the fairies and, by correspondent extension, Theseus and
Hippolyta.

Deprived of the technological control over nature implicit in their
occupations, the craftsmen perform an abstract form of labour 'in
their minds' (V.i.73); that is, they attempt to adopt the aristocratic
attitude toward nature, to control violence and passion through the
interpolation of the imagination, of rhetorical and verbal acts.
Bottom, unwilling to 'leave the killing out' of their play, declares:

> I have a device to make all well. Write me a prologue, and let the prologue seem to say we will do no harm with our swords, and that Pyramus is not kill'd indeed ... .
>
> (III.i.14,16–19)

So that the ladies will not be 'afeard of the lion', the actor who plays the part:

> must speak through, saying thus, or to the same defect: 'Ladies', or 'Fair ladies, I would wish you', or 'I would request you', or 'I would entreat you, not to fear, not to tremble: my life for yours'.
>
> (III.i.38–42)

Not only do the craftsmen attempt to replace violence with language, they plan to use language to recreate natural phenomena. Instead of bringing moonlight to their production by leaving 'a casement of the great chamber window (where we play) open; and the moon may shine in at the casement', they decide that 'one must come in with a bush of thorns and a lantern, and say he comes to disfigure, or to present, the person of Moonshine', (ll.56–61).

Each verbal interpolation, although comic in itself, occurs within a social context from which we should not isolate it: within the boundaries of *A Midsummer Night's Dream*, the craftsmen only serve to entertain and to divert the aristocracy. Consequently one cannot speak of any relation established in the play between the craftsmen and nature independent of the relation, the relation of use, established between the craftsmen and either the Athenian aristocracy or its spirit counterparts. The hilarity of the craftsmen's ineffective attempts to control nature through language measures the craftsmen's dependence on aristocratic patronage: the play furthers the aristocracy's fantasy of its absolute social predominance by replacing the craftsmen's physical control of nature in the performance of their work with their inept verbal control of nature in an artistic performance. This substitution removes from the craftsmen all of their implicit self-sufficiency as labourers and inverts the structure of the state: the state should depend on its foundation, those who work within the state and whose work creates the surplus and leisure time for those who rule. Here, with the craftsmen separated from the technical aspect of their work, they expect to thrive not on the objective, material products that they produce

but on the pleasure that their aesthetic actions elicit from the aristocratic audience:

> If our sport had gone forward, we had all been made men ... . O
> sweet bully Bottom! Thus hath he lost sixpence a day during his life;
> he could not have scap'd sixpence a day. And the Duke had not
> given him sixpence a day for playing Pyramus, I'll be hang'd.
>
> (IV.ii.17–23)

The craftsmen can be 'made men' only as a direct consequence of
their subservience to the ruling class and of the suppression of their
autonomy in the dramatic roles they play in 'Pyramus and Thisbe'.

The craftsmen, in effect, get incorporated into the ruling-class
vision of society by exclusion from and reification by the ruling
class. Correspondent to aristocratic fantasies that the spiritual
world and the world of nature – the second world – confirm the
hierarchical vision of society arises the fantasy that no actions taken
within the primary world can have any intrinsic function or
purpose, that all primary-world actions derive significance and
motive from the need to offer service to the ruling class.

From Elliot Krieger, *A Marxist Study of Shakespeare's Comedies*
(London, 1979), pp. 37–61.

NOTES

[What is presented here as a self-contained essay is actually abstracted from
a somewhat longer chapter, which itself is integral to Elliot Krieger's book.
Trimming of the chapter (to conserve space) has been confined largely to
passages which introduce comparisons with other plays, not entirely relevant to this volume, to a few quotations which merely reiterate points
already well established, and to a final section ('Harmony'), much of which
is devoted to placing Krieger's own Marxist critique in relation to the arguments of earlier writers, most of whom had evaded the social and political
particularities of the Shakespearean text. Krieger is conventionally Marxist
in insisting that the nature of aristocratic power, and the ramifications of
class struggle, are the central concerns of the text (whatever the ostensible
subject of the plot), and also in his determination to examine sympatheti-
cally the condition of the Athenian/Elizabethan workers – not to treat them
merely as comic butts, as the aristocrats in the play, and so many traditional critics, are inclined to do, lumping them together in Puck's dismissive
phrase as 'rude mechanicals'. But he is ahead of his time in arguing that
power operates as much through the imaginations and subjectivities of the

governed as through the wealth and physical force of those who govern – hence his perception that the lovers never really escape from Theseus's power in the woods outside Athens, but reconstitute it in different terms. These are not precisely the formulations of modern subjectivity articulated by Michel Foucault (in works as various as *Madness and Civilisation: A History of Insanity in the Age of Reason,* tr. R. Howard [London, 1971], and *Discipline and Punish: The Birth of the Prison* [Harmondworth, 1979]), but they are adjacent to them. In this respect the essay is clearly a precursor of Louis Adrian Montrose's New Historicist essay, '"Shaping Fantasies"', later in this volume. Ed.]

1. R. Girard's discussion of 'mediated desire' in his *Violence and the Sacred,* tr. P. Gregory (1972; rpt. Baltimore, MD, 1977), has influenced my thinking here about the Athenian lovers.

2. R. W. Dent, 'Imagination in *A Midsummer Night's Dream',* *Shakespeare Quarterly,* 15 (1964), 115–29.

3. H. Nemerov, 'The Marriage of Theseus and Hippolyta', *Kenyon Review,* 18 (1956), 633–41.

4. C. L. Barber, *Shakespeare's Festive Comedy* (1959; rpt. Cleveland, 1963), p. 170.

3

Hermia's Dream

NORMAN N. HOLLAND

> Literature is a dream dreamed for us.
> (*The Dynamics of Literary Response*, 1968)

What could be more imaginary than a dream of a dream of a dream? Yet Hermia's dream is just that in *A Midsummer Night's Dream*. She dreams but later decides she was dreaming that she dreamed. Then, at the very end of the play, we, the audience, are told: 'You have but slumb'red here'; we dreamed that she dreamed that she dreamed.

A dream of a dream of a dream – surely this is what the comedy means when it tells how:

> ... as imagination bodies forth
> The forms of things unknown, the poet's pen
> Turns them to shapes, and gives to aery nothing
> A local habitation and a name.
> (V.i.14–17)[1]

The psychoanalyst and the literary critic do the same. In our effort to give imaginary dreams a local habitation and a name, those of us who use psychoanalysis to talk about literature have historically used several different approaches. The first is typical of the first phase of psychoanalysis: we would use Hermia's dream as an illustration of someone's unconscious made conscious. In the second phase, we would place her dream within a system of ego functions. Finally – today – we would use this airy nothing to symbolise ourselves to ourselves.

For the moment, though, let me go back to the circumstances that lead up to Hermia's dream. At the opening of the play, Duke Theseus hears a plea from Hermia's father, Egeus. Egeus wants the Duke to force Hermia to marry Demetrius, who loves Hermia and has the approval of Egeus. Hermia, however, loves Lysander, and he loves Hermia. Theseus nevertheless agrees with Egeus and promises to enforce the law of Athens, which provides that Hermia must either marry the man her father has chosen, or die, or vow to live the rest of her life as a nun, abjuring forever the society of men. This was a dreadful fate for a young lady even in Elizabethan times, but perhaps not so bad a fate when you see what men were available.

Hermia and Lysander decide that the best way to cope with this decree is to run away from Athens. They do so, but Lysander gets lost and Hermia becomes exhausted from wandering in the wood. They sleep and Hermia has her dream.

When we first hear the dream, it is still going on. That is, I think she is still dreaming when she first speaks about it. As with so many nightmares, she is having trouble waking:

> Help me, Lysander, help me! do thy best
> To pluck this crawling serpent from my breast!
> Ay me, for pity!

And only now, I think, is she beginning to come out of it:

> Ay me, for pity! what a dream was here!
> Lysander, look how I do quake with fear.
> Methought a serpent eat my heart away,
> And you sate smiling at his cruel prey.
> Lysander! what, remov'd? Lysander! lord!
> What, out of hearing gone? No sound, no word?
> Alack, where are you? Speak, and if you hear!
> Speak, of all loves! I swoon almost with fear.
> No? Then I well perceive you are not nigh.
> Either death, or you, I'll find immediately.
>   (II.ii.145–56)

In effect, as Hermia tells the dream, she splits it into two parts. In the first, we hear the dream actually taking place. In the second, Hermia reports the dream to us after it is over. In the first part she makes a plea for help, but in the second we learn that Lysander wasn't interested in helping at all – he was just smiling and watching the serpent eat Hermia. Further, if we take the most obvious Freudian meaning for that serpent – a penis or phallus – the masculinity in the dream is split between the attacking, crawling serpent and her lover Lysander, smiling at a distance.

Among the fifty-one topics Erikson suggest considering in a full dream analysis, let me be merciful and select just one: 'methods of defence, denial, and distortion', which might be considered a variation on another topic, 'mechanisms of defence', itself a subtopic of 'ego identity and lifeplan'.[2] I see in this dream something I think is fundamental to Hermia's character.

If I go back to the first things Hermia says and look just at her speeches as an actor would, I see a recurring pattern.[3] After hearing her father, Theseus admonishes her, 'Demetrius is a worthy gentleman', and Hermia replies with her first words in the play, 'So is Lysander' (an alternative). But, replies Theseus, since Demetrius has your father's approval, he 'must be held the worthier'. 'I would my father look'd but with my eyes', answers Hermia. Next she begins a long speech by begging Theseus' pardon, wondering why she is bold, and worrying lest, by revealing her thoughts, she impeach her modesty. But, she says:

> ... I beseech your Grace that I may know
> The worst that may befall me in this case,
> If I refuse to wed Demetrius.
> (I.i.62–4)

I hear in all these speeches a distinct, recurring pattern. Call it a concern for alternatives, for other possibilities, or for an elsewhere: Lysander as alternative to Demetrius, her judgement as an alternative to her father's, her boldness contrasted with her modesty, or the alternatives the law allows her. We could say that Hermia's personal style or character consists (in the theoretical language of Heinz Kohut) of creating self-objects.[4] Thus, after her dialogue with Theseus, the lovers are left alone, and Hermia uses a variety of examples and legends from the elsewhere of classical mythology to illustrate and buttress their love. Then, to Helena, who loves Demetrius, she describes how she and Lysander will run away, again looking for an elsewhere, an alternative to Athens: 'To seek new friends and stranger companies.' I would phrase Hermia's personal style as the seeking of some alternative in order to amend something closer to herself.

Her last speeches as well as her first show this sense of alternatives. Theseus, Egeus, and the rest have come upon the lovers and wakened them. However, the lovers are not sure they aren't still dreaming. Says Hermia:

> Methinks I see these things with parted eye,
> When every thing seems double.
> (IV.i.189–90)

Demetrius starts checking reality and asks: 'Do you not think/The Duke was here, and bid us follow him?' And Hermia, for her last word in the play, offers one final alternative: 'Yea, and my father.'[5]

Her dream dramatises her 'parted eye' in all its divisions, in the double telling, in the here and there of Lysander and the serpent, and in the very content of the dream – her effort to save herself by getting the serpent away and bringing Lysander closer. I think I could show the same theme of amendment by alternative if I were to trace through the dream the various levels of this adolescent girl's development: oedipal, phallic, anal, and oral.

Following the symbols (like that snake) and the libidinal levels of Hermia's dream would be the first and classical way of analysing the dream, provided we ground the analysis on the free associations of the dreamer. Alas, however, this being a literary dream, we do not have associations in the way they usually float up from the couch. Nevertheless, we can analyse the dream in the classic way by inferring Hermia's associations.

I

We can begin by guessing at the day residue of Hermia's dream – a conversation she has with Lysander just before they lie down to go to sleep:

> *Enter Lysander and Hermia.*
> **Lysander**   Fair love, you faint with wand'ring in the wood;
>   And to speak troth I have forgot our way.
>   We'll rest us, Hermia, if you think it good,
>   And tarry for the comfort of the day.
> **Hermia**   Be't so, Lysander. Find you out a bed;
>   For I upon this bank will rest my head.
> **Lysander**   One turf shall serve as pillow for us both,
>   One heart, one bed, two bosoms, and one troth.

Hermia   Nay, good Lysander. For my sake, my dear,
  Lie further off yet. Do not lie so near.
Lysander   O, take the sense, sweet, of my innocence!
  Love takes the meaning in love's conference.
  I mean that my heart unto yours is knit
  So that but one heart we can make of it;
  Two bosoms interchained with an oath,
  So then two bosoms and a single troth.
  Then by your side no bed-room me deny;
  For lying so, Hermia, I do not lie.
Hermia   Lysander riddles very prettily.
  Now much beshrew my manners and my pride,
  If Hermia meant to say Lysander lied.
  But, gentle friend, for love and courtesy,
  Lie further off, in humane modesty;
  Such separation as may well be said
  Becomes a virtuous bachelor and a maid,
  So far be distant; and good night, sweet friend.
  Thy love ne'er alter till thy sweet life end!
Lysander   Amen, amen, to that fair prayer, say I,
  And then end life when I end loyalty.
  Here is my bed; sleep give thee all his rest!
Hermia   With half that wish the wisher's eyes be pressed!
                              [*They sleep.*]
                              (II.ii.35–65)

(Notice how she closes by alternating Lysander's wish.)

   Their conversation concerns just exactly the question of separation, as in 'lie further off', and the danger of union, Hermia's fear for her maidenly modesty if Lysander comes too close. If I think about Hermia's dream in the general framework of an adolescent girl's oedipal fears and wishes about the opposite sex, particularly in the light of this conversation, I see her imagining Lysander in two aspects. First, there is the Lysander who is physically close to her, and in the conversation they had before sleeping this is a sexual Lysander, one whom she feels is a threat to her maidenly virtue. The other is a Lysander at a distance, and him she associates with love, courtesy, humane modesty, and loyalty. In the dream, she will image this distant Lysander as smiling. Not so the nearer. In the day residue, the Lysander trying to get close proclaims that 'my heart unto yours is knit,/So that but one heart we can make of it'. In the dream, this sexual union of hearts becomes a snake eating her heart away. The dream separates these two aspects of Lysander, the sexual and the affectionate, but has images of both as hostile.

By her waking cry for Lysander to help her, Hermia tries to put them back together in a more benevolent, pitying way, but reality fails her in this. While she dreamed, Lysander left her for Helena.

The next time we see Hermia, she has managed to track down the missing Lysander by his voice. Lysander has been following Helena because, while he and Hermia were briefly asleep, Puck dropped on his eyes the 'love-juice' or 'this flower's force in stirring love', which made Lysander fall in love with the next being he saw. While Hermia was sleeping, Helena came in and woke Lysander. He promptly fell madly in love with her and followed her off into the forest. Thus when Hermia woke from her nightmare, she could not find him.

We have no way of knowing how much Hermia has heard through her sleep of Puck's talk about the charm for Lysander's eyes or of the ensuing dialogue between Helena and Lysander, but I am willing to assume that some of this talk has percolated into her dream. In particular I think she may have heard Puck speaking about the charm and may have drawn on the idea of a special fluid in representing the oedipal Lysander as a snake with its venom. She may also have heard Lysander declare his love for Helena, and that is why she shows him in the dream as hurting her and as a double person, that is, one who lies. This is a key word not only because his name is 'Lies-ander', but also because he made all those puns on 'lie' during the dialogue before their nap. As he said, 'for lying so [close to you], Hermia, I do not lie'. Puns and lies, in which one word carries two meanings, might have helped Hermia to split and so double her representation of Lysander, especially Lysander as a snake.

In a true free association, the next time we see Hermia, she misunderstands Demetrius and thinks he has killed Lysander while he was sleeping. She promptly compares Demetrius to a snake:

> O brave touch!
> Could not a worm, an adder, do so much?
> An adder did it! for with doubler tongue
> Than thine, thou serpent, never adder stung.
> (III.ii.70–3)

In other words, Hermia's free association for falseness while sleeping is a snake, and her free association to the snake is the doubleness of its tongue. As one of the fairies had sung earlier, 'you spotted snakes with double tongue' (II.ii.9).

Both in the doubleness and in the tonguiness, the snake says what Hermia might well want to say about her now false Lysander. Moreover, the serpent fits Hermia's thoughts in another curious way. Twice in Shakespeare's works (although not, as it happens, in *A Midsummer Night's Dream*) we are told that the adder is deaf. So in Hermia's dream, Lysander does not seem to hear her cries for help.

In yet another way, then, Hermia applies her characteristic personal style to the sexual problems imaged in her dream. She separates the oedipal Lysander into two aspects: a sexual, hostile, intrusive being right on top of her and a milder but also hostile man at some distance. In the same way, her dream shifts its sensory mode (to return to another of Erikson's topics for dream analysis). She begins with something touching her – the serpent crawling on her breast. She shifts to looking: 'Lysander, look how I do quake with fear.' Then she looks for Lysander and does not find him: 'What, remov'd?' Then she calls to him, but he does not answer: 'What, out of hearing gone?' She has moved from the immediate sense of touch to the more distant senses of sight and hearing. Interestingly, Hermia comments on – or if you will, associates to – just this shift when next we see her. The very words she speaks when she finds her lost Lysander are:

> Dark night, that from the eye his function takes,
> The ear more quick of apprehension makes.
> Wherein it [night] doth impair the seeing sense,
> It pays the hearing double recompense.
> Thou art not by mine eye, Lysander, found;
> Mine ear, I thank it, brought me to thy sound.
> (III.ii.177–82)

Again, with her doubling and with the ear gaining what the eye loses at night, she shows her characteristic concern with alternatives, particularly one alternative compensating for another.

Sight takes on still more importance if we can imagine that Hermia has unconsciously overheard Lysander falling in love with Helena. Puck has just dropped the love-juice into Lysander's eyes. Further, when Helena comes upon the sleeping Hermia and Lysander right after Puck leaves, she is complaining that her eyes will not attract Demetrius the way Hermia's eyes do. Then, almost the first thing Lysander says when he awakes and falls in love with Helena is:

> Transparent Helena, nature shows art,
> That through thy bosom makes me see thy heart.
>   (II.ii.104–5)

Hermia seems to me to take this image of complete truth or candour and dream it into a snake eating her own heart, an emblem of doubleness, treachery, and hostility.

If we were to limit ourselves to the old, rigid, one-to-one symbolism of early psychoanalysis, we would say simply that the snake is a symbol for a penis or a phallus. Rather than call it simply phallic, though, I would like to go beyond the symbolic code to a more human meaning for that stinging, biting snake. I can find it in Erikson's modal terms *intrusive* or *penetrating*. Hermia expresses that intrusion into her body as eating. In other words, she has built into the oedipal or phallic levels of the dream (the dream considered as an expression of an adolescent girl's attitude toward male sexuality) a regression to earlier levels of development. In yet another way, Hermia has provided an alternative – namely, anal and oral significances – to her own oedipal and phallic sexuality.

For example, one of the issues raised by the serpent in Hermia's dream is possession in contrast to true love. The serpent proposes to eat Hermia's heart, to make it a prey – in other words, to possess it. Earlier that day Hermia's father, Egeus, had accused Lysander: 'With cunning hast thou filch'd my daughter's heart' (I.i.36), just as he had given her bracelets and rings, knick-knacks and nosegays. Lysander partly replies by insisting that he has just as much money and land as Demetrius. Finally, when Hermia sees that Lysander has fallen in love with Helena, she cries:

> What, have you come by night
> And stol'n my love's heart from him?
>   (III.ii.283–4)

False love is treating a heart like a possession that can be stolen. In true love, by contrast, hearts fuse and become one, as in Lysander's plea for Hermia to lie down by him: 'My heart unto yours is knit,/So that but one heart we can make of it.' Similarly, Helena recalls that she and Hermia were such close friends they had 'two seeming bodies, but one heart' (III.ii.212).

Yet it is precisely this fusion of hearts that Hermia refused when she would not let Lysander lie down with her. She left herself open to the other, possessive kind of love. Now, after her dream, she pleads to Lysander: 'Do thy best/To pluck this crawling serpent from my breast!' In other words, make an effort to get this repellent, crawling thing away – and I hear the faintest trace of an excremental metaphor here: make an effort to push this disgusting thing out of you or me.

'Crawling' she calls it, a word she uses only one other time in the play, much later, when Puck has thoroughly befuddled all four lovers, leading them on a wild goose chase through the woods. Finally, each collapses, with Hermia saying:

> I can no further crawl, no further go;
> My legs can keep no pace with my desires.
> (III.ii.444–5)

Legless crawling is something less than fully human. Crawling suggests a desire for possession almost disembodied from the human, a desire that in life she has kept within 'humane modesty' but which in her dream she feels as overpowering.

At the deepest level of the dream, that desire for possession becomes eating and thus both fusing with and taking away a person's essence: 'Methought a serpent eat my heart *away*.' Phallic intrusion and possession become a hostile, consuming oral possession. The dominant image of the dream seems to me to be the mouth: the serpent's eating and Lysander's smiling. Hermia's thought moves in the direction of sublimation from the eating to the smiling, from her being the serpent's 'prey', to 'pray' in the other sense, her prayer to Lysander to help her. Similarly, in the dream she moves from being eaten to being looked at: 'Lysander, *look* how I do quake ... ' The day before, she had parted from Lysander by saying that, 'we must starve our sight / From lovers' food till morrow deep midnight' (I.i.222–3). The sight of the beloved is lovers' food. We should perhaps hear a pun in Hermia's exclamation during her dream: 'Ay me, for pity!' 'Ay me' includes 'Eye me', look at me, as well as 'I–me', a blurting out of her dual self. Again, Hermia has defended by setting up alternatives. She deals with the nightmare by saying she is both in the dream and out of it.

In the same way, when she cannot find Lysander, she cries 'alack', and I hear the word in its original sense – just that, a lack: something is missing, taken away, dissociated. Her characteristic defence of providing an alternative can lead to a tragic separation – here it is Lysander's going off after the alternative, Helena.

Doubleness thus takes on a special charge for Hermia because it plays into her characteristic mode of defences and adaptation: the providing of alternatives. Now, finally, I can surmise why out of all the materials that might have been important to her – her meeting with the Duke, the argument with her father, her flight by night – she dreams about the conversation she has with Lysander before they lie down to go to sleep. That conversation hinges on precisely the key issue for Hermia: one and two. Lysander wants them to have 'one turf ... /One heart, one bed, two bosoms, and one troth', but this idea Hermia finds threatening, not only for the ordinary reasons a young girl of the gentry in the English Renaissance would, but because such a fantasy would deprive her of her customary mode of adaptation. At all levels of her dream, she is working out a theme of love within her characteristic way of dealing with inner and outer reality, namely, by finding alternatives. Union in love is one possibility, but she dreams about her fear of it as a deadly possession that would prey upon and eat away her very being. However, the other alternative, separation, leads to another kind of cruelty through distance and indifference and – alack! – a loss.

The sexual symbolism of her dream thus rests upon a far deeper doubleness, her wish and her fear that alternatives won't work, that she will have to settle for just one thing: one intrusive, penetrating, possessive lover. In a psychoanalytic context, we can guess that the adolescent Hermia is working out with Lysander a much earlier, more formative relationship with a figure never seen, never even mentioned, in this comedy: her mother.

II

When we come to mother, we come to both the beginning and the end of this kind of dream analysis. What you have just read is an analysis of this fictitious dream as if I were doing it ten years ago. I have been thinking about Hermia's dream mostly as though it were an event 'out there' in a play 'out there', wholly separate from me. I have been tracing her associations through deeper and earlier phases of her development.

In the earliest years of psychoanalysis, when people turned to invented dreams like Hermia's, they did so for two reasons. Either they were going to use the insight of the poet to confirm the views of the scientist, or they were going to use the ideas of the scientist to understand what the poet had done. One could use Hermia's dream to confirm various ideas about dreaming: that associations explain dreams, that dreams express character structure, that dreams work at a variety of developmental levels, and so on. Then one could say: 'See, Shakespeare knew this intuitively. Now psychoanalysis has shown it scientifically.' Alternatively, the psychoanalytic literary critic might say, 'Here is all this scientific knowledge about dreams. If we apply it to Hermia's dream, we shall see what an extraordinarily rich and complex thing it is.' In effect, the Shakespearean critic got a boost from psychoanalysis, and the psychoanalyst got a lift from Shakespeare.

Both these approaches, however, rest on the assumption that we can treat the dream Shakespeare invented for Hermia like a real dream. We are assuming that a play is an exact representation of reality, which obeys the same laws as reality and to which we can apply the same rules for interpretation that we would apply in real life. We can have free associations and symbols and oedipal, phallic, anal, and oral levels in Hermia's dream just as in any real adolescent girl's dream.

Such an assumption is, of course, one way of relating to a play, and some psychoanalytic criticism is still written this way, but few indeed are the literary critics who would settle for this one way. For some four decades now, literary people have been insisting that literary works are not meant to be looked through so as to discover some other, imagined reality they portray. Rather, they are to be looked at as ends in themselves. They are artifacts, just like paintings or sculpture, but made of words instead. This non-representational attitude, furthermore, is part and parcel of the whole twentieth-century concept of art. As Matisse replied to a lady who complained that the arm of a woman in one of his paintings was too long: 'Madame, you are mistaken. That is not a woman, that is a picture'. So here Hermia is not an adolescent girl – she is a character in a remarkably artificial comedy, so artificial, in fact, that she states her dream in rhymed couplets. How many patients in real life do *that*?

Some ten or twenty years ago, we psychoanalytic literary critics shifted our objective. No longer did we want to treat Hermia like a literal adolescent. Instead, we wanted to understand her as one part fitted into the total play, as the arm fits into Matisse's painting. Both the character and the play are sequences of words that we understand by giving them meaning. Treating Hermia as a real person leads, of course, to one possible meaning, but a very closely limited one, and literary critics prefer to find a larger, more general meaning through themes.

For example, most literary critics treat Hermia's dream as simply 'an accurate, if symbolic, account of what has just happened'.[6] In that sense, the dream fits into the play's major theme: revelations through vision, like watching plays or seeing fairies or falling in love with someone you look at.

At least two Shakespeareans, however, have found their way to larger themes by treating Hermia's dream more dreamily. Marjorie Garber analyses this dream as part of her study of all Shakespeare's dreams and dream imagery.[7] She sees Hermia as afraid of the doubleness she represents in the snake. Hermia separates Lysander as beloved from the sexuality and violation she associates with the serpent. Yet, in the context of the play as a whole, says Garber, Hermia should not be afraid of ambiguity or double meanings, for that is what this play is. She should take doubleness rather as a form of creativity, for in this play the dream – and that includes the whole play – is truer than reality.

Melvin D. Faber has analysed this dream, too. The strength of his analysis lies in the thoroughness with which he has followed out every symbolic and associative possibility. The limitation comes from resting the analysis on the overly simple one-to-one symbolic equations so popular in the first exuberant years of applying psychoanalytic symbolism. Thus the snake is Lysander's penis, dissociated from Lysander, thereby making him less sexual, and therefore less dangerous. Hermia's heart stands for her genitals, and the serpent's eating symbolises (but regressively disguises) genital sex. Thus, concludes Faber, the dream fulfils Hermia's wish for sex with Lysander, and Lysander's smiling expresses his satisfied desire and Hermia's as well.

Faber sees in the play as a whole Shakespeare's effort to establish masculine control over unruly impulses associated with the lack of proper boundaries between male and female. The play establishes control by dissociating the conscious, social part of the mind from the unconscious, sexual, and dreamlike part – as, says Faber, Hermia does in miniature in her dream.[8]

As for my own themes for this comedy, I see the questions of separation and fusion that appear in Hermia's dream permeating the play. That is, *A Midsummer Night's Dream* begins with the separation of lovers. Theseus and Hippolyta have to wait out the four days till their wedding, the fairy King and Queen, Oberon and Titania, have quarrelled, and, of course, the lovers have tangled up their affections and drawn down the threats of the Duke and the father.

The end of the comedy brings all these lovers together and in between, what has happened is *our* dream. Puck says in the epilogue:

> Think ...
> That you have but slumb'red here
> While these visions did appear.
> And this weak and idle theme,
> No more yielding but a dream ...
> (V.i.424–8)

Hermia's dream is, as we have seen, a dream within a dream, a wish therefore that what she dreams of were a wish like the dream around it, therefore the truest part of the play. What, then, is the truth she dreams? She dreams of the doubleness of lovers and the separation of the two aspects of her own lover. As in our word *duplicity*, this doubleness connotes his falseness, as perhaps his name also does: 'Lie-sander'. One part of him wishes to fuse sexually with her, and she turns to a more separate part of him for help. But, divided this way, both parts of Lysander are cruel, one more physically so than the other.

Cruelty pervades this comedy. As Theseus says to his fiancée in the opening lines:

> Hippolyta, I woo'd thee with my sword,
> And won thy love doing thee injuries.
> (I.i.16–17)

You could say the same of Oberon, who humiliates Titania, or of either of our two young men, each of whom deserts and reviles and threatens his future wife. Throughout the play, the ruler, the father, the lovers, the King of the fairies, the amateur actors, and even the audience at the play within the play – all proclaim love, but they also threaten violence or humiliation. The play within the play focuses this ambivalence: it is a 'very tragical mirth' (V.i.55), and 'the most lamentable comedy and most cruel death of Pyramus and Thisby' (I.ii.11–12) is both the funniest and the bloodiest part of the play.

This comical tragedy within the comedy comes about because the lover Pyramus, separated from his love Thisby and confused in the dark (like our four lovers), believes a lion has eaten her. That lion in Renaissance symbology provides the opposite to Hermia's snake.[9] The royal beast takes his prey in the open, by force and grandeur. The low serpent sneaks his prey by stealth and cunning. Thus the lion in the clowns' broad farce causes right before your eyes a bloody fusion of lovers as Pyramus stabs himself over Thisby's bloody mantle and Thisby stabs herself over Pyramus' bloody body. By contrast, the snake in Hermia's dream images a much subtler cruelty, the desertion and indifference of these not-so-courtly lovers.

This is a second way, then, to read Hermia's dream. The first way is as a clinical study of an adolescent girl. This second, larger reading sets Hermia's dream in the whole atmosphere and development of ambivalence in the comedy. We move beyond the nineteenth and early twentieth-century concern with realism toward a more contemporary interest in theme. Instead of treating the various levels (oedipal, phallic, anal, and oral) as aspects of some particular adolescent girl, I would see them all as variations on the comedy's theme of ambivalence, separations that are both loving and cruel.

Yet both these methods treat Hermia or her dream or her play as though they were 'out there', as though I were distant and indifferent to them except for a coolly intellectual curiosity. Both readings pretend the dream and the play are not connected to any me 'in here' who shapes and recreates both the dream and the comedy to fit my own character or, as I prefer to say, my identity. Rather, an abstractly skilled interpreter finds 'the' meaning of the dream and fits it to 'the' meaning of the play.

III

In the ten years since I wrote such externalised dream analyses, most of us in literature and psychology have come to feel that same new interest in the self that has quickened psychoanalytic theory throughout the world: in Paris through the writings of Lacan, in London in the object-relations theory of Milner and Winnicott and others, or in Chicago in the remarkable technical and theoretical studies of Heinz Kohut. Rather than simply look for an abstract theme 'out there' in *A Midsummer Night's Dream*, we have become more interested in how a self – my self, for example – uses the text of the play or the dream as an object to establish a self-structuring relation.

Clearly, the kind of level-by-level exegesis you have just read makes up part of that relation: working out the implications of the dream through such schemes as Erikson's for analysing the interaction of manifest and latent content or the classic psychoanalytic scheme of developmental levels. But this kind of analysis leaves out a great deal. It ignores, for example, my feelings as I hear this dream. It ignores the personal quality of my reading, which makes it different from Professor Faber's or Professor Garber's.

Ten years ago, psychoanalytic literary critics cared little about the personal qualities that set one interpretation off from another, partly because we believed there was a best reading (a 'the' reading) that would rise to the top as we refined our literary ideas, and the other readings left in the pot simply wouldn't matter very much. Partly, too, we ignored the personal element because we had no way of talking about it. Now, however, we are less confident that there is some best reading, and we have a way of talking about the personal quality of a response.

That is, we have identity theory. We have a way of conceptualising each new thing someone does as new, yet stamped with the same personal style as all the other actions chosen by that person. Each of us is a mixture of sameness and difference. We detect the sameness by seeing what persists within the constant change of our lives. We detect the difference by seeing what has changed against the background of sameness.

The most powerful way I know to think of that dialectic of sameness and difference is the one suggested by Heinz Lichtenstein: to see identity as a theme and variations like a musical theme and variations. Think of the sameness as a theme, an 'identity theme'. Think of the differences as variations on that identity theme. That is the way I have read Hermia's character, for example. She creates an alternative that will amend the original possibility. That is her identity theme, and we have seen her work out variations on it in her opening plea to Theseus, in her witty dialogue with Lysander before they lie down to sleep, and, above all, in her dream. These are all various ways by which she tries to amend through an alternative.

Now, just as Hermia develops a variation on her identity theme when she dreams, so you and I develop variations on our identity theme when we read her dream. Thus we arrive at a new kind of psychoanalytic method with literature. Our group at Buffalo calls it 'transactive criticism'. We actively create, we *transact* – for example, Hermia's dream and *A Midsummer Night's Dream*. As critics, it is our job to articulate the relation of those two explicitly.

For me, the two images of Hermia's dream, the eating snake and the smiling lover, evoke large questions of fidelity and possession between men and women that I find puzzling and troubling as I watch my students struggling to find and maintain stable relationships or as I see in my own generation yet another friend's marriage break up. That is, Hermia's dream, her very presence in the forest with Lysander, builds on the mutual promises she and Lysander made, a contract sealed by a dangerous elopement, a pledge of faith that her lover, at the very moment of her dream, has abandoned. Her dream begins from his infidelity.

As I visualise the dream, I see a small snake at a distance – yes, like a penis in the classic Freudian symbolism – but I also remember a picture from a book of nature photographs of a snake's wide open mouth with long, curved fangs under a pink, arched palate, one demonic eye showing behind the furious jaws. The head is all mouth, really, there is so little else besides that act of biting. Hermia describes the snake as 'crawling', and we have already guessed at her associations. Mine are to a baby who is all helpless, inarticulate demand. For me, then, Hermia's image of the snake sets up the idea of possession, the way a lover or a penis can make a total demand as an animal or a baby demands food.

Curiously, food comes up again when Shakespeare has the two men explain why they switched partners. When Demetrius announces he is back in love with Helena, he says:

> ... like a sickness did I loathe this food [Helena],
> But, as in health, come to my natural taste,
> Now I do wish it, love it, long for it,
> And will forevermore be true to it.
>
> (IV.i.173–5)

The first time Shakespeare explains the switching of affections, it is Lysander who has suddenly fallen in love with Helena just before Hermia's dream. He looks at the sleeping Hermia and says:

> For as a surfeit of the sweetest things
> The deepest loathing to the stomach brings,

...
So thou, my surfeit and my heresy,
Of all be hated, but most of me!
                    (II.ii.137–42)

Both times Shakespeare has his lovers refer emotional love to oral appetite, and an appetite of total desire or total rejection, fidelity to one girl meaning disgust at all others – at least for a time.

As we have seen, mouths appear twice in Hermia's dream, once in the serpent's eating and once when Hermia says of Lysander, 'You sate smiling'. For me, there is a great cruelty in that smile, just as there is in his radical rejection of Hermia as a 'surfeit' that brings 'deepest loathing to the stomach'. I feel hatred in that smile and in that imagery of disgust, a hatred that psychoanalysis, in one of its hardest truths, asks us to believe tinges every human relationship. As the tough-minded La Rochefoucauld put it once and for all, 'In the misfortune of our best friends we always find something that is not entirely displeasing.'[10]

In other words, if I bring my own associations to Hermia's dream and its context, I begin to read the comedy of which it is a part as a rather uncomfortable hovering between different views of love. In one view, love is a total, consuming desire like a baby's for food. In the other, the relation is less demanding: it admits a change of heart or appetite. Yet so cool a lover may be hateful in his very smiling, just as hateful as the snake is in his eating.

Nowadays, people reject the idea that love entitles you to possess another person. I too reject that kind of possessiveness – at least I consciously do. Yet the opposite possibility, a cool distant love, does not satisfy me as a solution. I believe in a fidelity of mutual trust, an exchange of promises that I will be true to you and you will be true to me. I realise that contemporary patterns of marriage and sex deeply question this style of relationship. Many people believe they can and do love more than one person passionately and sexually at the same time.

No matter how contemporary I like to think myself in sexual matters, however, I have to admit that, deep down, I do not feel that the mutual pledge of loving or of sexual promises is the kind of contract one can negotiate like a lease on an apartment, with provisions for termination, renegotiation, or repairs. Nor do I believe one can hold several such leases at once. To be intimate is to risk oneself with another, and it is difficult, for me at least, to feel free to open myself up to another person without being able to feel that that opening up will be one-to-one, that neither of us will compromise our intimacy by sharing it with some third person. Somewhere inside me I deeply fear that I would be made small and ridiculous, like a child, were my lover to share our one-to-oneness with another lover. Hence I perceive Lysander's smiling as a cruel ridicule.

The comedy, however, like today's lovers, rejects possessiveness. Hermia's father states the theme: 'As she is mine, I may dispose of her.' The comedy as a whole moves away from this dehumanising possessiveness, when what the play will substitute is not exactly clear. At the end, Duke Theseus rules:

> Egeus, I will overbear your will;
> For in the temple, by and by, with us
> These couples shall eternally be knit.
> (IV.i.179–81)

They will be married, and the power of the Duke will knit them together as couples and as his subjects.

Paradoxically, though, the comedy arrives at this knitting by a system of separations and infidelities. At first Demetrius had been in love with Helena, but at the opening of the play he has fallen in love with Hermia. Then, when Lysander's eyes are charmed, *he* falls in love with Helena. Later, the same thing happens to Demetrius: his eyes are drugged and he too falls in love with Helena. Finally, Puck uncharms Lysander, and the lovers fall into their natural pairs. The Polish critic, Jan Kott, urges us to think of this part of the comedy as a drunken switch party on a hot night, in which all the scantily clad lovers are interchangeable objects of desire who exchange with one another, finally waking up the next morning hung over, exhausted, and ashamed.[11]

Perhaps Kott takes too extreme a view, but the comedy does seem to say the lovers learn fidelity through their infidelities. Yet very little is said about how his union comes about. After they all wake up, Demetrius says of the events of the night before: 'These things seem small and indistinguishable' (IV.i.187). And once they are reunited with their proper lovers, the two girls say not another word for the whole long last scene of the comedy.

In other words, the comedy is silent just at the point where I, with my puzzling about fidelity, am most curious. How do these lovers, who now pledge to be true to one another, derive fidelity from their previous infidelity? The play doesn't say. I feel it is up to us as readers and critics to find a solution. One distinguished Shakespearean, Norman Rabkin, writes:

> In *A Midsummer Night's Dream* Shakespeare opposes reason to the folly of lovers whose choices are often magically induced and always wilful, only to make us realise that those choices are ultimately right and of the same order as that anti-rational illusion-mongering, the performing and watching of plays, which, depending on the charitable suspension of disbelief ... nevertheless tells us truths of which reason is incapable.[12]

Rabkin suggests a parallel between the lovers falling in love and the way the rest of us give ourselves to plays. Illusions, fancies, fictions – if we can tolerate them, even lies – can lead us to a higher truth, a loving experience beyond reason. In psychoanalytic terms, I think this transcending corresponds to the basic trust we must all have developed in translating an imagining of a mother's nurturing presence into a confidence that she would really be there when needed. By not being there, she is unfaithful, but out of that first infidelity, most of us made the most basic of fidelities.

Thus I read Hermia's dream as having three parts. First, the snake preys on a passive Hermia's heart in an act of total, painful, destructive possession – hard on Hermia, but satisfying to that masculine snake. That possessiveness is one possibility open to me in relating to a woman or a play.

Second, Lysander smilingly watches the woman he so recently loved being possessed by another. His smile signals to me another kind of cruelty – dispassion, distance, indifference – another way of relating to a play or a lover. The snake is fantastic and symbolic, whereas Lysander presents a far more realistic lover whom I can interpret all too well through our century's alternatives to romantic commitment.

Then there is a third aspect to the dream, as I view it. It is a nightmare. The dream has aroused anxieties too great for Hermia to sleep through. She wakes, and we never learn how she might have dreamed that a loving Lysander plucked away a possessive snake. Instead, we are left with his deserting her for another woman.

For me, the sense of incompleteness is particularly strong, because I very much need to see a coherence and unity in human relations. I want a happy ending for this comedy. I want these couples married at the end, but I don't see – I don't trust, really – the way the comedy gets them together. Out of infidelity comes fidelity – but how? Hermia trusts Lysander, but he is unfaithful and leaves her alone and terrified: 'I swoon almost with fear.' It is hard for me to trust that there will be a happy outcome despite his cruel and contemptuous abandonment.

When I confess my uneasiness because the dream is incomplete and the play is silent on the creation of trust, I am working through something about myself I have faced many times before. It's hard for me simply to trust and to tolerate uncertainty or absence or silence. I question both Hermia's dream and the sexual revolution of our own time because I need to *know* things, particularly about human relations. I need to feel certain.

None of this, of course, do Lysander or the other lovers say. They talk about feelings of love and jealousy we can all share, but they do so within the conventions of Renaissance marriage. You and I, however, read what they say from a perch in our own culture, with its many marital and non-marital and extra-marital possibilities, all challenging the traditional limits on relations between the sexes. Where Shakespeare's lovers proceeded in their own day to a sure and socially structured Renaissance conclusion, now I feel they are opening up all kinds of twentieth-century uncertainties without, naturally, saying much about them. In particular, Hermia's dream images the tension between possessiveness and distance and the – to me at least – unknown way trust will resolve that tension.

Often, I think, we Shakespeareans teach Shakespeare as though we were ourselves unaffected by any of the changes in the relations between men and women that have happened since the days of Queen Elizabeth or A. C. Bradley. We are reading Shakespeare's romantic comedies in the middle of a sexual revolution. It would make sense to come to grips with the way our own feelings about that revolution shape our perception of episodes like Hermia's dream (or, even more drastically, Kate's anti-feminist speech at the end of *The Taming of the Shrew*). That assertion of our selves is the new direction psychoanalytic literary criticism has begun to take.[13]

In acknowledging my role in bringing these twentieth-century issues to this comedy of 1594, I am discovering through Hermia's dream how I am unconsciously or half-consciously possessive, even though I consciously aspire to an ethic of mutual trust. More generally, I am discovering that Hermia's dream takes its life not from some fictitious dreamer, but from my own concern with relations between men and women in my own time and my own hopes for those relations. I read Hermia's dream as an emblem of two human problems. One is an American problem of the 1970s and 1980s. Can one separate love from trust? The other is a universal human question: how can we establish trust with another being whom we partly trust and partly mistrust? Reading Hermia's dream this way, I – or you and I, if you will go along with me – can go beyond the earlier relationships with literature that psychoanalysis made possible.

At first we treated the unconscious processes in literary characters as though they were fact, not fiction, happening 'out there', separate from us dispassionate observers. Then we set the character into an ego process embodied in the play as a whole. We began to acknowledge that we were included in that process, too, as we lent ourselves to the play. Now we have begun to make explicit the self-discovery that was only implicit and silent in those two earlier methods.

We can learn how each of us gives life to Shakespeare's imaginings 'out there' through our own times and lives, our wishes and fears and defences 'in here'. Through psychoanalytic identity theory, we can understand how we are able to talk about the words of another through ourselves and, in doing so, talk about ourselves through the words of another – even if they are as airy a nothing as dream of dream of dream. When we do, we each continue Shakespeare's achievement in and through ourselves. Just as self and object constitute each other in human development, so in the literary transaction the reader constitutes text so that text may constitute its reader. In this mutuality, Hermia's dream is not simply a dream dreamed for us. Rather, we dream her dream for ourselves, and as we know ourselves so we know the dream, until its local habitation is here and its name is us.

From *Annual of Psychoanalysis*, 7(1979), 369–89.

NOTES

[What is most striking about Holland's essay is the fullness with which it discusses its own developing strategies; rather like a postmodern building, all the plumbing, communications and life-support systems are conspicuously on view. This is of a piece with the almost confessional mode with which he concludes, after expounding a personalised history of psychoanalytic criticism. Holland is one of the foremost exponents of such criticism, though in the American tradition of ego-psychology closely aligned with clinical practice rather than of more abstract psychoanalytic theory. He has recently made no bones about 'using a psychology closer to that of the consulting room than to the increasingly abstract psychologies in contemporary literary theory' (Introduction to *Shakespeare's Personality*, ed. Norman N. Holland, Sidney Homan and Bernard J. Paris [Berkeley, CA, 1990], p.3). This is not a direct attack on arguably the most influential of recent psychoanalytic critics, Jacques Lacan, but it clearly has in view some of his less imaginative followers. Lacan challenged (from a poststructuralist perspective) the fundamental Freudian tenet of the ego as a stable entity, albeit one that progresses through stages of development which may be distorted by traumatic stress. He argued rather that the subjective self has no fixed identity, but constructs the fictive illusion of one through a process of misrecognitions or misidentifications (*méconnaissances*) – a process readily identifiable with the interaction of characters in plays and novels, especially romantic comedies which explore the seductive illusions and overpowering certainties of eros. In the present essay Holland locates Lacan's argument as one strand of modern identity-theory, but significantly advances his own alternative version (one more in tune with 'transactive criticism') in his closing section. The emphasis on 'transactive criticism', linking the functions of clinical analyst and literary critic, explains why Holland is often also characterised as a 'subjective' reader-response critic, who sees interpretation as a function of the identity process. This proposition was spelled out in an influential – if controversial – essay, 'Unity Identity Text Self', *PMLA*, 90 (1975), 813–20. Ed.]

1.   Throughout, I am relying on the text of *The Riverside Shakespeare*, ed. G. Blakemore Evans et al. (Boston, 1974), although I occasionally repunctuate it.

2.   Erik H. Erikson, 'The Dream Specimen of Psychoanalysis', in *Psychoanalytic Psychiatry and Psychology: Clinical and Theoretical Papers, Austen Riggs Center*, ed. Robert P. Knight and Cyrus R. Friedman (New York, 1954), pp. 131–70, 144–5.

3.   For a more elaborate example of this method, see Norman N. Holland, 'A Touching of Literary and Psychiatric Education', *Seminars in Psychiatry*, 5 (1973), 287–99.

4.   Heinz Kohut, *The Analysis of the Self: A Systematic Approach to the Psychoanalytic Treatment of Narcissistic Personality Disorders* (New York, 1971), pp. xiv–xv and passim.

5.   Most Shakespeareans regard Hermia and Helena as interchangeable, except for height and colour (III.ii.290ff. and II.ii.114). Reading their

'sides', though, as an actress would (see n. 3 above), I detect a characterological difference. As in the text, Hermia speaks and acts through 'amendment by alternative' (to compress her identity into a theme). Helena tries to cope (I think) by establishing a contradiction or opposition and then seeking to become that opposite. See, for example, her speeches in I.i.: 'Call you me fair? That fair again unsay', and 'O that your frowns would teach my smiles such skill.' She would give everything, she tells her rival Hermia, 'to be you translated'. And she adds: 'How happy some o'er other some can be.' All these lead to her explication of the emblem of Cupid in terms of reversals and her decision at the end of the scene to convert Demetrius' pursuit of Hermia in the wood to his presence with herself. Compare her last words in the play, 'And Hippolyta' (Theseus' opposite) to Hermia's, 'and my father' (Theseus' parallel).

6. David P. Young, *Something of Great Constancy: The Art of 'A Midsummer Night's Dream'* (New Haven, CT, 1966), p. 120.

7. Marjorie B. Garber, *Dream in Shakespeare: From Metaphor to Metamorphosis* (New Haven, CT, 1974), pp. 72–4.

8. Melvin D. Faber, 'Hermia's Dream: Royal Road to *A Midsummer Night's Dream*', *Literature and Psychology*, 22 (1972), 179–90.

9. See the similar juxtaposition of lion and snake threatening a sleeper in *As You Like It* (IV.iii.106–18).

10. La Rochefoucauld, *Maximes*, ed. F. C. Green (Cambridge, 1946), maxime 583, p. 138 (my translation).

11. Jan Kott, *Shakespeare Our Contemporary*, trans. Boleslaw Taborski (Garden City, NY, 1964), pp. 210–16.

12. Norman Rabkin, *Shakespeare and the Common Understanding* (New York, 1967), p. 74; see also pp. 201–5 and 234n.

13. For a particularly fine example of this new mode, applied to a number of Shakespearean plays, see Murray M. Schwartz, 'Shakespeare through Contemporary Psychoanalysis', *Hebrew University Studies in Literature*, 5 (Autumn 1977).

4

A *Midsummer Night's Dream:* 'Jack shall have Jill;/Nought shall go ill'

SHIRLEY NELSON GARNER

> Jack shall have Jill;
> Nought shall go ill;
> The man shall have his mare again,
> and all shall be well.[1]

More than any of Shakespeare's comedies, *A Midsummer Night's Dream* resembles a fertility rite, for the sterile world that Titania depicts at the beginning of Act II is transformed and the play concludes with high celebration, ritual blessing, and the promise of regeneration.[2] Though this pattern is easily apparent and has often been observed, the social and sexual implications of the return of the green world have gone unnoticed. What has not been so clearly seen is that the renewal at the end of the play affirms patriarchal order and hierarchy, insisting that the power of women must be circumscribed, and that it recognises the tenuousness of heterosexuality as well.[3] The movement of the play toward ordering the fairy, human, and natural worlds is also a movement toward satisfying men's psychological needs, as Shakespeare perceived them, but its cost is the disruption of women's bonds with each other.

I

Regeneration finally depends on the amity between Titania and Oberon. As she tells him, their quarrel over possession of an Indian boy has brought chaos, disease, and sterility to the natural world:

> And this same progeny of evils comes
> From our debate, from our dissension;
> We are their parents and original.
>   (II.i.115–17)

The story of the 'lovely boy' is told from two points of view, Puck's and Titania's. Puck tells a companion fairy that Oberon is 'passing fell and wrath' because Titania has taken as her attendant 'a lovely boy, stolen from an Indian king'; he continues:

> She never had so sweet a changeling.
> And jealous Oberon would have the child
> Knight of his train, to trace the forests wild.
> But she perforce withholds the lovèd boy,
> Crowns him with flowers, and makes him all her joy.
> And now they never meet in grove or green,
> By fountain clear, or spangled starlight sheen,
> But they do square, that all the elves for fear
> Creep into acorn cups and hide them there.
>   (II.i.18–31)

Shortly afterward, when Oberon tells Titania that it is up to her to amend their quarrel and that he merely begs 'a little changeling boy' to be his 'henchman', she retorts, 'Set your heart at rest./The fairy land buys not the child of me.' Then she explains the child's origin, arguing her loyalty to the child's mother to be the reason for keeping him:

> His mother was a vot'ress of my order,
> And, in the spicèd Indian air, by night,
> Full often hath she gossiped by my side,
> And sat with me on Neptune's yellow sands,
> Marking th' embarkèd traders on the flood;
> When we have laughed to see the sails conceive
> And grow big-bellied with the wanton wind;
> Which she, with pretty and with swimming gait
> Following – her womb then rich with my young squire –

> Would imitate, and sail upon the land,
> To fetch me trifles, and return again,
> As from a voyage, rich with merchandise.
> But she, being mortal, of that boy did die;
> And for her sake do I rear up her boy,
> And for her sake I will not part with him.
> (II.i.121–37)

Both accounts affirm that the child has become the object of Titania's love, but the shift in emphasis from one point of view to the other is significant. Puck describes the child as 'stolen from an Indian king', whereas Titania emphasises the child's link with his mother, her votaress. Puck's perspective, undoubtedly close to Oberon's, ignores or suppresses the connection between Titania and the Indian queen, which, in its exclusion of men and suggestion of love between women, threatens patriarchal and heterosexual values.[4]

Titania's attachment to the boy is clearly erotic. She 'crowns him with flowers, and makes him all her joy', according him the same attentions as those she bestows on Bottom when, under the spell of Oberon's love potion, she falls in love with the rustic-turned-ass. She has 'forsworn' Oberon's 'bed and company' (II.i.62). Whatever the child is to her as a 'lovely boy' and a 'sweet' changeling, he is ultimately her link with a mortal woman whom she loved. Oberon's passionate determination to have the child for himself suggests that he is both attracted to and jealous of him. He would have not only the boy but also the exclusive love of Titania.[5] He needs to cut her off from the child because she is attracted to him not only as boy and child, but also as his mother's son. Oberon's need to humiliate Titania in attaining the boy suggests that her love for the child poses a severe threat to the fairy king.

Puck's statement that Oberon wants the child to be 'knight of his train' and Oberon's that he wants him to be his 'henchman' have led some critics to argue that the fairy king's desires to have the boy are more appropriate than the fairy queen's. Oberon's wish to have the boy is consistent with the practice of taking boys from the nursery to the father's realm so that they can acquire the character and skills appropriate to manhood.[6] But Puck describes Oberon as 'jealous', and his emphasis on the 'lovely boy', the 'sweet' changeling, and the 'lovèd boy' (II.ii.20–7) suggests that Oberon, like Titania, is attracted to the child. There is no suggestion that Oberon wants to groom the child for manhood; he wants him rather 'to trace the forests wild' (l.25) with his fairy band. Those

critics who attribute moral intentions to Oberon, arguing for his
benevolent motives in taking the boy from Titania, overlook that
Oberon has no intention of returning him to his father, with whom
he, as a human child, might be most properly reared. When we last
hear of the boy, Titania's fairy has carried him to Oberon's 'bower'
(IV.i.62).

Oberon's winning the boy from Titania is at the centre of the
play, for his victory is the price of amity between them, which in
turn restores the green world. At the beginning, Oberon and Titania
would seem to have equal magical powers, but Oberon's power
proves the greater. Since he cannot persuade Titania to turn over
the boy to him, he humiliates her and torments her until she does
so. He uses the love potion not simply to divert her attention from
the child, so that he can have him, but to punish her as well.[7] As he
squeezes the love flower on Titania's eyes, he speaks a charm – or
rather a curse – revealing his intention:

> What thou see'st when thou dost wake,
> Do it for thy truelove take;
> Love and languish for his sake.
> Be it ounce, or cat, or bear,
> Pard, or boar with bristled hair,
> In thy eye that shall appear
> When thou wak'st, it is thy dear.
> Wake when some vile thing is near.
> (II.ii.27–34)

When Puck tells him that Titania is 'with a monster in love'
(III.ii.6), he is obviously pleased: 'This falls out better than I could
devise' (1.35).

Though the scenes between Titania and Bottom are charming and
hilarious, Titania is made ridiculous. Whereas her opening speech is
remarkable for its lyric beauty, and her defence of keeping the
Indian boy has quiet and dignified emotion power, now she is
reduced to admiring Bottom's truisms and his monstrous shape:
'Thou art as wise as thou art beautiful' (III.i.147). However enjoy-
able the scenes between her and Bottom, however thematically satisfying in their representation of the marriage of our animal and
spiritual natures, Titania, free of the influence of Oberon's love
potion, says of Bottom, 'O, how mine eyes do loathe his visage
now!' (V.i.80). By his own account, Oberon taunts Titania into
obedience; he tells Puck:

> See'st thou this sweet sight?
> Her dotage now I do begin to pity:
> For, meeting her of late behind the wood,
> Seeking sweet favours for this hateful fool,
> I did upbraid her, and fall out with her.
> For she his hairy temples then had rounded
> With coronet of fresh and fragrant flowers;
> And that same dew, which sometime on the buds
> Was wont to swell, like round and orient pearls,
> Stood now within the pretty flouriet's eyes,
> Like tears, that did their own disgrace bewail.
> When I had at my pleasure taunted her,
> And she in mild terms begged my patience,
> I then did ask of her her changeling child;
> Which straight she gave me, and her fairy sent
> To bear him to my bower in fairy land.
> And now I have the boy, I will undo
> This hateful imperfection of her eyes.
>
> (IV.i.47–64)

Oberon gains the exclusive love of Titania and also possession of the boy to whom he is attracted. But his gain is Titania's loss: she is separated from the boy and, in that separation, further severed from the woman whom she had loved. Oberon can offer ritual blessing at the play's end because he has what he wanted from the beginning: Titania obedient and under his control and the beautiful Indian boy in his bower.

II

Like the fairy king, the two men in power in the human world, Theseus and Egeus, want to attain the exclusive love of a woman and, also, to accommodate their homoerotic desires.[8] In order to do so, they, like Oberon, attempt to limit women's power, and their success or failure to do so affects their participation in the comic world.

The opening of *A Midsummer Night's Dream* puts Hippolyta's subjugation in bold relief as Theseus reminds his bride-to-be:

> Hippolyta, I wooed thee with my sword,
> And won thy love, doing thee injuries;
> But I will wed thee in another key,
> With pomp, with triumph, and with revelling.
>
> (I.i.16–19)

Capturing Hippolyta when he defeated the Amazons, Theseus has abducted her from her Amazon sisters to bring her to Athens and marry her. Though most directors play Hippolyta as a willing bride, I once saw San Francisco's Actors' Workshop, following the cues of Jan Kott, bring her on stage clothed in skins and imprisoned in a cage.[9] The text invites such a rendering, for almost immediately it sets her apart from Theseus by implying that she sides with Hermia and Lysander against Egeus and Theseus, when he sanctions Egeus's authority. After Theseus tells Hermia to prepare to marry Demetrius or 'on Diana's altar to protest/For aye austerity and single life' (I.i.89–90) and then beckons Hippolyta to follow him offstage, he undoubtedly notices her frowning, for he asks, 'What cheer, my love?' (I.i.122). Shakespeare heightens her isolation by presenting her without any Amazon attendants.

Though Theseus is less severe than Egeus, he is, from the outset, unsympathetic toward women. The first words he speaks, voicing the play's first lines and first image, must be taken as a sign: the moon 'lingers' his desires, he tells Hippolyta, 'Like a stepdame, or a dowager,/Long withering out a young man's revenue.' He utterly supports Egeus as patriarch, telling Hermia:

> To you your father should be as a god,
> One that composed your beauties; yea, and one
> To whom you are but as a form in wax
> By him imprinted and within his power
> To leave the figure or disfigure it.
>
> (I.i.47–51)

As a ruler, he will enforce the law, which gives Egeus control over Hermia's sexuality and embodies patriarchal order. Though he has heard that Demetrius has won Helena's heart but now scorns her, and has meant to speak to him about it, 'My mind did lose it' (I.i.114). A lover-and-leaver of women himself, he undoubtedly identifies with Demetrius and forgets his duty toward Helena. He exits inviting Egeus and Demetrius to follow and talk confidentially with him, suggesting his spiritual kinship with them.

Whatever other associations Theseus had for Shakespeare's audience, he was notorious as the first seducer of Helen.[10] As early as Act II, Oberon recalls Theseus's reputation as a deserter of women.[11] When Titania accuses Oberon of infidelity, asking rhetorically why he was in Athens if not to see Hippolyta, 'the bouncing Amazon,/Your buskined mistress and your warrior love' (II.i.70–1), he accuses her of loving Theseus:

> Didst not thou lead him through the glimmering night
> From Perigenia, whom he ravishèd?
> And make him with fair Aegles break his faith,
> With Ariadne and Antiopa?
>
> (ll.77–80)

It is significant that the woman whom he at last will marry is not traditionally feminine. She has been a warrior, and in her new role as the fiancée of the Athenian Duke, we see her as a hunter. Nostalgically, she recalls her past experiences:

> I was with Hercules and Cadmus once,
> When in a wood of Crete they bayed the bear
> With hounds of Sparta. Never did I hear
> Such gallant chiding; for, besides the groves,
> The skies, the fountains, every region near
> Seemed all one mutual cry. I never heard
> So musical a discord, such sweet thunder.
>
> (IV.i.113–19)

Her androgynous character appears to resolve for Theseus the apparent dissociation of his romantic life, the sign of which is his continual desertion of women who love him.[12]

Having found an androgynous woman, Theseus captures her and brings her home to be his wife. By conquering and marrying this extraordinarily powerful woman, he fulfils his need for the exclusive love of a woman while gratifying his homoerotic desires.[13] Unlike Oberon, however, he finds satisfaction for his desires merged in one person. If we imagine Hippolyta played by a male actor who, though cast as a woman, dresses and walks like a man ('buskined mistress', 'bouncing Amazon'), Hippolyta and Theseus must have looked more like homosexual than heterosexual lovers. Hippolyta's androgynous appearance is further confirmed by the fact that in Renaissance fiction and drama men were occasionally disguised as Amazons, e.g. lovers, like Sidney's Zelmane, in the *Arcadia*, who wished to be near his lady.[14] Hippolyta, like Viola and Rosalind in disguise, fulfils a male fantasy, and more happily so since she is not in disguise. Because Theseus's romantic life is fortunately resolved once the young lovers have paired themselves off anew, with Demetrius loving Helena, he can sanction their preferences and ignore Egeus's persistent demand that Hermia marry Demetrius.[15]

By insisting that Hermia marry Demetrius, Egeus hopes to keep his daughter rather than lose her and to have Demetrius near him as well. Shakespeare makes Egeus's motives suspect by creating him foolishly comic, treating him more harshly than he does his other controlling and possessive fathers – Lear, Capulet, Brabantio, Shylock, Prospero. Unable to make his daughter marry where he wishes, Egeus turns to the law to enforce his will. More outrageous than Brabantio, he turns Lysander's courtship of his daughter into a series of crimes: Lysander has 'bewitched the bosom' of Hermia, 'stol'n the impression of her fantasy', 'filched' her heart (I.i.26–38). As Shakespeare depicts the two lovers who compete over Hermia, he is careful to draw them so that Egeus's choice is irrational and not in Hermia's best interests. Lysander states his case before Theseus:

> I am, my lord, as well derived as he [Demetrius],
> As well possessed; my love is more than his;
> My fortunes every way as fairly ranked
> (If not with vantage) as Demetrius';
> And, which is more than all these boasts can be,
> I am beloved of beauteous Hermia.
> (I.i.99–104)

Lysander continues to accuse Demetrius of making love to Helena, who now 'dotes in idolatry,/Upon this spotted and inconstant man' (109–10). His accusation is evidently founded, for Theseus confesses that he has 'heard so much' (l.111) and Demetrius does not deny it or defend himself. Later, Demetrius admits that he was betrothed to Helena before he saw Hermia (IV.i.172–3). Egeus chooses badly for his daughter unless he wishes to keep her for himself, as I think he does. By insisting that she marry a man whom she does not love and one who may be unfaithful to her besides, if his present conduct is a gauge, Egeus assures that she will always love her father; that she will never really leave him.

There are suggestions, as well, that Egeus has a particular affection for Demetrius. Shakespeare does not leave us to assume that Egeus's preference for Demetrius is simply proprietary, i.e. since Hermia is his, he may give her as he chooses; or that it is simply an affirmation of male bonding, like Capulet's demand that Juliet marry Paris, 'And you be mine, I'll give you to my friend' (*Romeo and Juliet,* III.v.193). Lysander's sarcasm defines Egeus's feeling for Demetrius:

> You have her father's love, Demetrius;
> Let me have Hermia's: do you marry him
> (I.i.93–4)

And Egeus immediately affirms:

> True, he hath my love,
> And what is mine, my love shall render him.

Even after Demetrius has fallen in love with Helena, Egeus continues to pair himself with him. When the lovers are discovered asleep in the forest coupled 'right' at last and Lysander begins to explain what Theseus calls their 'gentle concord', Egeus urges:

> Enough, enough, my lord; you have enough.
> I beg the law, the law, upon his head.
> They would have stol'n away; they would, Demetrius,
> Thereby to have defeated you and me,
> You of your wife and me of my consent,
> Of my consent that she should be your wife.
>   (IV.i.55–60)

Egeus would draw Demetrius back to him, realigning the original *we* against *them*.

Egeus, then, has hoped to have the exclusive love of Hermia and to accommodate his homoerotic feelings by binding Demetrius to him. To give up Hermia and accept that Demetrius loves Helena would defeat him doubly. Consequently, he leaves the stage unreconciled. Had it been left to him to affirm the comic resolution, we would have none.

III

Whereas the separation of Hippolyta and Titania from other women is implied or kept in the background, the breaking of women's bonds is central in the plot involving the four young lovers.[16] Demetrius and Lysander are divided at the outset, but the play dramatises the division of Hermia and Helena. Furthermore, their quarrelling is more demeaning than the men's. And once Demetrius and Lysander are no longer in competition for the same woman, their enmity is gone. Hermia and Helena, on the contrary, seem permanently separated and apparently give over their power to the men they will marry. Once their friendship is undermined and their power diminished, they are presumably 'ready' for marriage.

Hermia's fond recollection of her long-standing and intimate friendship with Helena calls attention to Helena's disloyalty, occasioned by the latter's desire to win Demetrius's thanks and to be near him. Telling her friend that she intends to run away with Lysander, Hermia recalls:

> And in the wood, where often you and I
> Upon faint primrose beds were wont to lie,
> Emptying our bosoms of their counsel sweet,
> There my Lysander and myself shall meet.
> (I.i.214–17)

Just as Helena breaks her faith with Hermia to ingratiate herself with Demetrius, so later she will believe that Hermia has joined with men against her. Deeply hurt, Helena chastises Hermia:

> Is all the counsel that we two have shared,
> The sister's vows, the hours that we have spent,
> When we have chid the hasty-footed time
> For parting us – O, is all forgot?
> All school days friendship, childhood innocence?
> We, Hermia, like two artificial gods,
> Have with our needles created both one flower,
> Both on one sampler, sitting on one cushion,
> Both warbling of one song, both in one key;
> As if our hands, our sides, voices, and minds,
> Had been incorporate. So we grew together,
> Like to a double cherry, seeming parted,
> But yet an union in partition,
> Two lovely berries moulded on one stem;
> So, with two seeming bodies, but one heart;
> Two of the first, like coats in heraldry,
> Due but to one and crownèd with one crest.
> And will you rent our ancient love asunder,
> To join with men in scorning your poor friend?
> It is not friendly, 'tis not maidenly.
> Our sex, as well as I, may chide you for it,
> Though I alone do feel the injury.
> (III.ii.198–219)

In a scene that parallels in its central position Titania's wooing of Bottom, the rupture of their friendship becomes final. They accuse and insult each other, with Hermia calling Helena a 'juggler', 'canker blossom', 'thief of love', 'painted maypole'; and Helena naming her a 'counterfeit' and a 'puppet' (III.ii.282–96). Their quarrel becomes absurd as it turns on Hermia's obsession, taken up by both Lysander and Helena, that Lysander has come to prefer

Helena because she is taller. Though no other women characters in Shakespeare's plays come close to fighting physically, Hermia threatens to scratch out Helena's eyes (III.ii.297–8). Her threat is serious enough to make Helena flee (ll.340–3). Lysander is made equally ridiculous in his abrupt change of heart; yet he and Demetrius are spared the indignity of a demeaning quarrel and leave the stage to settle their disagreement in a 'manly' fashion, with swords. Even though Puck makes a mockery of their combat through his teasing, they are not so thoroughly diminished as Hermia and Helena.

In the course of the play, both Hermia and Helena suffer at the hands of their lovers. Betrothed to Helena, Demetrius deserts her for Hermia. When she pursues him, he tells her that she makes him sick (II.i.212) and threatens to rape her (ll.214–19). By doggedly following him, she maintains a kind of desperate power over him. She will not play Dido to his Aeneas. Consequently, he cannot sustain the image of the romantic rake, whose women pine and die, commit suicide, or burn themselves on pyres when he leaves them. Disappointed in his love for Hermia, he cannot get loose from Helena. Yet her masochism undercuts her power:

> I am your spaniel; and, Demetrius,
> The more you beat me, I will fawn on you.
> Use me but as your spaniel, spurn me, strike me,
> Neglect me, lose me; only give me leave,
> Unworthy as I am, to follow you.
> What worser place can I beg in your love –
> And yet a place of high respect with me –
> Than to be usèd as you use your dog?
> (II.1.202–10)

When Helena is in a position of positive power with both Lysander and Demetrius in love with her, she cannot take advantage of it because she assumes that she is the butt of a joke. And of course, in a sense, she is right: she is the victim of either Puck's prank or his mistake. Hermia must also bear Lysander's contempt. In the forest, he insists that he 'hates' her (III.ii.270, 281) and calls her outrageous names: 'cat', 'burr', 'vile thing', 'tawny Tartar', 'loathed med'cine', 'hated potion', 'dwarf', 'minimus, of hind'ring knotgrass made', 'bead', 'acorn' (ll.260–4, 328–30). While both women protest their lovers' treatment of them, neither can play Beatrice to her Benedick. Both more or less bear their lovers' abuses.

After the four lovers sleep and awaken coupled as they will marry, Hermia and Helena do not reconcile. Once they leave the forest, they lose their voices. Neither of them speaks again. Recognising that it is difficult for an actor to be on stage without any lines, as Helena and Hermia are for almost all of Act V, Shakespeare was undoubtedly aware that he was creating a portentous silence. Since Helena and Hermia are evidently married between Acts IV and V, their silence suggests that in their new roles as wives they will be obedient, allowing their husbands dominance.

IV

The end of *A Midsummer Night's Dream* is as fully joyous as the conclusion of any of Shakespeare's comedies. No longer angry with each other, Oberon and Titania bring blessing to the human world:

> Hand in hand, with fairy grace,
> Will we sing, and bless this place.
> (V.i.398–9)

Though Oberon calls up dark possibilities, he offers a charm against them. The prospect of love, peace, safety, prosperity is as promising as it ever will be. The cost of this harmony, however, is the restoration of patriarchal hierarchy, so threatened at the beginning of the play. This return to the old order depends on the breaking of women's bonds with each other and the submission of women, which the play relentlessly exacts. Puck's verse provides the paradigm:

> Jack shall have Jill;
> Nought shall go ill;
> The man shall have his mare again,
> and all shall be well.

If we turn to some of Shakespeare's comedies in which women's bonds with each other are unbroken and their power is left intact or even dominates, the tone of the ending is less harmonious or even discordant.[17] In *The Merchant of Venice*, for example, where Portia is in control and she and Nerissa triumph over Gratiano and Bassanio, there is no ritual celebration. Portia directs the scene and carefully circumscribes her marriage with Bassanio to close out Antonio. When she and Nerissa reveal their identities as the doctor and the clerk, they make clear their extraordinary power to outwit and deceive, calling up women's ultimate destructive power in marriage and love – to cuckold. The final moments of the play move toward reconciliation, but not celebration. The last line, a bawdy joke, is spoken by Gratiano, the most hate-filled character in the play, and reminds us of men's fear of women and their need to control them: 'While I live I'll fear no other thing/So sore, as keeping safe Nerissa's ring' (V.i.306–7).

In *Love's Labour's Lost*, where the women remain together and in control, there is no comic ending.[18] Echoing Puck, Berowne makes the point as he speaks to the King of Navarre:

> Our wooing doth not end like an old play;
> Jack hath not Jill. These ladies' courtesy
> Might well have made our sport a comedy.

When the King replies, 'Come, sir, it wants a twelvemonth and a day,/And then 'twill end', Berowne answers, 'That's too long for a play' (V.ii.872–6). The refrains of the closing songs call forth images of cuckolding and of 'greasy Joan' stirring the pot.

The pattern of these comic endings suggests that heterosexual bonding is tenuous at best. In order to be secure, to enjoy, to love – to participate in the celebration that comedy invites – men need to maintain their ties with other men and to sever women's bonds with each other. The implication is that men fear that if women join with each other, they will not need men, will possibly exclude them or prefer the friendship and love of women. This is precisely the threat of the beautiful scene that Titania describes between herself and her votaress. This fear may be based partially on reality, but it is also partially caused by projection: since men have traditionally had stronger bonds with other men than with women and have excluded women from participation in things about which they cared most, they may assume that women, granted the opportunity, will do the same. Given this possibility or likelihood, Shakespeare's male characters act out of a fear of women's bonding with each other and a feeling of sexual powerlessness. The male characters think they can keep their women only if they divide and conquer them. Only then will Jack have Jill; only then will their world flourish.

From *Women's Studies*, 9 (1981), 48–63.

NOTES

[*A Midsummer Night's Dream* has received less attention from feminists than some other Shakespearean comedies, like *The Taming of The Shrew*, where female subservience is so blatantly an issue, and those where the cross-dressing of the heroines – notably *The Merchant of Venice*, *As You Like It* and *Twelfth Night* – foregrounds gender-definition (see Further Reading, 'Feminist Approaches', for specific names and texts associated with this note). Yet the action revolves around disjunctive father–daughter and husband–wife relationships, and the resistance of the women to 'normal' male authority, as Garner clearly demonstrates. In this she is neither concerned to highlight Shakespeare's portrayal of resourceful and strong-minded women, as some earlier feminists had done, nor to explore the ways in which these gender narratives are in any way peculiar to the sixteenth century; Louis Adrian Montrose (in a note to the next essay in this volume) describes her article as 'ahistorical' precisely because it does not address this issue. Some feminists have seen the Renaissance as an almost pre-lapsarian era, where gender roles were much freer and more fluid than they were to become under capitalist and bourgeois societies (and Shakespeare has been given some credit for reflecting this fluidity); others – increasingly preponderant – have seen the early modern era as just another chapter in the remorseless history of patriarchy, interesting because it set the terms for gender relations in the modern world (and Shakespeare is deemed complicit in the world he depicts). Garner sees the play rather as exploring some universal psychological facets of male–female relations, concentrating in particular on the male weaknesses implicitly exposed in the patriarchal exercise of power. Shakespeare is neither hero nor villain in this scenario; in fact, he takes something of a bit part. Once she has established that 'The movement of the play toward ordering the fairy, human, and natural world is also a movement toward satisfying men's psychological needs, as Shakespeare perceived them ... ', she treats the play as a free-standing narrative, almost an objective case study, rather than one in which the author is personally implicated. Ed.]

1. William Shakespeare, *The Complete Signet Classic Shakespeare*, ed. Sylvan Barnet (New York, 1972), *MND*, III.ii.461–4. Subsequent quotations from Shakespeare are from this edition.

2. C. L. Barber, *Shakespeare's Festive Comedy; A Study Of Dramatic Form and its Relation to Social Custom*, 2nd edn (1959; rpt. Cleveland, OH, 1963), pp. 119–24, 127.

3. In 'Hermia's Dream: Royal Road to *A Midsummer Night's Dream*', *Literature and Psychology*, 22 (1972), 188–9, M. D. Faber has ob-

served that 'the order for which the play strives is a severely patriarchal one which, by its very nature, engenders ambivalence and hostility in women, and thus produces a constant straining toward disorder'. Yet Faber's insistence that Theseus, 'a governor of strength and understanding', has transcended rigid patriarchal attitudes, and his suggestion that women are responsible for disorder make clear that our arguments are substantially different.

4. Describing Titania's lines as 'one of the most bravura speeches', Barber remarks that the moment is 'a glimpse of women who gossip alone, apart from men and feeling now no need of them, rejoicing in their own special part of life's power' (pp. 136–7).

5. Some male critics regard Titania's love as Oberon's right; Melvin Goldstein writes: 'We know also that Titania violates natural order by making the changeling child "all her joy", when her joy should be Oberon' ('Identity Crisis in a Midsummer Nightmare: Comedy as Terror in Disguise', *Psychoanalytic Review*, 60 [1973], 189).

6. Goldstein argues for example, that Titania 'needs to give up the boy not only for Oberon's and for her sake, but for the boy's sake. The danger is that in her company and that of her women friends she will feminise him' (p. 189). In his introduction to the New Arden edition of *A Midsummer Night's Dream* (London, 1979), Harold F. Brooks states, 'It is perhaps (Puck may imply this) high time the boy was weaned from maternal dandling to be bred a knight and huntsman' (p. cvi).

7. Jan Kott, *Shakespeare our Contemporary*, tr. Boleslaw Taborski (Garden City, NY, 1966), p. 227.

8. I use 'homoerotic desires' to mean unconsummated homosexual feelings, which may or may not be recognised.

9. Allan Lewis describes John Hancock's even more extreme presentation of Hippolyta in his production of the play in Greenwich Village in 1967: 'She was brought back from captivity, robed in leopard skins, was caged and guarded' ('*A Midsummer Night's Dream* – Fairy Fantasy or Erotic Nightmare?', *Educational Theatre Journal*, 21 [1969], 251).

10. References to Theseus and Helen are commonplace in the Renaissance. George Gascoigne, who uses the most ordinary classical allusions, addresses Paris in 'Dan Bartholmew his first Triumphe', one of the poems from *Dan Bartholomew of Bathe*:

> 'Alas, she made of thee, a nodye for the nonce,
> For *Menelaus* lost hir twise, though thou hir found but once.
> But yet if in thine eye, shee seemed a peereless peece,
> Aske *Theseus* the mighty Duke, what town she knew in *Greece*?
> Aske him what made hir leave hir wofull aged sire,

And steale to *Athens* gyglot like: what? what but foule desire?'
(*The Posies*, ed. John W. Cunliffe [Cambridge, 1907], I.101).

11. In an excellent article, '"Unkinde" Theseus: A Study in Renaissance Mythography' (*ELR*, 4[1973], 276–98), D'Orsay W. Pearson outlines classical and Renaissance traditions that depict Theseus's darker side, particularly his treacherous and abusive treatment of women. Shakespeare's audience would have been familiar with these traditions. If in remembering Theseus's heroic exploits, they forgot his 'unkindness', Shakespeare was careful to remind them by recalling women Theseus had loved and left. Pearson also analyses Theseus's opening speech, describing ways in which it suggests his negative Renaissance stereotype (p. 292).

12. In his frequent desertion of women, Theseus acts similarly to men Freud describes as evincing a dissociated erotic life. See 'A Special Type of Choice of Object Made by Men' and 'On the Universal Tendency to Debasement in the Sphere of Love', *The Standard Edition of The Complete Psychological Works of Sigmund Freud*, tr. James Strachey (London, 1957), XI, 166–7, 182–3.

13. In 'The Sexual Aberrations', the first of his *Three Contributions on the Theory of Sex*, Freud comments that a large proportion of male homosexuals 'retain the mental quality of masculinity ... and that what they look for in their real sexual object are in fact feminine mental traits'. Their 'sexual object is not someone of the same sex, but someone who combines the characters of both sexes ... a union of both sex characteristics, a compromise between an impulse that seeks for a man and one that seeks for a woman' (VII, 144–5).

14. Celeste Turner Wright, 'The Amazons in Elizabethan Literature' (*SP*, 37 [1940], 439).

15. E. K. Chambers notices that Theseus's marriage to Hippolyta evinces a change in character: 'Theseus has had his wayward youth; ... Moreover, in his passion for Hippolyta he has approached her through deeds of violence; he has "won her love, doing her injuries". But now, like Henry the Fifth of whom he is the prototype, he has put away childish things; he stands forth as the serene law-abiding king, no less than the still loving and tender husband' (*Shakespeare: A Survey* [London, 1925], pp. 84–5). Chambers is right in observing that Theseus has changed. I suggest that the change is not one of character but a result of altered situation: i.e. he has captured a woman who at last can fulfil his romantic needs, which until now have been disparate.

16. In considering the modification Shakespeare made in his construction of the plot involving the Athenian lovers, Chambers points especially to his 'making the broken friendship that of women, not that of men' (p. 82). In Chaucer's *Knight's Tale*, which Shakespeare drew on, Palomon's and Arcite's common love of Emilia breaks their friendship.

In *The Two Gentlemen of Verona*, in which the relation of Proteus and Valentine corresponds to that of Palomon and Arcite, the friendship between the two men is disrupted though two women, rather than one, are involved. Shakespeare's alteration of Chaucer's tale and variation on his former pattern in *A Midsummer Night's Dream* suggests that the disruption of women's bonds was a significant theme.

17. In a fine essay, 'Sexual Politics and the Social Structure in *As You Like It*', Peter B. Erickson argued similarly, in comparing the endings of *As You Like It* and *Love's Labour's Lost*: 'The ending of *As You Like It* works smoothly because male control is affirmed and women are rendered non-threatening, whereas in *Love's Labour's Lost* women do not surrender their independence and the status of patriarchy remains in doubt.' In *As You Like It*, he writes, 'Festive celebration is now possible because a dependable, that is patriarchal, social order is securely in place' (unpublished paper delivered at the session on 'Marriage and the Family in Shakespeare', sponsored by the Shakespeare Division, at the annual meeting of MLA, 1979, pp. 3, 15; forthcoming in the *Massachusetts Review*).

18. See Peter Erickson, 'The Failure of Relationship Between Men and Women in *Love's Labour's Lost*', *Women's Studies*, 9 (1981).

5

'Shaping Fantasies': Figurations of Gender and Power in Elizabethan Culture

LOUIS ADRIAN MONTROSE

I

Shakespeare's Duke Theseus formulates policy when he proclaims that 'The lunatic, the lover, and the poet / Are of imagination all compact'; that 'Lovers and madmen have such seething brains, / Such shaping fantasies, that apprehend / More than cool reason ever comprehends.'[1] The social order of Theseus' Athens depends upon his authority to name the forms and his power to control the subjects of mental disorder. The ruler's tasks is to *comprehend* – to understand and to encompass – the energies and motives, the diverse, unstable, and potentially subversive *apprehensions* of the ruled. But the Duke – so self-assured and benignly condescending in his comprehension – might also have some cause for apprehension: he himself and the fictional society over which he rules have been shaped by the imagination of a poet. My intertextual study of Shakespeare's *Midsummer Night's Dream* and symbolic forms shaped by other Elizabethan lunatics, lovers, and poets construes the play as calling attention to itself, not only as an end but also as a source of cultural production. Thus, in writing of 'shaping fantasies', I mean to suggest the dialectical character of cultural representations: the fantasies by which the text of *A Midsummer Night's Dream* has been shaped are also those to which it gives shape. I explore this dialectic within a specifically Elizabethan context of cultural production: the interplay between representations of gender and power in a stratified society in which authority is everywhere invested in men – everywhere, that is, except at the top.

In the introduction to his recent edition of *A Midsummer Night's Dream*, Harold Brooks summarises the consensus of modern criticism: 'Love and marriage is the [play's] central theme: love aspiring to and consummated in marriage, or to a harmonious partnership within it' (p. cxxx). But, as Paul Olson suggested some years ago, the harmonious marital unions of *A Midsummer Night's Dream* are in harmony with doctrines of Tudor apologists for the patriarchal family: marital union implies a domestic hierarchy; marital harmony is predicated upon the wife's obedience to her husband.[2] Brook's romantic view and Olson's authoritarian one offer limited but complementary perspectives on the dramatic process by which *A Midsummer Night's Dream* figures the social relationship between the sexes in courtship, marriage, and parenthood. The play imaginatively embodies what Gayle Rubin has called a 'sex–gender system': a socio-historical construction of sexual identity, difference and relationship; an appropriation of human anatomical and physiological features by an ideological discourse; a culture-specific fantasia upon Nature's universal theme.[3]

As has long been recognised, *A Midsummer Night's Dream* has affinities with Elizabethan courtly entertainments. In his edition of the play, Harold Brooks cautiously endorses the familiar notion that it was 'designed to grace a wedding in a noble household'. He adds that 'it seems likely that Queen Elizabeth was present when the *Dream* was first acted ... She delighted in homage paid to her as the Virgin Queen, and receives it in the myth-making about the imperial votaress' (pp. liii, lv). Although attractive and plausible, such topical connections must remain wholly conjectural. The perspective of my own analysis of the play's court connection is dialectical rather than causal, ideological rather than occasional. For, whether or not Queen Elizabeth was physically present at the first performance of *A Midsummer Night's Dream*, her pervasive *cultural presence* was a condition of the play's imaginative possibility. This is not to imply that *A Midsummer Night's Dream* is merely an inert 'product' of Elizabethan culture. The play is rather a new *production* of Elizabethan culture, enlarging the dimensions of the cultural field and altering the lines of force within it. Thus, in the sense that the royal presence was itself *re*-presented within the play, it may be said that the play henceforth conditioned the imaginative possibility of the Queen. In what follows, I shall explore how Shakespeare's play and other Elizabethan texts figure the Elizabethan sex–gender system and the queen's place within it.

II

I would like to recount an Elizabethan dream – not Shakespeare's *Midsummer Night's Dream*, but one dreamt by Simon Forman on 23 January 1597. Forman – a professional astrologer and physician, amateur alchemist, and avid playgoer – recorded in his diary the following account:

> I dreamt that I was with the Queen, and that she was a little elderly woman in a coarse white petticoat all unready; and she and I walked up and down through lanes and closes, talking and reasoning of many matters. At last we came over a great close where were many people, and there were two men at hard words. One of them was a weaver, a tall man with a reddish beard, distract of his wits. She talked to him and he spoke very merrily unto her, and at last did take her and kiss her. So I took her by the arm and put her away; and told her the fellow was frantic. And so we went from him and I led her by the arm still, and then we went through a dirty lane. She had a long, white smock, very clean and fair, and it trailed in the dirt and her coat behind. I took her coat and did carry it up a good way, and then it hung too low before. I told her she should do me a favour to let me wait on her, and she said I should. Then said I, 'I mean to wait *upon* you and not under you, that I might make this belly a little bigger to carry up this smock and coats out of the dirt'. And so we talked merrily and then she began to lean upon me, when we were past the dirt and to be very familiar with me, and methought she began to love me. And when we were alone, out of sight, methought she would have kissed me.[4]

It was then that Forman awoke.

Within the dreamer's unconscious, the 'little elderly woman' who was his political mother must have been linked to the mother who had borne him. In an autobiographical fragment, Forman repeatedly characterises himself as unloved and rejected by his mother during his childhood and youth: he writes of himself, that 'Simon, being a child of six years old, his father loved him above all the rest, but his mother nor brethren loved him not ... After the father of Simon was dead, his mother, who never loved him, grudged at his being at home, and what fault soever was committed by any of the rest he was beaten for it'.[5] Forman's mother was still alive at the date of his dream, a very old woman. C. L. Barber has suggested that 'the very central and problematical role of women in Shakespeare – and in Elizabethan drama generally – reflects the fact that Protestantism did away with the cult of the Virgin Mary. It meant the loss of ritual resource for dealing with the internal residues in all of us of the once all-powerful and all-inclusive mother.'[6] What Barber fails to note is that a concerted effort was in fact made to appropriate the symbolism and the affective power of the suppressed Marian cult in order to foster an Elizabethan cult. Both the internal residues and the religious rituals were potential resources for dealing with the political problems of the Elizabethan regime. Perhaps, at the same time, the royal cult may also have provided Forman and other Elizabethans with a resource for dealing with the internal residues of their relationships to the primary maternal figures of infancy. My concern is not to psychoanalyse Forman but rather to emphasise the historical specificity of psychological processes, the politics of the unconscious. Whatever the place of this dream in the dreamer's interior life, the text in which he represents it to himself allows us to glimpse the cultural contours of an Elizabethan psyche.

The virginal sex-object of Forman's dream, the 'little elderly woman' scantily clad in white, corresponds with startling accuracy to descriptions of Elizabeth's actual appearance in 1597. In the year that Forman dreamt his dream, the ambassador extraordinary of the French King Henri IV described the English Queen in his journal. At his first audience, he recorded:

> She was strangely attired in a dress of silver cloth, white and crimson ... She kept the front of her dress open, and one could see the whole of her bosom, and passing low, and often she would open the front of this robe with her hands as if she was too hot ... Her bosom is somewhat wrinkled ... but lower down her flesh is exceeding white and delicate, so far as one could see. As for her face, it is and appears to be very aged. It is long and thin, and her teeth are very yellow and unequal ... Many of them are missing so that one cannot understand her easily when she speaks quickly.[7]

For the ambassador's second audience, the Queen appeared

clad in a dress of black taffeta, bound with gold lace ... She had a
petticoat of white damask, girdled, and open in front, as was also her
chemise, in such a manner that she often opened this dress and one
could see all her belly, and even to her navel ... When she raises her
head, she has a trick of putting both hands on her gown and opening
it insomuch that all her belly can be seen.

(pp. 36–7)

In the following year, another foreign visitor who saw the Queen
noted that 'her bosom was uncovered, as all the English ladies have
it till they marry'.[8]

Elizabeth's display of her bosom signified her status as a maiden. But,
as in Spenser's personification of Charity as a nursing mother or in the
popular emblem of the life-rendering Pelican (which Elizabeth wore as
a pendant upon her bosom in one of her portraits), her breasts were
also those of a selfless and bountiful mother. The image of the Queen
as a wetnurse may have had some currency. Of the Earl of Essex's
insatiable thirst for those offices and honours which were in the
Queen's gift, Naunton wrote that 'my Lord ... drew in too fast, like a
childe sucking on an over-uberous Nurse'.[9] The Queen was the source
of her subjects' social sustenance, the fount of all preferments; she was
represented as a virgin-mother – part Madonna, part Ephesian Diana.
Like her bosom, Elizabeth's belly must have figured her political
motherhood. But, as the French ambassador insinuates, these conspicuous self-displays were also a kind of erotic provocation. The
official portraits and courtly blazons that represent the splendour of
the Queen's immutable body politic are nicely complemented by the
ambassador's sketches of the Queen's sixty-five year old body natural.
His perceptions of the vanity and melancholy of this personage in no
way negate his numerous observations of her grace, vitality, and
political cunning. Indeed, in the very process of describing the
Queen's preoccupation with the impact of her appearance upon her
beholders, the ambassador demonstrates its impact upon *himself*.

So, too, the aged Queen's body exerts a power upon the mind of
Doctor Forman; and, in his dream, he exerts a reciprocal power
upon the body of the Queen. The virginal, erotic, and maternal
aspects of the Elizabethan feminine that the royal cult appropriates
from the domestic domain are themselves appropriated by one of
the Queen's subjects and made the material for his dreamwork. At
the core of Forman's dream is his joke with the Queen: 'I told her
she should do me a favour to let me wait on her, and she said I

should. Then said I, "I mean to wait *upon* you and not under you, that I might make this belly a little bigger to carry up this smock and coats out of the dirt".' The joke – and, in a sense, the whole dream – is generated from Forman's verbal quibble: to *wait* upon/to *weight* upon. Within this subversive pun is concentrated the reciprocal relationship between dependency and domination. With one vital exception, all forms of public and domestic authority in Elizabethan England were vested in men: in fathers, husbands, masters, teachers, magistrates, lords. It was inevitable that the rule of a woman would generate peculiar tensions within such a 'patriarchal' society.[10] Forman's dream epitomises the indissolubly political and sexual character of the cultural forms in which such tensions might be represented and addressed. In Forman's wordplay, the subject's desire for employment (to *wait* upon) coexists with his desire for mastery (to *weight* upon); and the pun is manifested physically in his desire to inseminate his sovereign, which is at once to serve her and to possess her. And because the figures in the dream are not only subject and prince but also man and woman, what the *subject* desires to perform, the *man* has the capacity to perform: for Forman to raise the Queen's belly is to make her female body to bear the sign of his own potency. In the context of the cross-cutting relationships between subject and prince, man and woman, the dreamer insinuates into a gesture of homage, a will to power.

It is strange and admirable that the dreamer's rival for the Queen should be a weaver – as if Nick Bottom had wandered out of Shakespeare's *Dream* and into Forman's. Forman's story of the night does indeed have affinities with the 'most rare vision' (IV.i.203) that Shakespeare grants to Bottom. Bottom's dream, like Forman's, is an experience of fleeting intimacy with a powerful female who is at once lover, mother, and queen. The liaison between The Fairy Queen and the assified artisan is an outrageous theatrical realisation of a personal fantasy that was obviously not Forman's alone. Titania treats Bottom as if he were both her child and her lover. And she herself is ambivalently nurturing and threatening, imperious and enthralled. She dotes upon Bottom, and indulges in him all those desires to be fed, scratched, and coddled that make Bottom's dream into a parodic fantasy of infantile narcissism and dependency. The sinister side of Titania's possessiveness is manifested in her binding up of Bottom's tongue, and her intimidating command, 'Out of this wood do not desire to go:/Thou shalt remain here, whether thou wilt or no' (III.i.145–6). But if Titania manipulates Bottom, an artisan and amateur actor, she herself is manipulated by Oberon, a 'King of shadows' (III.ii.347) and the play's internal dramatist. A fantasy of male dependency upon woman is expressed and contained within a fantasy of male control over woman; the social reality of the player's dependency upon a Queen is inscribed within the imaginative reality of the dramatist's control over a Queen. Both Forman's private dream-text and Shakespeare's public play-text embody a culture-specific dialectic between personal and public images of gender and power; both are characteristically *Elizabethan* cultural forms.

III

The beginning of *A Midsummer Night's Dream* coincides with the end of a struggle in which Theseus has been victorious over the Amazon warrior:

> Hippolyta, I woo'd thee with my sword,
> And won thy love doing thee injuries;
> But I will wed thee in another key,
> With pomp, with triumph, and with revelling.
>   (I.i.16–19)

Descriptions of the Amazons are ubiquitous in Elizabethan texts. For example, all of the essentials are present in popular form in William Painter's 'Novel of the Amazones', which opens the second book of *The Palace of Pleasure* (1575). Here we read that the Amazons 'were most excellent warriors'; that 'they murdred certaine of their husbands' at the beginning of their gynaecocracy; that, 'if they brought forth daughters, they norished and trayned them up in armes, and other manlik exercises ... If they were delivered of males, they sent them to their fathers, and if by chaunce they kept any backe, they murdred them, or else brake their armes and legs in sutch wise as they had no power to beare weapons, and served for nothynge but to spin, twist, and doe other feminine labour.'[11] The Amazons' penchant for male infanticide is complemented by their obvious delight in subjecting powerful heroes to their will. Spenser's Artegall, hero of the Legend of Justice, becomes enslaved to Radigund, 'A Princesse of great powre, and greater pride, / And Queene of Amazons, in armes well tride' (*The Faerie Queene*,

V.4.33). Defeated by Radigund in personal combat, Artegall must undergo degradation and effeminisation of the kind endured by Hercules and by the Amazons' maimed sons.

Sixteenth-century travel narratives often recreate the ancient Amazons of Scythia in South America or in Africa. Invariably, the Amazons are relocated just beyond the receding boundary of *terra incognita*. Thus, in Sierra Leone in 1582, the chaplain of an English expedition to the Spice Islands recorded the report of a Portuguese trader that 'near the mountains of the moon there is a queen, empress of all these Amazons, a witch and a cannibal who daily feeds on the flesh of boys. She ever remains unmarried, but she has intercourse with a great number of men by whom she begets off-spring. The kingdom, however, remains hereditary to the daughters, not to the sons.'[12] This cultural fantasy assimilates Amazonian myth, witchcraft, and cannibalism into an anti-culture which precisely inverts European norms of political authority, sexual licence, marriage practices, and inheritance rules. The attitude toward the Amazons expressed in such Renaissance texts is a mixture of fascination and horror. Amazonian mythology seems symbolically to embody and to control a collective anxiety about the power of the female not only to dominate or reject the male but to create and destroy him. It is an ironic acknowledgement by an androcentric culture of the degree to which men are in fact dependent upon women: upon mothers and nurses, for their birth and nurture; upon mistresses and wives, for the validation of their manhood.

Shakespeare engages his wedding play in a dialectic with this mythological formation. The Amazons have been defeated before the play begins; and nuptial rites are to be celebrated when it ends. *A Midsummer Night's Dream* focuses upon different crucial transitions in the male and female life cycles: the fairy plot, upon taking 'a little changeling boy' from childhood into youth, from the world of the mother into the world of the father; the Athenian plot, upon taking a maiden from youth into maturity, from the world of the father into the world of the husband. The pairing of the four Athenian lovers is made possible by the magical powers of Oberon and made lawful by the political authority of Theseus. Each of these rulers is preoccupied with the fulfilment of his own desires in the possession or repossession of a wife. Only after Hippolyta has been mastered by Theseus may marriage seal them 'in everlasting bond of fellowship' (I.i.85). And only after 'proud Titania' has been degraded by 'jealous Oberon' (II.i.60, 61), has 'in mild terms begg'd' (IV.i.57) his patience, and has readily yielded the changeling boy to him, may they be 'new in amity' (IV.i.86).

The diachronic structure of *A Midsummer Night's Dream* eventually restores the inverted Amazonian system of gender and nurture to a patriarchal norm. But the initial plans for Theseus' triumph are immediately interrupted by news of yet another unruly female. Egeus wishes to confront his daughter Hermia with two alternatives: absolute obedience to the paternal will, or death. Theseus intervenes with a third alternative: if she refuses to marry whom her father chooses, Hermia must submit

> Either to die the death or to abjure
> Forever the society of men.
> ...
> For aye to be in shady cloister mew'd,
> Chanting faint hymns to the cold, fruitless moon.
> Thrice blessed they that master so their blood
> To undergo such maiden pilgrimage;
> But earthlier happy is the rose distill'd
> Than that which, withering on the virgin thorn,
> Grows, lives, and dies, in single blessedness.
> (I.i.65–6, 71–8)

Theseus has characteristically Protestant notions about the virtue of virginity: maidenhood is a phase in the life-cycle of a woman who is destined for married chastity and motherhood. As a permanent state, 'single blessedness' is mere sterility. Theseus expands Hermia's options only in order to clarify the constraints. In the process of tempering the father's domestic tyranny, the Duke affirms his own interests and authority. He represents the life of a vestal as a *punishment*, and it is one that fits the nature of Hermia's crime. The maiden is surrounded by men, each of whom – as father, lover, or lord – claims a kind of property in her. Yet Hermia dares to suggest that she has a claim to property in herself: she refuses to 'yield [her] virgin patent up / Unto his lordship whose unwished yoke / [Her] soul consents not to give sovereignty' (I.i.80–2). Like Rosalind, in *As You Like It*, Hermia wishes the limited privilege of giving herself. Theseus appropriates the source of Hermia's fragile power: her ability to deny men access to her body. He usurps the power of virginity by imposing upon Hermia his own power to deny her the use of her body. If she will not submit to its use by her father and by Demetrius, she must 'abjure forever the society of men', and 'live a barren sister all [her] life' (I.i.65–6, 72). Her own words suggest that the female body is a supreme form of property and a locus for the contestation of authority. The self-possession of single blessdness is a form of power against which are opposed the marriage doctrines of Shakespeare's culture and the very form of his comedy.

In devising Hermia's punishment, Theseus appropriates and parodies the very condition which the Amazons sought to enjoy. They rejected marriages with men and alliances with patriarchal societies because, as one sixteenth-century writer put it, they esteemed 'that Patrimonie was not a meane of libertie but of thraldome'.[13] The separatism of the Amazons is a repudiation of men's claims to have property in women. But if Amazonian myth figures the inversionary claims of matriarchy, sisterhood, and the autonomy of women, it also figures the *repudiation* of those claims in the act of Amazonomachy. Painter recounts the battle between the Amazons, led by Menalippe and Hippolyta (both sisters of Queen Antiopa) and the Greeks, led by Hercules and Theseus. Hercules returned Menalippe to Antiopa in exchange for the Queen's armour, 'but Theseus for no offer that she coulde make, woulde he deliver Hippolyta, with whom he was so farre in love, that he carried her home with him, and afterward toke her to wyfe, of whom hee had a sonne called Hipolitus' (*The Palace of Pleasure*, 2:163). Theseus' violent and insatiable lust – what North's Plutarch suggestively calls his 'womannishenes' – divorced Hippolyta from her sisters and from the society of Amazons.[14]

Shakespeare's play naturalises Amazonomachy in the vicissitudes of courtship. Heterosexual desire disrupts the innocent pleasures of Hermia's girlhood: 'What graces in my love do dwell, / That he hath turn'd a heaven unto a hell!' (I.i.206–7). Hermia's farewell to Helena is also a farewell to their girlhood friendship, a delicate repudiation of youthful homophilia:

> And in the wood, where often you and I
> Upon faint primrose beds were wont to lie,
> Emptying our bosoms of their counsel sweet,
> There my Lysander and myself shall meet;
> And thence from Athens turn away our eyes,
> To seek new friends, and stranger companies.
> (I.i.214–19)

Before dawn comes to the forest, the 'counsel' shared by Hermia and Helena, their 'sisters' vows ... school-days' friendship, childhood innocence' (III.ii.198, 199, 202), have all been torn asunder, to be replaced at the end of the play by the primary demands and loyalties of wedlock. On the other hand, by dawn the hostilities between the two male youths have dissolved into 'gentle concord' (IV.i.142). From the beginning of the play, the relationship between Lysander and Demetrius has been based upon aggressive rivalry for the same object of desire: first for Hermia, and then for Helena. Each youth must despise his previous mistress in order to adore the next; and a change in one's affections provokes a change in the other's. R. W. Dent has pointed out that the young women do not fluctuate in their desires for their young men, and that the ending ratifies their constant if inexplicable preferences.[15] It should be added that the maidens remain constant to their men at the cost of inconstancy to each other. If Lysander and Demetrius are flagrantly inconstant to Hermia and Helena, the pattern of their inconstancies nevertheless keeps them constant to each other. The romantic resolution transforms this constancy from one of rivalry to one of friendship by making each male to accept his own female. In Puck's charmingly crude formulation:

> And the country proverb known,
> That every man should take his own,
> In your waking shall be shown:
> Jack shall have Jill,
> Nought shall go ill:
> The man shall have his mare again, and all shall be well.
>
> (III.ii.458–63)

At the end of *A Midsummer Night's Dream*, as at the end of *As You Like It*, the marital couplings dissolve the bonds of sisterhood at the same time that they forge the bonds of brotherhood.[16]

According to the paradigm of Northrop Frye, Shakespearean comedy 'normally begins with an anti-comic society, a social organisation blocking and opposed to the comic drive, which the action of the comedy evades or overcomes. It often takes the form of a harsh or irrational law, like ... the law disposing of rebellious daughters in *A Midsummer Night's Dream* ... Most of these irrational laws are preoccupied with trying to regulate the sexual drive, and so work counter to the wishes of the hero and heroine, which form the main impetus of the comic action'.[17] Frye's account of Shakespearean comic action emphasises intergenerational tension at the expense of those other forms of social and familial tension from which it is only artificially separable; in particular, he radically un-

dervalues the centrality of sexual politics to these plays by unques-
tioningly identifying the heroines' interests with those of the heroes.
The interaction of characters in the fictive societies of
Shakespearean drama – like the interaction of persons in the society
of Shakespeare's England – is structured by the complex interplay
among culture-specific categories, not only of age and gender but
also of kinship and class. The 'drive toward a festive conclusion'
(Frye, p. 75) which liberates and unites comic heroes and heroines
also subordinates wives to husbands and confers the responsibilities
and privileges of manhood upon callow youths. What Frye calls
'the main impetus' of Shakespearean comic action is not so much to
liberate 'the sexual drive' from 'irrational laws' as it is to fabricate
a temporary accommodation between law and libido. In *A
Midsummer Night's Dream*, as in other Shakespearean comedies,
the 'drive toward a festive conclusion' is, specifically, a drive
toward a wedding. And in its validation of marriage, the play is less
concerned to sacrimentalise libido than to socialise it.

In the opening scene, Egeus claims that he may do with Hermia
as he chooses because she is his property: 'As she is mine, I may
dispose of her' (I.i.142). This claim is based upon a stunningly
simple thesis: she is his because he has *made* her. Charging that
Lysander has 'stol'n the impression' (I.i.32) of Hermia's fantasy,
Egeus effectively absolves his daughter from responsibility for her
affections because he cannot acknowledge her capacity for volition.
If she does not – cannot – obey him, then she should be destroyed.
Borrowing Egeus' own imprinting metaphor, Theseus explains
to Hermia the ontogenetic principle underlying her father's
vehemence:

> To you your father should be as a god:
> One that compos'd your beauties, yea, and one
> To whom you are but as a form in wax
> By him imprinted, and within his power
> To leave the figure or disfigure it.
> (I.i.47–51)

Theseus represents paternity as a cultural act, an art: the father is a
demiurge or *homo faber*, who composes, in-forms, imprints himself
upon, what is merely inchoate matter. Conspicuously excluded
from Shakespeare's play is the relationship between mother and
daughter – the kinship bond through which Amazonian society reproduces itself. The mother's part is wholly excluded from this

account of the making of a daughter. Hermia and Helena have no mothers; they have only fathers. The central female characters of Shakespeare's comedies are not mothers but mothers-to-be, maidens who are passing from fathers to husbands in a world made and governed by men.

In effect, Theseus' lecture on the shaping of a *daughter* is a fantasy of male parthenogenesis. Titania's votaress is the only biological mother in *A Midsummer Night's Dream*. But she is an absent presence who must be evoked from Titania's memory because she has died in giving birth to a *son*. Assuming that they do not maim their sons, the Amazons are only too glad to give them away to their fathers. In Shakespeare's play, however, Oberon's paternal power must be directed against Titania's maternal possessiveness:

> For Oberon is passing fell and wrath,
> Because that she as her attendant hath
> A lovely boy, stol'n from an Indian king–
> She never had so sweet a changeling;
> And jealous Oberon would have the child
> Knight of his train to trace the forest wild;
> But she perforce withholds the loved boy,
> Crowns him with flowers, and makes him all her joy.
>   (II.i.20–7)

A boy's transition from the female-centred world of his early childhood to the male-centred world of his youth is given a kind of phylogenetic sanction by myths recounting a cultural transition from matriarchy to patriarchy. Such a myth is represented at the very threshold of *A Midsummer Night's Dream*: Theseus' defeat of the Amazonian matriarchate sanctions Oberon's attempt to take the boy from an infantilising mother and to make a man of him. Yet 'jealous' Oberon is not only Titania's rival for the child but also the child's rival for Titania: making the boy 'all her joy', 'proud' Titania withholds herself from her husband; she has 'forsworn his bed and company' (II.i.62–3). Oberon's preoccupation is to gain possession, not only of the boy but of the woman's desire and obedience; he must master his own dependency upon his wife.

Titania has her own explanation for her fixation upon the changeling:

> His mother was a votress of my order
> And in the spiced Indian air, by night,
> Full often hath she gossip'd by my side;

> And sat with me on Neptune's yellow sands,
> Marking th'embarked traders on the flood:
> When we have laugh'd to see the sails conceive
> And grow big-bellied with the wanton wind;
> Which she, with pretty and with swimming gait
> Following (her womb then rich with my young squire),
> Would imitate, and sail upon the land
> To fetch me trifles, and return again
> As from a voyage rich with merchandise.
> But she, being mortal, of that boy did die;
> And for her sake do I rear up her boy;
> And for her sake I will not part with him
>   (II.i.123–37)

Titania's attachment to the changeling boy embodies her attachment to the memory of his mother. What Oberon accomplishes by substituting Bottom for the boy is to break Titania's solemn vow. As in the case of the Amazons, or of Hermia and Helena, the play again enacts a male disruption of an intimate bond between women: first by the boy, and then by the man. It is as if, in order to be freed and enfranchised from the prison of the womb, the male child must *kill* his mother: 'She, being mortal, of that boy did die.' Titania's words suggest that mother and son are potentially mortal to each other: the matricidal infant complements the infanticidal Amazon. As is later the case with Bottom, Titania both dotes upon and dominates the child, attenuating his imprisonment to the womb: 'And for her sake I will not part with him.' Thus, within the changeling plot are embedded transformations of the male fantasies of motherhood which are figured in Amazonian myth.

Titania represents her bond to her votaress as one that is rooted in an experience of female fecundity, an experience for which men must seek merely mercantile compensations. The women 'have laugh'd to see the sails conceive / And grow big-bellied with the wanton wind'; and the votaress has parodied such false pregnancies by sailing to fetch trifles while she herself bears riches within her very womb. The notion of maternity implied in Titania's speech counterpoints the notion of paternity formulated by Theseus in the opening scene. In Theseus' description, neither biological nor social mother – neither *genetrix* nor *mater* – plays a role in the making of a daughter; in Titania's description, neither *genitor* nor *pater* plays a role in the making of a son. The father's daughter is shaped from without; the mother's son comes from within her body: Titania dwells upon the physical bond between mother and child, as manifested in pregnancy and parturition. Like an infant of the Elizabethan upper classes, however, the changeling is nurtured not by his natural mother but by a surrogate. By emphasising her own role as a foster mother to her gossip's offspring, Titania links the biological and social aspects of parenthood together within a wholly maternal world, a world in which the relationship between women has displaced the relationship between wife and husband. Nevertheless, despite the exclusion of a paternal role from Titania's speech, Shakespeare's embryological notions remain distinctly Aristotelian, distinctly phallocentric: the mother is represented as a *vessel*, as a container for her son; she is not his *maker*. In contrast, the implication of Theseus' description of paternity is that the male is the only begetter; a daughter is merely a token of her father's potency. Thus these two speeches may be said to formulate in poetic discourse, a proposition about the genesis of gender and power: men make women, and make themselves through the medium of women. Such a proposition reverses the Amazonian practice, in which women use men merely for their own reproduction. But much more than this, it seems an overcompensation for the *natural* fact that men do indeed come from women; an overcompensation for the *cultural* facts that consanguineal and affinal ties *between* men are established through mothers, wives, and daughters. *A Midsummer Night's Dream* dramatises a set of claims which are repeated throughout Shakespeare's canon: claims for a spiritual kinship among men that is unmediated by women; for the procreative powers of men; and for the autogeny of men.

It may be relevant to recall that what we tend to think of as the 'facts of life' have been established as *facts* relatively recently in human history, with the development of microbiology that began in Europe in the late seventeenth century. Of course, that seminal and menstrual fluids are in some way related to generation, and that people have both a father and a mother are hardly novel notions. My point is that, in Shakespeare's age, they remained *merely* notions. Although biological maternity was readily apparent, biological paternity was a cultural construct for which ocular proof was unattainable. More specifically, the evidence for *unique* biological paternity, for the physical link between a particular man and child, has always been exiguous. And, in Shakespearean drama, this link is frequently a focus of anxious concern, whether the concern is to validate paternity or to call it in question. Thus, Lear tells Regan that if she were *not* glad to see him, 'I would divorce me from thy mother's tomb, / Sepulchring an adult'ress' (*King Lear*, II.iv.131–2). And Leontes exclaims, upon first meeting Florizel, 'Your mother was most true to wedlock, Prince, / For she did print your royal father off, / Conceiving you' (*The Winter's Tale*, V.i.124–6). In the former speech, a vulnerable father invokes his previously unacknowledged wife precisely when he wishes to repudiate his child; while in the latter, a vulnerable husband celebrates female virtue as the instrument of male self-reproduction.

The role of genetrix is self-evident but the role of genitor is not. As Launcelot Gobbo puts it, in *The Merchant of Venice*, 'it is a wise father that knows his own child' (*MV*, II.ii.76–7). This consequence of biological asymmetry calls forth an explanatory – and compensatory – asymmetry in many traditional embryological theories: paternity is procreative, the formal and/or efficient cause of generation; maternity is nurturant, the material cause of generation. For example, according to *The Problemes of Aristotle*, a popular Elizabethan medical guide that continued to be revised and reissued well into the nineteenth century,

> The seede [i.e. of the male] is the efficient beginning of the childe, as the builder is the efficient cause of the house, and therefore is not the materiall cause of the childe … . The seedes [i.e. both male and female] are shut and kept in the wombe: but the seede of the man doth dispose and prepare the seed of the woman to receive the forme, perfection, or soule, the which being done, it is converted into humiditie, and is fumed and breathed out by the pores of the matrix, which is manifest, bicause onely the flowers [i.e. the menses] of the woman are the materiall cause of the yoong one.[18]

Conflating Aristotelian and Galenic notions, the text registers some confusion about the nature of the inseminating power and about its attribution to the woman as well as to the man. Although the contributions of both man and woman are necessary, the female seed is nevertheless materially inferior to that of the male. The notion of woman as an unperfected, an inadequate, imitation of man extends to the analogy of semen and menses: 'The seede … is white in man by reason of his greate heate, and because it is digested better … . The seede of a woman is red … because the flowers is corrupt, undigested blood' (*Problemes of Aristotle*, sig. E3ʳ). Whether in folk medicine or in philosophy, notions of maternity have a persistent natural or physical bias, while notions of paternity have a persistent social or spiritual bias. And such notions are articulated within a belief-system in which nature is subordinated to society, and matter is subordinated to spirit. The act of generation brings man and woman into a relationship that is both complementary and hierarchical. Thus, there exists a homology between the cultural construction of sexual generation and the social institution of marriage: genitor is to genetrix as husband is to wife.

While Shakespeare's plays reproduce these legitimating structures, they also reproduce challenges to their legitimacy. For, like the ubiquitous jokes and fears about cuckoldry to which they are usually linked, the frequent allusions within Shakespeare's texts to the incertitude of paternity point to a source of tension, to a potential contradiction, within the ostensibly patriarchal sex–gender system of Elizabethan culture. Oberon's epithalamium represents procreation as the union of man and woman, and marriage as a relationship of mutual affection:

> To the best bride-bed will we,
> Which by us shall blessed be;
> And the issue there create
> Ever shall be fortunate.
> So shall all the couples three
> Ever true in loving be.
> (V.i.389–94)

This benign vision is predicated upon the play's reaffirmation of the father's role in generation and the husband's authority over the wife. But at the same time that the play reaffirms essential elements of a patriarchal ideology, it also calls that reaffirmation in question; irrespective of authorial intention, the text intermittently undermines its own comic propositions. Oberon assures himself that, by the end of the play, 'all things shall be peace' (III.ii.377). But the continuance of the newlyweds' loves and the good fortune of their issue are by no means assured. Indeed, as soon as the lovers have gone off to bed, Puck begins to evoke an uncomic world of labour, fear, pain, and death (V.i.357–76). This invocation gives some urgency to Oberon's subsequent ritual blessing: the dangers are imminent and the peace is most fragile. *A Midsummer Night's Dream* ends, not only with the creation of new children but with the creation of new mothers and new fathers; it ends upon the threshhold of another generational cycle, which contains *in potentia* a renewal of the strife with which the play began. The status of 'jealous' Oberon and 'proud' Titania as personifications of forces in Nature at once sanctions and subverts the doctrine of domestic hierarchy. For, as personified in Shakespeare's fairies, the divinely ordained imperatives of Nature call attention to themselves as the humanly constructed imperatives of Culture: Shakespeare's naturalisation and legitimation of the domestic economy deconstructs itself. The all-too-human struggle between the play's already married couple provides an ironic prognosis for the new marriages.

The promised end of romantic comedy is not only undermined by dramatic ironies but also contaminated by a kind of inter-textual irony. The mythology of Theseus is filled with instances of terror, lust, and jealousy which are prominently recounted and censured by Plutarch in his *Life of Theseus* and in his subsequent comparison of Theseus with Romulus. Shakespeare uses Plutarch as his major source of Theseus-lore but does so highly selectively, excluding those events 'not sorting with a nuptial ceremony' (V.i.55) nor with a comedy. Nevertheless, as Harold Brooks' edition has now conclusively demonstrated, the text of Shakespeare's play is permeated by echoes not only of Plutarch's parallel lives of Theseus and Romulus but also of Seneca's *Hippolitus* and his *Medea* – by an archaeological record of the texts which shaped the poet's fantasy as he was shaping his play. Thus, sedimented within the verbal texture of *A Midsummer Night's Dream* are traces of those forms of sexual and familial violence which the play would suppress: acts of bestiality and incest, of parricide, uxoricide, filicide, and suicide; sexual fears and urges erupting in cycles of violent desire – from Pasiphae and the Minotaur to Phaedra and Hippolitus. The seductive and destructive powers of women figure centrally in Theseus' career; and his habitual victimisation of women, the chronicle of his rapes and disastrous marriages, is a discourse of anxious misogyny which persists as an echo within Shakespeare's text, no matter how much it has been muted or transformed.[19]

The play actually calls attention to the mechanism of mythological suppression by an ironically meta-dramatic gesture: Theseus demands 'some delight' with which to 'beguile / The lazy time' (V.i.40–1) before the bedding of the brides. The list of available entertainments includes 'The battle with the Centaurs, to be sung / By an Athenian eunuch to the harp', as well as 'The riot of the tipsy Bacchanals, / Tearing the Thracian singer in their rage' (V.i.44–5, 48–9). Theseus rejects both – because they are already too familiar.

These brief scenarios encompass the extremes of reciprocal violence between the sexes. The first performance narrates a wedding that degenerates into rape and warfare; the singer and his subject – Athenian eunuch and phallic Centaur – are two antithetical kinds of male-monster. In the second performance, what was often seen as the natural inclination of women toward irrational behaviour is manifested in the Maenads' terrible rage against Orpheus. The tearing and decapitation of the misogynistic Ur-Poet at once displaces and vivifies the Athenian singer's castration; and it also evokes the fate of Hippolytus, the misogynistic offspring of Theseus and Hippolyta. It is in its intermittent ironies, dissonances, and contradictions that the text of *A Midsummer Night's Dream* discloses – perhaps, in a sense, despite itself – that patriarchal norms are compensatory for the vulnerability of men to the powers of women.

IV

Such moments of textual disclosure also illuminate the interplay between sexual politics in the Elizabethan family and sexual politics in the Elizabethan monarchy: for the woman to whom *all* Elizabethan men were vulnerable was Queen Elizabeth herself. Within legal and fiscal limits, she held the power of life and death over every Englishman; the power to advance or frustrate the worldly desires of all her subjects. Her personality and personal symbolism helped to mould English culture and the consciousness of Englishmen for several generations.

Although the Amazonian metaphor might seem suited to strategies for praising a woman ruler, it was never popular among Elizabethan encomiasts. Its associations must have been too sinister to suit the personal tastes and political interests of the Queen. However, Sir Walter Ralegh did boldly compare Elizabeth to the Amazons in his *Discoverie of Guiana*.[20] In his digression on the Amazons, who are reported to dwell 'not far from Guiana', Ralegh repeats the familiar details of their sexual and parental practices, and notes that they 'are said to be very cruel and bloodthirsty, especially to such as offer to invade their territories' (p. 28). At the end of his narrative, Ralegh exhorts Elizabeth to undertake a conquest of Guiana:

> Her Majesty heereby shall confirme and strengthen the opinions of al nations, as touching her great and princely actions. And where the

south border of *Guiana* reacheth to the Dominion and Empire of the *Amazones*, those women shall heereby heare the name of a virgin, which is not onely able to defend her owne territories and her neighbors, but also to invade and conquere so great Empyres and so farre removed.

(p. 120)

Ralegh's strategy for convincing the Queen to advance his colonial enterprise is to insinuate that she is both like and unlike an Amazon; that Elizabethan imperialism threatens not only the Empire of the Guiana but the Empire of the Amazons; and that Elizabeth can definitively cleanse herself from contamination by the Amazons if she sanctions their subjugation. The Amazonomachy which Ralegh projects into the imaginative space of the New World is analogous to that narrated by Spenser within the imaginative space of Faeryland. Radigund, the Amazon Queen, can only be defeated by Britomart, the martial maiden who is Artegall's betrothed and the fictional ancestress of Elizabeth. Radigund is Britomart's double, split off from her as an allegorical personification of everything in Artegall's beloved which threatens him. Having destroyed Radigund and liberated Artegall from his effeminate 'thraldome', Britomart reforms what is left of Amazon society: she

> The liberty of women did repeale,
> Which they had long usurpt; and them restoring
> To mens subjection, did true Justice deale:
> That all they as a Goddesse her adoring,
> Her wisedome did admire, and hearkned to her loring.
> (*The Faerie Queene*, V.7.42)

Unlike some of the popular sixteenth-century forms of misrule so well discussed by Natalie Davis, this instance of sexual inversion, of Woman-on-Top, would seem to be intended as an exemplum 'of order and stability in a hierarchical society', which 'can clarify the structure by the process of reversing it'.[21] For Ralegh's Elizabeth, as for Spenser's Britomart, the woman who has the prerogative of a goddess, who is authorised to be out of place, can best justify her authority by putting other women in their places.

A few paragraphs before Ralegh exhorts Elizabeth to undertake an Amazonomachy, he exhorts his gentlemen-readers to commit a cultural rape:

> Guiana is a Countrey that hath yet her Maydenhead, never sackt, turned, nor wrought, the face of the earth hath not beene torne, nor the vertue and salt of the soyle spent by manurance, the graves have not beene opened for gold, the mines not broken with sledges, nor their Images puld down out of their temples. It hath never been entered by any armie of strength and never conquered and possessed by any Christian Prince.
>
> (p. 115)

Ralegh's enthusiasm is, at one and the same time, for the unspoiled quality of this world and for the prospect of despoiling it. Guiana, like the Amazons, is fit to be wooed with the sword and won with injuries. Such metaphors have a peculiar resonance in the context of an address to Elizabeth. Certainly, it is difficult to imagine Ralegh using them to represent the plantation of Virginia, which had been named by and for the Virgin Queen. When, in the proem to the second book of *The Faerie Queene*, Spenser conjoins 'the Amazons huge river' and 'fruitfullest Virginia' (*FQ*, II.Proem.2), he is invoking not only two regions of the New World but two archetypes of Elizabethan culture: the engulfing Amazon and the nurturing Virgin. Later in the same book, they are conjoined again: Belphoebe, the beautiful virgin huntress who figures Queen Elizabeth in her body natural, is introduced into the poem with an extended blazon (*FQ*, II.3.21–31) that insinuates sexual provocation into its encomium of militant chastity. The description concludes in a curiously ominous epic simile, in which the Amazonian image is at once celebrated and mastered: Belphoebe is compared both to the goddess Diana and to Penthesilea, 'that famous Queene / Of *Amazons*, whom *Pyrrhus* did destroy' (*FQ*, II.3.31). Women's bodies – and, in particular, the Queen's two bodies – provide a cognitive map for Elizabethan culture, a veritable matrix for the Elizabethan forms of desire.

The Queen herself was too politic, and too ladylike, to wish to pursue the Amazonian image very far. Instead, she transformed it to suit her purposes, representing herself as an androgynous marital maiden, like Spenser's Britomart. Such was her appearance at Tilbury in 1588, where she had come to review her troops in expectation of a Spanish invasion. On that momentous occasion, she rode a white horse and dressed in white velvet; she wore a silver cuirass on her breast and carried a silver truncheon in her hand. The theme of her speech was by then already familiar to her listeners: she dwelt upon the womanly frailty of her body natural and the masculine strength of her body politic – a strength deriving from the love of her people, the virtue of her lineage, and the will of her God: 'I have always so behaved myself that, under God, I have placed my chiefest strength and safeguard in the loyal hearts and good will of my subjects ... . I know I have the body of a weak and feeble woman, but I have the heart and stomach of a king, and of a king of England too.'[22] As the female ruler of what was, at least in theory, a patriarchal society, Elizabeth incarnated a contradiction at the very centre of the Elizabethan sex–gender system. When Spenser's narrator moralises on the negative example of the Amazons, he must be careful to provide himself with an escape clause at the end of his stanza:

> Such is the crueltie of womenkynd
> When they have shaken off the shamefast band,
> With which wise Nature did them strongly bynd,
> T'obay the heasts of mens well ruling hand,
> That then all rule and reason they withstand,
> To purchase a licentious libertie.
> But vertuous women wisely understand,
> That they were borne to base humilitie,
> Unlesse the heavens them lift to lawful soveraintie.
> (*FQ*,V.5.25)

After the death of their royal mistress, Cecil wrote to Harington that she had been 'more than a man, and, in troth, sometimes less than a woman'.[23] Queen Elizabeth was a cultural anomaly; and this anomalousness – at once divine and monstrous – made her powerful, and dangerous. By the skilful deployment of images that were at once awesome and familiar, this perplexing creature tried to mollify her male subjects while enhancing her authority over them.

At the beginning of her reign, Elizabeth formulated the strategy by which she turned the political liability of her gender to advantage for the next half century. She told her first parliaments that she was content to have as her epitaph 'that a Queen, having reigned such a time, lived and died a virgin'; that her coronation ring betokened her marriage to her subjects; and that, although after her death her people might have many stepdames, yet they should never have 'a more natural mother than [she] meant to be unto [them] all'.[24] One way in which she actualised her maternal policy was to sponsor more than a hundred godchildren, the off-spring of nobility and commoners alike.

In his memorial of Elizabeth, Bacon epitomised her policy on gender and power:

> The reigns of women are commonly obscured by marriage; their praises and actions passing to the credit of their husbands; whereas those that continue unmarried have their glory entire and proper to themselves. In her case this was more especially so; inasmuch as she had no helps to lean upon in her government, except such as she herself provided ... no kinsmen of the royal family, to share her cares and support her authority. And even those whom she herself raised to honour she so kept in hand and mingled one with the other, that while she infused into each the greatest solicitude to please her, she was herself ever her own mistress.[25]

As Elizabeth herself reportedly told the Earl of Leicester, 'I will have here but one Mistress, and no Master' (Naunton, *Fragmenta Regalia*, p. 17). To be her own mistress, her own master, the Queen had to be everyone's mistress and no one's. Lawrence Stone wryly remarks that 'things were not easy for lovers at the Court of Elizabeth'. She frequently intervened in the personal affairs of those who attended her, preventing or punishing courtships and marriages not to her liking. As Stone points out, 'her objections were based partly ... on a desire to preserve the Court as the focus of interest of every English man and woman of note. She was afraid, with reason, that marriage would create other interests and responsibilities, and replace the attendance of both husband and wife upon her Court and upon herself.'[26] It was this royal politics of centripetal force that Spenser imaged in the proem to his 'legend ... of Courtesie':

> Then pardon me, most dreaded Soveraine,
> That from yourselfe I doe this vertue bring,
> And to your self doe it returne againe:
> So from the Ocean all rivers spring,
> And tribute backe repay as to their King.
> Right so from you all goodly vertues well
> Into the rest, which round about you ring,
> Faire Lords and Ladies, which about you dwell,
> And doe adorne your Court, where courtesies excell.
> (*FQ*, VI.Proem.7)

In a royal household comprising some fifteen hundred courtiers and retainers, the Queen's female entourage consisted of merely a dozen ladies of high rank – married or widowed – and half a dozen maids of honour from distinguished families, whose conduct was of almost obsessive interest to their mistress. Sir John Harington, the Queen's godson and an acute observer of her ways, wrote in a letter that 'she did oft aske the ladies around hir chamber, If they lovede to thinke of marriage? And the wise ones did conceal well their liking hereto; as knowing the Queene's judgement in this matter.' He goes on to relate an incident in which one of the maids of honour, 'not knowing so deeply as hir fellowes, was asked one day hereof, and simply said – "she had thought muche about marriage, if her father did consent to the man she lovede".' Thereupon, the Queen obtained the father's consent that she should deal as she saw fit with her maid's desires. 'The ladie was called in, and the Queene tould her father had given his free consente. "Then, replied the ladie, I shall be happie and please your Grace." – "So thou shalte; but not to be a foole and marrye. I have his consente given to me, and I vow thou shalte never get it into thy possession ... . I see thou art a bolde one, to owne thy foolishnesse so readilye".'[27] The virgin Queen threatened her vestal with the prospect of living a barren sister all her life. Directly, in cases such as this, and indirectly through the operation of the Court of Wards, the Queen reserved to herself the traditional paternal power to give or withhold daughters. Among the aristocracy, marriage was not merely a legal and affective union between private persons but also a political and economic alliance between powerful families; it was an institution over which a careful and insecure monarch might well wish to exercise an absolute control. Behaviour which, in the context of Elizabeth's body natural, may have been merely peevish or jealous was, in the context of her body politic, politic indeed.

Elizabeth's self-mastery and mastery of others were enhanced by an elaboration of her maidenhood into a cult of virginity which 'allows of amorous admiration but prohibits desire' (Bacon, *In Felicem Memoriam*, p. 460); the displacement of her wifely duties from a household to a nation; and the sublimation of her temporal and ecclesiastical authority into a nurturing maternity. She appropriated not only the suppressed cult of the Blessed Virgin but also the Tudor conception of the Ages of Woman. By fashioning herself into a singular combination of Maiden, Matron, and Mother, the Queen transformed the normal domestic life-cycle of an Elizabethan female into what was at once a social paradox and a religious mystery. Her emblem was the phoenix; her motto, *semper eadem*. Because she was always uniquely herself, Elizabeth's rule was not intended to undermine the male hegemony of her culture. Indeed, the emphasis upon her *difference* from other women may have helped to reinforce it. As she herself wrote in response to Parliament in 1563, 'though I can think [marriage] best for a private woman, yet I do strive with myself to think it not meet for a prince' (Neale, *Elizabeth I and Her Parliaments 1559–1581*, p. 127). The royal exception could prove the patriarchal rule in society at large.

Nevertheless, from the very beginning of her reign, Elizabeth's parliaments and counsellors urged her to marry and produce an heir. There was a deeply felt and loudly voiced need to ensure a legitimate succession, upon which the welfare of the whole people depended. But there must also have been another, more obscure motivation behind these requests: the political nation, which was wholly a nation of men, seems at times to have found it frustrating or degrading to serve a female prince – a woman who was herself unsubjected to any man. Late in Elizabeth's reign, the French ambassador observed that 'her government is fairly pleasing to the people, who show that they love her, but it is little pleasing to the great men and nobles; and if by chance she should die, it is certain that the English would never again submit to the rule of a woman' (De Maisse, *Journal*, pp. 11–12). In the 1560s and 1570s, Elizabeth witnessed allegorical entertainments boldly criticising her attachment to a life of 'single blessedness'. For example, in the famous Kenilworth entertainments sponsored by the Earl of Leicester in 1575, Diana praised the state of fancy-free maiden meditation and condemned the 'wedded state, which is to thraldome bent'. But Juno had the last word in the pageant: 'O Queene, O worthy queene,/ Yet never wight felt perfect blis / But such as wedded beene.'[28] By the 1580s, the Queen was past childbearing; Diana and her virginal nymph, Eliza, now carried the day in such courtly entertainments as Peele's *Araygnment of Paris*. Although 'as fayre and lovely as the queene of Love', Peele's Elizabeth was also 'as chast as Dian in her chast desires'.[29] By the early 1590s, the cult of the unageing royal virgin had entered its last and most extravagant phase. In the 1590 Accession Day pageant, there appeared 'a Pavilion ... like unto the sacred Temple of the Virgins Vestal'.[30] Upon the altar there were presents for the Queen – offerings from her votaries. At Elvetham, during the royal progress of 1591, none other than 'the Fairy Queene' gave to Elizabeth a chaplet that she herself had received from 'Auberon, the Fairy King' (Nichols,

Progresses and Public Processions, 3:118–19). From early in the reign, Elizabeth had been directly engaged by such performances: debates were referred to her arbitration; the magic of her presence civilised savage men, restored the blind to sight, released errant knights from enchantment, and rescued virgins from defilement. These social dramas of celebration and coercion played out the delicately balanced relationship between the monarch and her greatest subjects. And because texts and descriptions of most of them were in print within a year of their performance, they may have had a cultural impact far greater than their occasional and ephemeral character might at first suggest.

A *Midsummer Night's Dream* is permeated by images and devices that suggest these characteristic forms of Elizabethan court culture. However, whether or not its provenance was in an aristocratic wedding entertainment, Shakespeare's play is neither focused upon the Queen nor structurally dependent upon her presence or her intervention in the action. On the contrary, it might be said to depend upon her absence, her exclusion. In the third scene of the play, after Titania has remembered her Indian votaress, Oberon remembers his 'imperial votaress'. He has once beheld

> Flying between the cold moon and the earth,
> Cupid all arm'd; a certain aim he took
> At a fair vestal, throned by the West,
> And loos'd his love-shaft smartly from his bow
> As it should pierce a hundred thousand hearts.
> But I might see young Cupid's fiery shaft
> Quench'd in the chaste beams of the watery moon;
> And the imperial votress passed on,
> In maiden meditation, fancy-free.
> Yet mark'd I where the bolt of Cupid fell:
> If fell upon a little western flower,
> Before milk-white, now purple with love's wound:
> And maidens call it 'love-in-idleness'.
> ...
> The juice of it, on sleeping eyelids laid,
> Will make or man or woman madly dote
> Upon the next live creature that it sees.
> (II.i.156–68, 170–2)

The evocative monologues of Titania and Oberon are carefully matched and contrasted: the fairy queen speaks of a mortal mother from the east; the fairy king speaks of an invulnerable virgin from the west. Their memories express two myths of origin: Titania's provides a genealogy for the changeling and an explanation of why she will not part with him; Oberon's provides an aetiology of the metamorphosed flower which he will use to make her part with him. The floral symbolism of female sexuality begun in this passage is completed when Oberon names 'Dian's bud' (IV.i.72) as the anti-dote to 'love-in-idleness'. With Cupid's flower, Oberon can make the Fairy Queen 'full of hateful fantasies' (II.i.258); and with Dian's bud, he can win her back to his will. The vestal's invulnerability to fancy is doubly instrumental to Oberon in his reaffirmation of ro-mantic, marital, and parental norms that have been inverted during the course of the play. Thus, Shakespeare's royal compliment re-mythologises the cult of the Virgin Queen in such a way as to sanc-tion a relationship of gender and power that is personally and politically inimical to Elizabeth.

Unlike the fair vestal, Shakespeare's comic heroines are in a tran-sition between the states of maidenhood and wifehood, daughter-hood and motherhood. These transitions are mediated by the wedding rite and the act of defloration, which are brought together at the end of A *Midsummer Night's Dream*: when the newlyweds have retired for the night, Oberon and Titania enter the court in order to bless the 'bride-bed' where the marriages are about to be consummated. By the act of defloration, the husband takes physical and symbolic possession of his bride. The sexual act in which the man draws blood from the woman is already implicit, at the begin-ning of the play, in Theseus' vaunt: 'Hippolyta, I woo'd thee with my sword, / And won thy love doing thee injuries.' The impending injury is evoked – and dismissed with laughter – in the play-within-the-play which wears away the hours 'between our after-supper and bedtime' (V.i.34): Pyramus finds Thisbe's mantle 'stain'd with blood', and concludes that 'lion vile hath here deflower'd [his] dear' (V.i.272, 281). The image in which Oberon describes the flower's metamorphosis suggests the immanence of defloration in the very origin of desire: 'the bolt of Cupid fell / ... Upon a little western flower, / Before milk-white, now purple with love's wound.' Cupid's shaft violates the flower when it has been deflected from the vestal: Oberon's purple passion flower is procreated in a dis-placed and literalised defloration.[31] Unlike the female *dramatis per-sonae*, Oberon's vestal virgin is *not* subject to Cupid's shaft, to the frailties of the fresh and the fancy. Nor is she subject to the mastery of men. Isolated from the experiences of desire, marriage and maternity, she is immune to the pains and pleasure of human mutability. But it is precisely her bodily and mental impermeability which make possible Oberon's pharmacopoeia. Thus, ironically, the vestal's very freedom from fancy guarantees the subjection of others. She is necessarily excluded from the erotic world of which her own chastity is the efficient cause.

Within *A Midsummer Night's Dream*, the public and domestic domains of Elizabethan culture intersect in the figure of the imperial votaress. When a female ruler is ostensibly the virgin mother of her subjects, then the themes of male procreative power, autogeny, and mastery of women acquire a seditious resonance. In royal pageantry, the Queen is always the cynosure; her virginity is the source of magical potency. In *A Midsummer Night's Dream*, however, magical power is invested in the King. Immediately after invoking the royal vestal and vowing to torment the Fairy Queen, Oberon encounters Helena in pursuit of Demetrius. In Shakespeare's metamorphosis of Ovid, 'the story shall be chang'd / Apollo flies, and Daphne holds the chase' (II.i.230–1). Oberon's response is neither to extinguish desire nor to make it mutual but to restore the normal pattern of pursuit: 'Fare thee well, nymph; ere he do leave this grove / Thou shalt fly him and he shall seek thy love' (II.i.245–6). Perhaps three or four years before the first production of *A Midsummer Night's Dream*, in a pastoral entertainment enacted at Sudeley during the royal progress of 1591, the Queen's presence had changed Ovid's story into an emblem of Constancy. The scenario might be seen as a benevolent mythological transformation of the Queen's sometimes spiteful ways with her maids of honour. Here it was in the power of the royal virgin to undo the metamorphosis, to *release* Daphne from her arboreal imprisonment and to protect her from the lustful advances of Apollo. Unlike Elizabeth, Oberon uses his mastery over Nature to subdue others to their passions. The festive conclusion of *A Midsummer Night's Dream* depends upon the success of a process by which the female pride and power manifested in misanthropic warriors, possessive mothers, unruly wives, and wilful daughters are brought under the control of lords and husbands. When the contentious young lovers have been sorted out into pairs by Oberon, then Theseus can invite them to share his own wedding day. If the Duke finally overbears Egeus' will (IV.i.178), it is because the father's obstinate claim to 'the ancient privilege of Athens' (I.i.41) threatens to obstruct the very process by which

Athenian privilege and Athens itself are reproduced. Hermia and Helena are granted their desires – but those desires have themselves been shaped by a social imperative. Thus, neither for Oberon nor for Theseus does a contradiction exist between mastering the desires of a wife and patronising the desires of a maiden. In the assertion of an equivalence between the patriarchal family and the patriarchal state, the anomalous Elizabethan relationship between gender and power is suppressed.

In his letters, Sir John Harington wrote of Elizabeth as 'oure deare Queene, my royale godmother, and this state's natural mother'; as 'one whom I both lovede and fearede too'. After her death, he reflected slyly on how she had manipulated the filial feelings of her subjects: 'Few knew how to aim their shaft against her cunninge. We did all love hir, for she saide she loved us, and muche wysdome she shewed in thys matter.'[32] So much for Elizabeth's maternal strategies. As for her erotic strategies, Bacon provides perhaps the most astute contemporary analysis:

> As for those lighter points of character, – as that she allowed herself to be wooed and courted, and even to have love made to her; and liked it; and continued it beyond the natural age for such vanities; – if any of the sadder sort of persons be disposed to make a great matter of this, it may be observed that there is something to admire in these very things, which ever way you take them. For if viewed indulgently, they are much like the accounts we find in romances, of the Queen in the blessed islands, and her court and institutions, who allows of amorous admiration but prohibits desire. But if you take them seriously, they challenge admiration of another kind and of a very high order; for certain it is that these dalliances detracted but little from her fame and nothing from her majesty, and neither weakened her power nor sensibly hindered her business.
>
> (*In Felicem Memoriam*, p. 460)

Bacon appreciates that the Queen's personal vanity and political craft are mutually reinforcing. He is alert to the generic affinities of the royal cult, its appropriation and enactment of the conventions of romance. And he also recognises that, like contemporaneous romantic fictions, the Queen's romance could function as a political allegory. However, symbolic forms may do more than *represent* power: they may actually help to *generate* the power that they represent. Thus – although Bacon does not quite manage to say so – the Queen's dalliances did not weaken her power but strengthened it; did not hinder her business but furthered it.

By the same token, the Queen's subjects might put the discourse of royal power to their own uses. Consider the extravagant royal entertainment of 1581, in which Philip Sidney and Fulke Greville performed as 'Foster Children of Desire'.[33] 'Nourished up with [the] infective milke' (p. 313) of Desire – 'though full oft that dry nurse Dispaier indevered to wainne them from it' (p. 314) – the Foster Children boldly claimed and sought to possess The Fortress of Perfect Beauty, an allegorical structure from within which Elizabeth actually beheld the 'desirous assault' (p. 317) mounted against her. The besieged Queen was urged that she 'no longer exclude vertuous Desire from perfect Beautie' (p. 314). During two days of florid speeches, spectacular self-displays, and mock combats, these young, ambitious, and thwarted courtiers acted out a fantasy of political demand, rebellion, and submission in metaphors of resentment and aggression that were alternately filial and erotic. They seized upon the forms in which their culture had articulated the relationship between sovereign and subjects: they demanded sustenance from their royal mother, favours from their royal mistress. The nobility, gentlemen, and hangers-on of the court generated a variety of pressures that constantly threatened the fragile stability of the Elizabethan regime. At home, personal rivalries and political dissent might be sublimated into the agonistic play-forms of courtly culture; abroad, they might be expressed in warfare and colonial enterprise – displaced into the conquest of lands that had yet their maidenheads.

The Queen dallied, not only with the hearts of courtiers but with the hearts of commoners, too. For example, in 1600, a deranged sailor named Abraham Edwardes sent 'a passionate ... letter unto her Majesty', who was then sixty-eight years old. Edwardes was later committed to prison 'for drawing his dagger in the [royal] presence chamber'. The Clerk of the Privy Council wrote to Cecil that 'the fellow is greatly distracted, and seems rather to be transported with a humour of love, than any purpose to attempt anything against her Majesty'. He recommended that this poor lunatic and lover 'be removed to Bedlam'.[34] By her own practice of sexual politics, the Queen may very well have encouraged the sailor's passion – in the same sense that her cult helped to fashion the courtly performances and colonial enterprises of courtiers like Sidney or Ralegh, the dream-life of Doctor Forman, the dream-play of Master Shakespeare. This being said, it must be added that the Queen was as much the creature of her image as she was its creator,

that her power to fashion her own strategies was itself fashioned by
her culture and constrained within its mental horizon. Indeed, in *A
Midsummer Night's Dream*, as in *The Faerie Queene*, the ostensible
project of elaborating Queen Elizabeth's personal mythology inex-
orably subverts itself – generates ironies, contradictions, resistances
which undo the royal magic. Such processes of disenchantment are
increasingly evident in Elizabethan cultural productions of the
1580s and 1590s. The texts of Spenser and other Elizabethan
courtly writers often fragment the royal image, reflecting aspects of
the Queen 'in mirrors more then one' (*FQ*, III.Proem.5). In a
similar way, Shakespeare's text splits the triune Elizabethan cult
image between the fair vestal, an unattainable *virgin*; and the Fairy
Queen, an intractable *wife* and a dominating *mother*. Oberon uses
one against the other in order to reassert male prerogatives. Thus,
the structure of Shakespeare's comedy symbolically neutralises the
forms of royal power to which it ostensibly pays homage. It would
be an oversimplification and a distortion to characterise such cultural processes merely as an allegorical encoding of political
conflict. The spiritual, maternal, and erotic transformations of
Elizabethan power are not reducible to instances of Machiavellian
policy, to intentional mystifications. Relationships of power and dependency, desire and fear, are inherent in both the public and
domestic domains. Sexual and family experience were invariably
politicised; economic and political experience were invariably eroti-
cised: the social and psychological force of Elizabethan symbolic
forms depended upon a thorough conflation of these domains.

V

Differences within the courtly and fairy groups of *A Midsummer
Night's Dream* are structured principally in terms of gender and
generation. When Bottom and his company are introduced into the
newly harmonised courtly milieu in the final scene, the striking difference *between* groups overshadows the previously predominant
differences *within* groups.[35] Like Bottom, in his special relationship
to Titania, the mechanicals are presented collectively in a child-like
relationship to their social superiors. (They characterise themselves,
upon two occasions, as 'every mother's son' [I.ii.73; III.i.69];
however, they hope to be 'made men' [IV.ii.18] by the patronage of
the Duke.) But differences of gender and generation have now been

reorganised in terms of a difference which is at once social and the-atrical: a difference between common artisan-actors and the leisured elite for whom they perform. In the mechanicals' play, *A Midsummer Night's Dream* internalises and distances its relation-ship to traditions of amateur and occasional dramatic entertain-ment. And in the attitudes of the play-within-the-play's courtly audience, *A Midsummer Night Dream* internalises and distances its relationship to the pressures and constraints of aristocratic patron-age. By incorporating and ironically circumscribing it, Shakespeare's professional theatre implicitly repudiates Theseus' attitude toward the entertainers' art: that performances should serve only as an in-nocuous distraction from princely cares or as a gratifying homage to princely power. In this dramatic context, Duke Theseus is not so much Queen Elizabeth's *masculine* antithesis as he is her *princely* surrogate.

The much-noted 'metadrama' of *A Midsummer Night's Dream* – its calling of attention to its own artifice, its own artistry – analo-gises the power of parents, princes, and playwrights; the fashioning of children, subjects, and plays. Shakespeare's text is a cultural pro-duction in which the processes of cultural production are them-selves represented; it is a representation of fantasies about the shaping of the family, the polity, and the theatre. When Oberon blesses the bride-beds of 'the couples three' (V.i.393), he metapho-rises the engendering of their offspring as an act of *writing*: 'And the blots of Nature's hand / Shall not in their issue stand' (V.i.395–6). And when Theseus wryly describes the poet's 'fine frenzy' (V.i.12), the text of *A Midsummer Night's Dream* obliquely represents the parthenogenetic process of its *own* creation:

> And as imagination bodies forth
> The forms of things unknown, the poet's pen
> Turns them to shapes, and gives to airy nothing
> A local habitation and a name.
>
> (V.i.14–17)

That the dramatic medium itself is thematised in Shakespeare's play does not imply a claim for the self-referentiality of the aesthetic object or the aesthetic act. On the contrary, it implies a claim for a dialectic between Shakespeare's profession and his society, a dialec-tic between the theatre and the world. In its preoccupation with the transformation of the personal into the public, the metamorphosis of dream and fantasy into poetic drama, *A Midsummer Night's Dream* does more than *analogise* the powers of prince and play-wright: it dramatises – or, rather, *meta*-dramatises – the relations of power *between* prince and playwright. To the extent that the cult of Elizabeth informs the play, it is itself transformed within the play. The play bodies forth the theatre poet's contest, not only with the generativity of Elizabethan mothers but with the generativity of the royal virgin; it contests the princely claim to cultural authorship and social authority. *A Midsummer Night's Dream* is, then, in a double sense, a *creation* of Elizabethan culture: for it also creates the culture by which it is created, shapes the fantasies by which it is shaped, begets that by which it is begotten.

From *Representations*, 1 (1983), 61–94.

NOTES

[This essay is one of a distinguished sequence of articles by Montrose on the place of Shakespeare's texts in the cultural and power-relations of Elizabethan England. They are central to the whole project of rehistoricising Renaissance literary studies which dominated this field of scholarship (along with the feminists) in the 1980s. Montrose is usually associated with Stephen Greenblatt, Richard Helgerson and others as a member of the American New Historicist wing of the project, as distinct from the cultural materialists who have flourished predominantly (but not exclusively) in Britain. He himself, however, has cautioned more than once against over-rigid demarcations of this kind, emphasising that 'the new historicism is the invention of its critics and commentators' rather than of its practitioners, and that it is at most an 'orientation' rather than a clearly defined pro-gramme or ideological project; it involves scholars with a variety of critical methodologies and ideological positions. (See Further Reading, 'Historicist Readings'.) This essay first appeared in print in the first issue of the New Historicist flagship journal, *Representations*, though it has been reprinted a number of times, sometimes in a shorter, altered (and occasionally retitled) version. The original version is the one reprinted here, trimmed only of some of the very extensive annotation for reasons of space. The author informs me that he is engaged in a revised and much enlarged study of *A Midsummer Night's Dream*, part of which will probably appear before this volume does as 'A Kingdom of the Shadows: Theatre, State and Society in Shakespeare's *A Midsummer Night's Dream*', in *The Theatrical City: London's Culture, Theatre and Literature, 1576–1640*, ed. David L. Smith, Richard Strier, and David Bevington (Cambridge, 1994/5). Ed.]

1. *A Midsummer Night's Dream (MND)*, V.i.7–8, 4–6. All quotations will follow *The Arden Shakespeare* edition of *MND*, ed. Harold F. Brooks (London, 1979), and will be cited in the text by act, scene, and line. Quotations from other Shakespearean plays follow the texts in *The Riverside Shakespeare*, G. Blakemore Evans, textual ed. (Boston, 1974).

2. Paul A. Olson, '*A Midsummer Night's Dream* and the Meaning of Court Marriage', *English Literary History*, 24 (1957), 95–119.

3. See Gayle Rubin, 'The Traffic in Women: Notes on the "Political Economy" of Sex', in *Toward an Anthropology of Women*, ed. Rayna R. Reiter (New York, 1975), pp. 157–210.

4. Quoted from manuscript in A. L. Rowse, *The Case Books of Simon Forman* (London, 1974), p. 31.

5. Excerpts from Forman's autobiography, diaries, and notes are printed in Rowse, *Case Books*, pp. 272–307. I quote from pp. 273, 276.

6. See C. L. Barber, 'The Family in Shakespeare's Development: Tragedy and Sacredness', in *Representing Shakespeare*, ed. Murray M. Schwartz and Coppélia Kahn (Baltimore, MD, 1980), pp. 188–202; quotation from p. 196.

7. André Hurault, Sieur de Maisse, *Journal* (1597), trans. and ed. G. B. Harrison and R. A. Jones (Bloomsbury, 1931), pp. 25–6.

8. 'Extracts from Paul Hentzner's Travels in England, 1598', in *England as seen by Foreigners in the Days of Elizabeth & James the First*, ed. William Brenchley Rye (1865; rpt. New York, 1967), pp. 104–5.

9. Sir Robert Naunton, *Fragmenta Regalia* (written ca. 1630; printed 1641), ed. Edward Arber (1870; rpt. New York, 1966), p. 51.

10. I use this term advisedly, to describe a specific household organisation in which authority resides in a male 'head': husband, father, and master of servants and apprentices.

11. William Painter, *The Palace of Pleasure* (1575), ed. Joseph Jacobs, 3 vols (1890; rpt. New York, 1966), vol. 2, pp. 159–61.

12. *An Elizabethan in 1582: The Diary of Richard Madox, Fellow of All Souls*, ed. Elizabeth Story Donno, Hakluyt Society, second ser., no. 47 (London, 1977), p. 183.

13. André Thevet, *The newe founde Worlde*, trans. (London: Henrie Bynneman for Thomas Hackett, 1568), p. 102ʳ.

14. Plutarch, *The Lives of the Noble Grecians and Romanes*, trans. Thomas North (1579), the Tudor Translations, 2 vols (1895; rpt. New York, 1967), vol. 1, p. 116.

15. Robert W. Dent, 'Imagination in *A Midsummer Night's Dream*', *Shakespeare Quarterly*, 15 (1964), 115–29; see p. 116.

16. For a detailed analysis, see Louis Adrian Montrose, ' "The Place of a Brother" in *As You Like It*: Social Process and Comic Form', *Shakespeare Quarterly*, 32 (1981), 28–54.

17. Northrop Frye, *A Natural Perspective* (New York, 1965), pp. 73–4.

18. *The Problemes of Aristotle, with other Philosophers and Phisitions* (London: Arnold Hattfield, 1597), sigs. E3^v–E4^r.

19. For a review and analysis of the play's sources and analogues, see Brooks' edition, pp. lviii–lxxxviii; 129–53; and the notes throughout the text. D'Orsay W. Pearson, ' "Unkinde Theseus": A Study of Renaissance Mythography', *English Literary Renaissance*, 4 (1974), 276–98, provides a richly informative survey of Theseus' 'classical, medieval, and Renaissance image as an unnatural, perfidious, and unfaithful lover and father' (p. 276).

Many details in the texts of Plutarch and Seneca that have not been considered previously as 'sources' for Shakespeare's play are nevertheless relevant to the problem of gender and filiation which seems to me to be central to *MND*. Here I can do no more than enumerate a few of these details. In his *Lives*, Plutarch relates that Theseus was 'begotten by stealth, and out of lawfull matrimony' (p. 30); that, 'of his father's side', he was descended from the 'Autocthones, as much to say borne of them selves' (p. 30); that, having been abandoned by Theseus on Cyprus, the pregnant Ariadne 'dyed ... in labour, and could never be delivered' (p. 48); that because the negligently joyful Theseus forgot to change his sail as a sign of success upon his return from Crete, his father Egeus, 'being out of all hope evermore to see his sonne againe, tooke such a griefe at his harte, that he threw him selfe headlong from the top of a clyffe, and killed him selfe' (p. 49).

In Seneca, as in Plutarch, the mother of Hippolytus is named Antiopa; Shakespeare's choice of the alternative – Hippolyta – obviously evokes Hippolytus, thus providing an ironic context for the royal wedding and the blessing of the bridal bed. (Similarly, the choice of Egeus for the Athenian patriarch whose will is overborne by Theseus effects a displacement within Shakespeare's comedy of Theseus' negligent parricide.) Seneca's *Hippolytus* emphasises Theseus' abuse of women – by this time, he has killed Antiopa/Hippolyta, married Phaedra, and gone off to the underworld to rape Persephone – and also gives voice to his victims in the invective of Phaedra. Hippolytus, as Phaedra's *nutrix* reminds him, is the only living son of the Amazons (577; here and following, *Seneca's Tragedies* are cited by line numbers from the Latin text in the Loeb edition, ed. F. J. Miller). In his very misogyny – his scorn of marriage, and his self-dedication to virginity, hunting, and the cult of Diana – Hippolytus proves himself his mother's son; he is '*genus Amazonium*' (231). Hippolytus reminds Phaedra that she has come from the same womb that bore the Minotaur; and that she is even worse than her mother Pasiphae (688–93). At the end of the play, Theseus' burden is to refashion ('*fingit*') his son from the '*disiecta ... membra*' of his torn body (1256–70). Now a filicide as well as a parricide and an uxoricide, Theseus has perverted and destroyed his own house (1166).

Seneca's *Medea* is clearly relevant to the subtext of *MND* in its domestic violence: in Medea's betrayal of her father: in the *sparagmos* of her brother, and, after Jason's unfaithfulness, in the slaughter of her two sons. But Medea also has a significant place in the history of Theseus, as recorded by Plutarch (*Lives*, p. 39) and by Seneca (*Hippolytus*, 696–7): fleeing Corinth after destroying Creusa and her own two boys, Medea sought asylum in Athens with old Egeus, whose power to beget offspring she promised to renew by her magic. Finding that young Theseus had come to Athens in disguise, Medea sought unsuccessfully to trick the suspicious Egeus into poisoning his own son. Thus as Seneca's Hippolytus points out, Medea has been to his father what Phaedra is to himself: the demonic, barbaric, passionate female who seeks to pervert the bonds between father and son, man and man.

20. *The discovery of the Large, Rich, and Beautiful Empire of Guiana* (1596), ed. Sir Robert H. Schomburgk, Hakluyt Society, first ser., no. 3 (1848; rpt. New York, n.d.).

21. See Natalie Zemon Davis, *Society and Culture in Early Modern France* (Stanford, CA, 1975), p. 130. Davis' own argument is that inversion phenomena may not only act as safety valves which renew the existing structures but as sources of cultural innovation and social change.

22. Quoted in Paul Johnson, *Elizabeth I: A Study in Power and Intellect* (London, 1974), p. 320.

23. Sir Robert Cecil to Sir John Harington, 29 May 1603, printed in John Harington, *Nugae Antiquae*, 3 vols (1779; rpt. Hildesheim, 1968), vol. 2, p. 264.

24. See J. E. Neale, *Elizabeth I and Her Parliaments 1559–1581* (New York, 1958), pp. 49, 109. Neale prints the full texts of these speeches.

25. *In Felisem Memoriam Elizabethae* (ca. 1608), in *The Works of Francis Bacon*, ed. James Spedding et al., 15 vols (Boston, 1860), vol. 11, pp. 425–42 (Latin text), 443–61 (English trans.); quotation from p. 450.

26. See Lawrence Stone, *The Crisis of the Aristocracy 1558–1641* (Oxford, 1965), pp. 605–6. Stone gives numerous examples of the Queen's interventions.

27. Letter to Robert Markham (1606), rpt. in *The Letters and Epigrams of Sir John Harington*, ed. N. E. McClure (Philadelphia, 1930), p. 124.

28. I quote the printed text of the Kenilworth entertainment (1576) from *The Complete Works of George Gasgoigne*, ed. J. W. Cunliffe, 2 vols (Cambridge, Eng., 1910), vol. 2, pp. 107, 120.

29. George Peele, *The Aragynment of Paris* (printed 1584), ed. R. Mark Benbow, in *The Dramatic Works of George Peele*, C. T. Prouty, gen. ed. (New Haven, 1970), lines 1172–3.

30. Described in Sir William Segar, *Honor Military and Civill* (1602), pp. 197–200; rpt. in John Nichols, *The Progresses and Public Processions of Queen Elizabeth*, 3 vols (1823; rpt. New York, 1966), vol. 3, pp. 41–50, quotation from Nichols, vol. 3, p. 46.

31. The change suffered by the flower – from the whiteness of milk to the purple wound of love – juxtaposes maternal nurturance and erotic violence. To an Elizabethan audience, the metamorphosis may have suggested not only the blood of defloration but also the blood of menstruation – and, perhaps, the menarche, which manifests the sexual maturity of the female, the advent of womanhood and potential motherhood. According to popular Elizabethan gynaecology, lactational amenorrhea is causally related to lactation, in that mother's milk is a transubstantiation and refinement of menstrual blood: 'Why have not women with childe the flowers? ... Because that then the flowers turne into milke, and into the nourishment of the childe' (*Problemes of Aristotle*, sig. E5r).

   An awareness that the commonest Elizabethan term for menses was 'flowers' (See *Oxford English Dictionary*, s.v. 'flower' sense 2.b.) adds a peculiar resonance to certain occurrences of flower imagery in Renaissance texts. This is especially the case in *MND*, in which flowers are conspicuously associated with female sexuality and with the moon. Consider Titania's observation:

   The moon, methinks, looks with a watery eye,
   And when she weeps, weeps every little flower,
   Lamenting some enforced chastity.
                                                                   (III.i.101–3)

   The answer to the question, 'Why do the flowers receive their name Menstrua, of this word Mensis a moneth?' constitutes a gloss on Titania's speech: 'Bicause it is a space of time which doth measure the Moone ... Now the Moone hath dominion over moist things, and bicause the flowers are an humiditie, they take their denomination of the moneth, and are called monethly termes: for moist things do increase as the Moone doth increase, and decrease as she doth decrease' (*Problemes of Aristotle*, sig. E5r). In the quoted passage, Brooks follows previous editors in glossing 'enforced' (line 193) as 'violated by force' (Brooks, *Arden* edn. of *MND*, p. 62; cf. p. cxxix). However, the opposite reading – 'enforced' as compulsory chastity – seems equally possible (see *Oxford English Dictionary*, s.v. 'enforced' sense 1: 'that is subjected to force or constraint'; and sense 2: 'That is forced upon or extracted from a person; that is produced by force'). In one sense, then, the allusion is to sexual violation; in the other it is to the injunction against sexual relations during menstruation (Leviticus 20:18; Ezekiel 18:6), which was commonly repeated by sixteenth- and seventeenth-century writers.

I raise the issue of menstrual symbolism here to suggest the degree to which an ambivalent discourse on female sexuality permeates Shakespeare's text. The imagery of the text insinuates that, whatever its provenance in horticultural lore, Oberon's maddening love-juice is a displacement of vaginal blood: a conflation of menstrual blood – which is the sign of women's generative power and of their pollution, their dangerousness to men – with the blood of defloration – which is the sign of men's mastery of women's bodies, of their generative powers and of their dangerousness. For a pertinent analogy to this dramatic process in tribal ritual, see J. S. La Fontaine, 'Ritualisation of Women's life-crises in Bugisu', in *The Interpretation of Ritual*, ed. J. S. La Fontaine (London, 1972), pp. 159–86. See Patricia Crawford, 'Attitudes to Menstruation in Seventeenth-Century England', *Past & Present*, 91 (May 1981), 47–73, for a useful introduction to this significant though neglected subject. Also see Barbara B. Harrell, 'Lactation and Menstruation in Cultural Perspective', *American Anthropologist*, 83 (1981), 796–818, for an interesting analysis of the interplay between physiological and cultural factors in the 'preindustrial reproductive cycle'.

32. Letters to Lady Mary Harington (1602) and Robert Markham (1606), rpt. in *The Letters and Epigrams of Sir John Harington*, pp. 96, 123–5.

33. Reprinted in Nichols, *Progresses and Public Processions*, vol. 2, pp. 312–29.

34. W. Wadd to Sir Robert Cecil, 3 June 1600, printed in *Calendar of the Manuscripts of … The Marquis of Salisbury … preserved at Hatfield House*, 18 vols (London: HMSO, 1883–1940), vol. 10, pp. 172–3.

35. Here I can do no more than briefly suggest how this vital aspect of the play impinges upon my immediate subject. The significance of the social dynamic among the play's character-groups is appreciated and analysed in Elliot Krieger, *A Marxist Study of Shakespeare's Comedies* (London, 1979), pp. 37–69.

6

Hippolyta's Silence and the Poet's Pen

PHILIP C. McGUIRE

I

The opening moments of *A Midsummer Night's Dream* include a silence – Hippolyta's – that has reverberations that, reaching beyond the scene of which it is a wordless yet crucial element, touch upon the issue of how much (and how little) the words Shakespeare penned reveal about the play. The first words of the play are those of Theseus telling Hippolyta of the approach of their wedding day:

> Now, fair Hippolyta, our nuptial hour
> Draws on apace. Four happy days bring in
> Another moon; but, O, methinks, how slow
> This old moon wanes! She lingers my desires,
> Like to a stepdame or a dowager
> Long withering out a young man's revenue.
>
> (I.i.1–6)

Hippolyta replies with the only words she speaks during the opening scene:

> Four days will quickly steep themselves in night,
> Four nights will quickly dream away the time;
> And then the moon, like to a silver bow
> New bent in heaven, shall behold the night
> Of our solemnities.
>
> (ll.7–11)

When Theseus says that, having conquered her in battle, he will now make her his wife 'in another key, / With pomp, with triumph, and with revelling' (ll.18–19), Hippolyta says nothing, and she maintains that silence the rest of the time she is onstage. The defeated Queen of the Amazons becomes a mute observer as the man who 'won' her love by doing her 'injuries' (l.17) rules that a young woman who is one of his subjects must die or live a life cloistered among women if she does not obey her father and enter into a marriage that she does not want.

The words Hippolyta does speak are of very limited use when we attempt to clarify the meanings and effects of her silence. What she says is part of a dialogue with Theseus that clearly reveals that each of them responds differently to the passage of time. For Theseus, time moves slowly toward their 'nuptial hour', but for Hippolyta times moves swiftly. He laments 'how slow / This old moon wanes', whereas she twice uses the word 'quickly' to describe the passing of time: 'Four days will quickly steep themselves in night, / Four nights will quickly dream away the time.'

The words that Shakespeare assigns to Theseus and Hippolyta allow us – if we wish – to see the differences in their temporal responses as facets of an underlying harmony. In emphasising how 'quickly' time will move, Hippolyta can be reassuring Theseus that the hour for which he longs will soon arrive, and her words of reassurance can also convey her own sense of excited anticipation. Theseus and Hippolyta have differing senses of time's pace, but each can be accurate. Time can move both quickly and slowly, travelling, as Rosalind notes in *As You Like It*, 'in divers paces with divers persons' (III.ii.293–4). The differences underscored by Hippolyta's use of 'quickly' can suggest that, when they are together, the Duke of Athens and the Queen of the Amazons have a fuller sense of the complexity of time than either does in isolation.[1] The 'nuptial hour' toward which each moves at a different pace becomes, then, a moment when they will complete a union that does not obliterate their differences but allows them to complement one another. Their differences become, in effect, the basis for a harmony that is more inclusive, more resilient, than would otherwise be possible.

The words Theseus and Hippolyta exchange at the start of the play permit us to see their differences as facets of an underlying harmony, but the words do not compel such a conclusion. The differences brought into focus by Hippolyta's use of 'quickly' can, without distorting the words of Shakespeare's playtext, just as plausibly be taken as reflecting a conflict between Theseus and her. If the nuptial hour approaches so slowly for Theseus because he desires it so much, then perhaps it approaches so quickly for Hippolyta, the newly conquered queen of a society of women who had long resisted male domination, precisely because she desires it so little. In explaining that 'time travels in divers paces with divers persons', Rosalind notes that it moves most swiftly for 'a thief [going] to the gallows; for though he go as softly as foot can fall, he thinks himself too soon there' (III.ii.293–4, 311–12). In contrast, time, which gallops by for the thief, moves at a trot, Rosalind says, for

> ... a young maid between the contract of her marriage and the day it is solemnised. If the interim be but a se'nnight, Time's pace is so hard that it seems the length of seven year.
>
> (ll.299–302)

The opening lines of *A Midsummer Night's Dream* reverse those relationships. Theseus feels time moving slowly as if he were a maid awaiting her wedding day, whereas the response of the woman whom he has taken to be his bride is like that of a thief approaching the gallows. For her, as for the thief, time moves 'quickly'. Before the scene concludes, Theseus decrees, in the presence of a silent Hippolyta, that the wedding day she said will 'quickly' arrive will also be the day on which Hermia must

> ... either prepare to die
> For disobedience to your father's will,
> Or else to wed Demetrius, as he would,
> Or on Diana's altar to protest
> For aye austerity and single life.
>
> (ll.86–90)

Theseus' decree means that Hippolyta's movement through time, toward what will be the day of her marriage, becomes congruent with Hermia's movement through time, toward the same day, which will find her facing an involuntary marriage, the single life, or death. Each woman might think herself, like the thief on his way to the gallows, 'too soon there'.

The more closely we analyse the opening exchange between Theseus and Hippolyta, the more likely we are to see it with what Hermia calls a 'parted eye, / When everything seems double'

(IV.i.188–9). As they exist on the printed page, the words that make up that exchange are 'double' in the sense of being radically ambiguous, of being equally capable of expressing harmony or conflict or even a combination of both. Because they are ambiguous, those words cannot provide the basis for specifying the precise meanings and effects of Hippolyta's silence. In fact, even if the meaning of the words were absolutely clear, they would not suffice as the basis for interpreting Hippolyta's silence. If, for example, we could determine beyond doubt that the dialogue between Theseus and Hippolyta established a fundamental harmony between them, Hippolyta's subsequent silence could indicate either a continuation of that harmony (since she utters no objection to what Theseus does) or a breakdown of that harmony (since she does not verbally agree with what he does). The converse is also true. If the opening dialogue were taken as establishing conflict between them, Hippolyta's ensuing silence could then reflect either the continuation of that conflict or, since she is no longer voicing any disagreement with Theseus, the cessation of that conflict.

Because no character comments upon Hippolyta's silence, there is no way to discriminate among the possibilities her silence allows by using a mode of analysis that focuses exclusively upon the words of *A Midsummer Night's Dream* and thus treats what is a play as if it were a work of literature. Hippolyta's silence is textually indeterminate. It is open in the sense that it is established by the words that constitute the playtext, but once established, it is capable of having meanings and effects that are not fixed by those words and that take on distinct form and shape only during performances of the play. We cannot probe her silence with any precision unless we attend to what has happened during performances.

II

Four specific productions of *A Midsummer Night's Dream* between 1959 and 1980 demonstrate the range of meanings and effects that Hippolyta's silence can generate without contradicting the words of Shakespeare's playtext. During Peter Hall's 1959 production at the Shakespeare Memorial Theatre in Stratford-upon-Avon, Hippolyta's silence confirmed the harmony between her and Theseus that was expressed during the opening dialogue.[2] She and Theseus sat side by side as he listened to Egeus' accusation and

Hermia's reply. After warning Hermia to 'take time to pause', Theseus stood and raised an unresisting Hippolyta to her feet. As they walked toward the staircase that dominated the set, Theseus stated that Hermia's decision must be made 'by the next new moon – / The sealing day betwixt my love and me / For everlasting bond of fellowship' (ll.83–5). They reached the staircase and stood there together while Theseus set forth the third of Hermia's alternatives: 'on Diana's altar to protest / For aye austerity and single life' (ll.89–90). The consistent pairing of Theseus and Hippolyta underscored the contrast between what that 'sealing day' would bring for Hippolyta and what it would bring for Hermia. Their movements together also established that both Theseus and Hippolyta were oblivious to the contrast.

That pairing was interrupted briefly later in the scene, when Theseus walked away from Hippolyta and toward Hermia while advising her to 'arm yourself / To fit your fancies to your father's will' (ll.117–18), but the interruption did not signify any breach in the relationship between Theseus and Hippolyta. Having warned Hermia that the Athenian law sentenced her 'to death or to a vow of single life' if she failed to obey her father, Theseus turned immediately to the woman who was soon to become his bride and said, 'Come, my Hippolyta' (l.122). Hippolyta's silent response was a model of the very type of obedience that Hermia had outspokenly refused to accept. Without hesitation, Hippolyta crossed toward Theseus and he toward her and, hands joined, they walked together toward the exit as he asked solicitously, 'What cheer, my love?' (l.122).

Hall's production, in which Hippolyta's silence conveyed her untroubled, obedient acquiescence in the sentence imposed on Hermia, stands in pointed contrast to the production of *A Midsummer Night's Dream* that John Hirsch directed at the Stratford (Ontario) Shakespearean Festival in 1968. In Hirsch's production, the opening exchange between Theseus and Hippolyta established that theirs was a relationship marked by conflict rather than by harmony. Theseus was a nearly doddering old man in military dress uniform of the late nineteenth century; Hippolyta was a desirable woman of middle years who entered carrying a red rose and wearing a black dress that, in contrast to what Hermia and Helena wore, showed her shoulders. As Hippolyta spoke of how quickly 'the night of our solemnities' would arrive, she stepped away from Theseus and stood, downstage right, on the lower of the two steps around most of the perimeter of the Festival Theatre's thrust stage. Theseus followed her, and when he ordered Philostrate to 'stir up the Athenian youth to merriments' (l.12) – an order that took on sexual overtones and stressed his own age – Hippolyta again distanced herself from him. Using the bottom step, she crossed to the downstage left corner, where she sat on the first step. Theseus followed her again and, dropping to his hands and knees, tried to kiss her at the conclusion of his pledge to wed her 'with pomp, with triumph, and with revelling'. Hippolyta avoided the kiss by drawing back without rising – a gesture that conveyed both her distaste and Theseus' awkward, futile amorousness as he sought to convert his military victory over the queen of the Amazons into a sexual conquest. The entrance of Egeus, Hermia, Demetrius, and Lysander caught Theseus unprepared. His failure as a wooer was obvious to them, and his subsequent exercise of ducal power became in part a compensation for that failure.

Hirsch's production intensified the conflict between Theseus and Hippolyta by using her silence to emphasise Hippolyta's recognition of the affinities between herself and Hermia. In this production, in contrast to Hall's, Hippolyta was not at Theseus' side as he listened to and acted upon Egeus' complaint against Hermia. Theseus, standing centre stage, addressed himself to Hermia, who stood at the downstage right corner while Hippolyta remained seated on the top step at the downstage left corner. That triangular configuration aligned the two women in their resistance to male authority, and that alignment eventually became a pairing. Hippolyta stood up when Demetrius called for Hermia to 'relent' (l.91), and when Lysander defiantly asked, 'Why should not I then prosecute my right?' (l.105), Hippolyta moved toward Hermia along the same step that she had earlier used to dodge Theseus. The pairing of the two women was completed following Hippolyta's response to Theseus' words, 'Come, my Hippolyta'. She crossed not to Theseus but to Hermia. Although he stood holding his hand out toward her, Hippolyta turned her back to him and handed to Hermia the red rose she had carried since her entrance. She then exited, leaving Theseus to ask, 'What cheer, my love?' to her departing back. Hippolyta's demonstration that she felt neither duty toward nor desire for Theseus gave a special flavour to the words Egeus used when he and Demetrius obeyed Theseus' order to accompany him as he exited after Hippolyta: 'With duty and desire we follow you' (l.127).

The rose that Hippolyta passed to Hermia extended the corre-spondences between the two women beyond the fact that both faced marriages that were being imposed on them by men whose control rested on law or military conquest. That rose made it easier for the audience to realise that Hippolyta's life among the Amazon women is analogous to that 'single life' available to Hermia if, re-sisting her father's will, she elects 'to abjure / For ever the society of men' (ll.65–6) and to live instead among women 'in shady cloister mewed' (l.71). The use of the rose to draw attention to the analogy was particularly appropriate because Theseus uses the rose metaphorically when he dismisses a life lived among women and without men:

> Thrice blessed they that master so their blood
> To undergo such maiden pilgrimage;
> But earthlier happy is the rose distilled
> Than that which, withering on the virgin thorn,
> Grows, lives, and dies in single blessedness.
> (ll.74–8)

Passed from Hippolyta to Hermia and then to Helena, the only woman in the opening scene whom no man seeks to marry, that rose came to signify the 'single blessedness' that Theseus dismisses. Hermia's response to his words is a defiant vow to undertake 'such maiden pilgrimage':

> So will I grow, so live, so die, my lord,
> Ere I will yield my virgin patent up
> Unto his lordship whose unwished yoke
> My soul consents not to give sovereignty
> (ll.79–82)

The sovereignty that Hermia explicitly refuses to accept is the sov-ereignty that, in Hirsch's production, the conquered Queen of the Amazons resisted in silence, and the life of 'a barren sister' (l.72) that Hermia prefers to wedded life with Demetrius points toward the life in sisterhood that Hippolyta lost when Theseus triumphed in battle.

Celia Brannerman's 1980 production of *A Midsummer Night's Dream* for the New Shakespeare Company at the Open Air Theatre in Regent's Park, London, endowed Hippolyta's silence with quite different meanings and effects. Theseus once again wore a military dress uniform of the late nineteenth century, but he was middle-aged and vigorous; Hippolyta wore vaguely near-Eastern garb, including what one reviewer called 'Turkish harem pants'.[3] Hippolyta did not move away when, kneeling on one knee, Theseus declared, 'But I will wed thee in another key, / With pomp, with triumph, and with revelling.' That posture suggested that the conqueror was submitting to the conquered, and thus Theseus' words became a conciliatory pledge rather than a self-aggrandising announcement of his capacity to shift styles as martial affairs gave way to marital concerns.

Standing side by side, Theseus and Hippolyta both found Egeus' complaint against Hermia and Lysander amusing at first. Egeus concluded his initial speech by opening a book he carried and citing the law that entitled him, as Hermia's father, to 'beg the ancient privilege of Athens':

> As she is mine, I may dispose of her,
> Which shall be either to this gentleman
> Or to her death, according to our law
> Immediately provided in that case.
> (ll.41–5)

Theseus himself checked Egeus' citation and handed the book, still open, to Hippolyta, before he turned to Hermia and said, 'Be advised, fair maid, / To you your father should be as a god' (ll.46–7). As Theseus listened to Hermia's reply, Hippolyta stood slightly away from him studying the book of laws. When Hermia asked to 'know / The worst that may befall me in this case / If I refuse to wed Demetrius', Theseus replied, 'Either to die the death, or to abjure / For ever the society of men' (ll.62–6). Having different characters consult the book of laws brought into focus the fact that Theseus here allows Hermia an alternative that her father had not mentioned when he called for either her obedience or her death, 'according to our law / Immediately provided in that case'. In offering Hermia the opportunity to live a life outside 'the society of men', Theseus made the first of several efforts to mollify the silent woman who would soon be his wife and who had been until very recently the head of a society that consisted entirely of women.

On hearing Theseus fix as Hermia's deadline 'the sealing day betwixt my love and me / For everlasting bond of fellowship', Hippolyta angrily and loudly snapped shut the book of laws – a gesture sharply different from the actions of Hippolyta and Theseus at the comparable point in Hall's production, when their gestures demonstrated their unbroken fellowship. Theseus rose and raised Hippolyta to her feet, after which they walked hand in hand toward the staircase as he set the deadline. The Theseus of Brannerman's production tried again to mollify a Hippolyta whose displeasure was unspoken but also unconcealed as he spoke his final words of counsel to Hermia:

> For you, fair Hermia, look you arm yourself
> To fit your fancies to your father's will;
> Or else the law of Athens yields you up
> (Which by no means we may extenuate)
> To death, or to a vow of single life.
>
> (ll.117–21)

In most productions of *A Midsummer Night's Dream*, the words 'which by no means we may extenuate' are spoken to Hermia and emphasise the certainty of 'death' or 'single life' if she persists in defying her father's will. Brannerman's Theseus, however, addressed the words to Hippolyta rather than to Hermia, and they become, because of that interpretation, an effort by Theseus to ease Hippolyta's displeasure by explaining his own inability to mitigate the workings of Athenian legal processes. The effort failed. Hippolyta responded to the next words Theseus spoke ('Come, my Hippolyta') by stepping toward him, slapping the book of laws into his hands, and proceeding to exit without him. He was left to ask after her, in a last, futile effort at reconciliation, 'What cheer, my love?' In Brannerman's production, Hippolyta's silence was part of a process whereby, as she witnessed Theseus' handling of Hermia's predicament, Hippolyta suspended her initial receptiveness to marriage with Theseus.

In his much acclaimed 1970 production of *A Midsummer Night's Dream* for the Royal Shakespeare Company (RSC), Peter Brook used Hippolyta's silence to deepen a split between her and Theseus that was present but muted during the play's opening dialogue.[4] Theseus and Hippolyta stood together during that exchange, and Hippolyta did not give the word 'quickly' an overtly hostile emphasis, but she walked away, crossing from stage right to stage left after Theseus voiced his pledge to wed her 'with pomp, with triumph, and with revelling'.

When Egeus presented his case against Hermia and Lysander, Theseus and Hippolyta remained apart, seated downstage right and downstage left, respectively. That configuration fixed and empha-

sised their separation.[5] Hippolyta stayed seated until after Hermia's
declaration that she would not marry Demetrius, to 'whose un-
wishèd yoke / My soul consents not to give sovereignty'. A sustained pause followed the word 'sovereignty', during which no one
moved or spoke. Then Hippolyta rose to her feet. The timing of her
movement brought into focus her unspoken resistance to the sovereignty over her that Theseus had won in battle and would now exercise in marriage. That resistance, in turn, sharpened the words
with which Theseus broke the stillness that followed the word 'sovereignty'. 'Take time to pause', he cautioned Hermia. He then set
the deadline for Hermia's decision, and in the specific context of
Brook's production, this announcement of that deadline was also a
declaration of his resolve to demonstrate his sovereignty over
Hippolyta. Hermia must decide 'by the next new moon', which
would also be, Theseus stressed, 'the sealing day betwixt my love
and me / For everlasting bond of fellowship.'

Another distinct pause followed Theseus' final warning to
Hermia that if she chose to resist her father's authority and did not
marry Demetrius, the law of Athens would yield her up 'to death,
or to a vow of single life'. That pause ended when Theseus said,
'Come, my Hippolyta'. Hippolyta, however, stood motionless as
Theseus crossed toward her, and before reaching her, he stopped to
ask, 'What cheer, my love?' When she still did not step toward him
or speak, he turned in embarrassed anger to address Demetrius and
Egeus. The Queen of the Amazons continued to stand motionless
and silent as he spoke to the two men, and she did not join Theseus
when he exited through the door upstage right. Instead, Hippolyta
walked alone toward the door upstage left, silently challenging
Theseus' claim that she is '*my* Hippolyta', '*my* love' (emphasis
added). On reaching the doors, Theseus and Hippolyta stopped and
looked briefly at one another before each exited separately. With
'duty and desire', Egeus and Demetrius then followed Theseus
through the door upstage right. Their eager compliance with his
order to 'go along' gave a final definition to Hippolyta's silent and
Hermia's explicit refusal to submit to the sovereignty that men
claimed over them.

Another way of demonstrating the impact that Hippolyta's
silence can have is to consider a production – Elijah Moshinsky's
in 1981 for BBC-TV – that obliterated it. Moshinsky split
Shakespeare's single opening scene into several 'scenes' set in differ-

ent locations. The first of Moshinsky's scenes opened by having the camera show Hippolyta, dressed in black, pacing restlessly, even angrily, in front of a line of attendants who stood along one wall of a room. The voice of Theseus speaking the play's first lines intruded as the audience watched Hippolyta. Then the camera showed him, still wearing armour, standing in front of his attendants, ranged along the opposite wall. Facing him across that intervening space, Hippolyta replied without in any way narrowing the distance, both physical and emotional, between them. After Hippolyta finished speaking, Theseus first ordered Philostrate to 'stir up the Athenian youth to merriments', then crossed until he stood face to face with an unsmiling, defiant Hippolyta. In an assertion of his will and dominance, he declared to her his resolve to wed her 'with pomp, with triumph, and with revelling'.

Moshinsky's production then shifted directly to the arraignment of Hermia, which, set in a different room, became a scene distinct from the exchange between Theseus and Hippolyta that began the play. Hippolyta was not present during this second scene to watch in silence as Theseus heard the 'complaint' against Hermia and passed judgement. Her absence negated all possibility of establishing visual correspondences between Hippolyta's situation and Hermia's, and Moshinsky squandered the potential established by his interpretation of the opening dialogue between Theseus and Hippolyta. Moshinsky thus wasted the opportunity presented by the silence that Shakespeare's words impose on Hippolyta – the same opportunity that Hall, Hirsch, Brannerman, and Brook exploited in sharply divergent ways.

III

The diverse meanings and effects that Hippolyta's silence yields have an impact that reaches beyond the opening scene. Her silence can be the primary factor in defining the nature of her relationship with Theseus, and that relationship in turn can shape the alignments among the various characters and even alter the structure of the play. Consider the possible consequences of endowing Hippolyta's silence with meanings and effects that establish – as Hall's production did – that the relationship between Theseus and Hippolyta is harmonious from the start of the play. Their harmony then contrasts with the discord that characterises the relationship between

Oberon and Titania and the interactions of Hermia, Lysander, Demetrius, and Helena.

After exiting mid-way through the opening scene, Theseus and Hippolyta do not again appear onstage until the fourth act, when they enter as, or directly after, Oberon and Titania, 'new in amity' (IV.i.86), exit. The placement of the entrance that ends their long absence illustrates how the Duke of Athens and the Queen of the Amazons, who are soon to be married, can function as a mean between the King and Queen of the Fairies, who are already married, and the four young Athenians who are seeking spouses. Theseus and Hippolyta are present when those youngsters awake to find themselves paired, after the confusions of the night, in mutually desired combinations, which Theseus, overruling Egeus's desires,[6] then validates: 'in the temple, by and by, with us, / These couples shall eternally be knit' (ll.179–80).

In productions such as Hall's, the harmony that Oberon and Titania attain is the harmony that Theseus and Hippolyta have enjoyed since the opening moments of the play, and it is through Oberon's manipulations that the four young lovers find their affections realigned in ways that allow them to participate in that harmony. If Hippolyta's silence signifies concord between Theseus and Hippolyta, *A Midsummer Night's Dream* becomes a play whose structure is based on the principle of repetition. The opening exchange between Theseus and Hippolyta establishes the harmony that emerges from conflict, the amity in union that follows enmity in battle. The audience then watches a variety of characters go through variations of the same change from discord to concord.

If, however, Hippolyta's silence signifies a conflict with Theseus, alignments among the various characters shift. The relationship between Theseus and Hippolyta at the start of the play does not establish a concordant order in which other characters eventually participate. Instead, the conflict between the Duke of Athens and the Queen of the Amazons is the initial manifestation of a more fundamental disorder that surfaces again in the quarrel between father and daughter and in the squabbling over which young man will be paired with Hermia and which with Helena. The source of that disorder lies, one learns at the start of Act II, outside the human realm, in the battle under way between the King and Queen of the Fairies that disrupts everything from the cycle of the seasons to the patterns of the Morris dancers. 'And this same progeny of evils comes', Titania advises Oberon,

From our debate, from our dissension;
We are their parents and original.
(II.i.115–17)

The occasion of their quarrel is Titania's refusal to give to Oberon the changeling boy whom she prizes because of her affection for his mother, who died giving birth to him: 'And for her sake,' Titania tells Oberon, 'do I rear up her boy; / And for her sake I will not part with him' (II.i.136–7). In her insistence on keeping the boy, Titania, like Hermia, explicitly refuses to submit to a male who claims authority over her. She defies her husband just as Hermia defies both her father and her duke. In performance, Hippolyta's silent defiance of the man who has conquered her and will be her husband can be just as pointed, even if unspoken. In her silence the defeated Queen of the Amazons can even convey a commitment, like Titania's, to the primacy of the bonds that link one woman to another – a commitment that marriage does not extinguish. The pattern of resistance to an authority figure can be extended to include the scenes involving the 'rude mechanicals' (III.ii.9), during which Bottom and to a lesser extent the other would-be actors repeatedly challenge Quince's decisions as director.

Peter Brook's production of *A Midsummer Night's Dream* illustrates the force such parallels can exert. He had the same actor play both Egeus and Quince, thus linking the father who tries to force his daughter to fit her fancies to his will and the novice director who struggles to force his performers to make their various and erratic fancies conform with his befuddled conception of dramatic order. Brook also doubled the roles of Oberon and Theseus, of Hippolyta and Titania, and of the courtiers and fairies. Probably the most striking instance of doubling involved Philostrate, the official charged with providing entertainment to the Athenian court, and Puck, the agent through whom Oberon seeks to execute his designs and the figure through whom, in the Epilogue, Shakespeare articulates the correspondence between what happens to the characters and what happens to the audience during the play:

If we shadows have offended,
Think but this, and all is mended –
That you have but slumb'red here
While these visions did appear.
And this weak and idle theme,
No more yielding but a dream,

Gentles, do not reprehend.
(V.i.412–18)

The extensive doubling enabled Brook to use the process of seeing to give non-verbal but compelling confirmation to Puck's summary of the dreamlike visions experienced by the theatre audience during *A Midsummer Night's Dream*. How audiences saw during performances of Brook's production was similar to how Hermia says she sees on awakening after her night in the forest: 'Methinks I see these things with parted eye, / When everything seems double.'[7]

When Hippolyta's silence is used to establish or to deepen her conflict with Theseus, the structure of *A Midsummer Night's Dream* changes accordingly. The principle of repetition is replaced by the principle of gradual intensification, followed by sudden, almost explosive transformation.[8] In the first four acts, the prevailing movement is toward disorder, which becomes ever more baffling to those caught up in it. At the moment during Act IV, scene i when that disorder seems greatest, it is – to use Quince's not inappropriate malapropism – 'translated' into order.[9] Titania awakes to find herself loathing the man with the head of the ass, whom she has taken to her bed, and willing to join hands and dance with Oberon without any thought of the changeling boy or his mother. The four young Athenians, each of whose last conscious memories were of hunting a member of the same sex in order to do battle,[10] awake to find themselves peacefully paired, male and female. With Theseus, Hippolyta, and Egeus standing before them, they learn, to their own amazement, that the answer to Theseus' question ('Begin these woodbirds but to couple now,' l.139) is yes. His affections changed 'I wot not by what power' (l.163), Demetrius, dazed but certain, declares that he now loves Helena, leaving Egeus with no one whom he can compel Hermia to marry. The process of 'translation' even touches Theseus. Overruling Egeus, he sets aside without explanation the law whose validity he had upheld during the opening scene while Hippolyta looked on in silence, and he sanctions the union of Hermia with Lysander and of Helena with Demetrius.

The decision to have Hippolyta's silence convey that she and Theseus are (or come to be) in conflict during the opening scene requires that another decision be made about when that conflict ends, allowing Theseus and Hippolyta to participate in the 'amity' engendered by the reconciliation of Oberon and Titania. One possibility is that the conflict has already ended when Theseus and Hippolyta enter in Act IV, scene i, immediately after Oberon and Titania have exited together 'new in amity'. Theseus says,

> We will, fair Queen, up to the mountain's top
> And mark the musical confusion
> Of hounds and echo in conjunction.
>   (ll.108–10)

Then Hippolyta speaks for the first time since falling silent during the opening scene. The very fact that she breaks her silence can testify to a reconciliation with Theseus, and that possibility is strengthened when one considers that what she says can be an endorsement of Theseus' sense of the thrill of the hunt:

> I was with Hercules and Cadmus once
> When in a wood of Crete they bayed the bear
> With hounds of Sparta. Never did I hear
> Such gallant chiding; for, besides the groves,
> The skies, the fountains, every region near
> Seemed all one mutual cry. I never heard
> So musical a discord, such sweet thunder.
>   (ll.111–17)

However, the words Hippolyta speaks when she breaks her silence – like those she uttered at the start of the play before falling silent – need not necessarily signify harmony with Theseus. Twice she uses the word 'never' ('Never did I hear' and 'I never heard'), each time in a phrase that can convey her belief that the hunting that Theseus now proposes cannot measure up to what she has known in the past. Delivered with a sceptical or belittling edge, her words can convey continuing discord with Theseus, and if they do, the moment when she and Theseus are joined in amity must come later in the scene, perhaps after Theseus says, 'Egeus, I will overbear your will' (l.178) and gives his approval to the marriages of Hermia with Lysander and Demetrius with Helena. With that decision Theseus disregards the Athenian law defining Egeus' paternal rights over Hermia, a law that, he had earlier said, 'by no means we may extenuate'. In Brannerman's production especially, those words emphasised Theseus' respect for Athenian law. By exploiting the parallels between the exit Theseus and Hippolyta make in this scene and the exit they make during the opening scene, Brannerman had their reconciliation flow directly from Theseus' refusal to heed Egeus' call for 'the law, the law' (l.154). When Theseus said, after announcing the triple marriages, 'Come, Hippolyta' (l. 185), Hippolyta's reaction was very different from her reaction when he said, 'Come, my Hippolyta' during the opening scene. She responded not by slapping the book of Athenian laws into Theseus' hands and exiting without him, but by taking first Egeus' hand and then Theseus', after which the three of them exited together.

If Hippolyta and Theseus are in harmony when they enter, the rest of Act IV, scene i shows order and the awareness of order emerging in a clearly hierarchical pattern – beginning with the King and Queen of the Fairies, followed by Theseus and Hippolyta, and finally by the four young lovers. A different pattern develops, however, if the reconciliation between Theseus and Hippolyta is delayed until Theseus affirms the lovers' pairings. Theseus' willingness to make that affirmation becomes, in effect, a condition for the reconciliation, and the movement from disorder to order does not proceed hierarchically, but rather from Oberon and Titania, to the four young lovers, to Theseus and Hippolyta. The Duke of Athens and the Queen of the Amazons – recent foes in actual battle – are the last to share in the concord that can result from the union of male and female.

The latest that the reconciliation between Theseus and Hippolyta can occur is the start of Act V, which opens with Hippolyta saying, 'Tis strange, my Theseus, what these lovers speak of'. This is the first time during the play that she addresses Theseus by name, and her use of 'my', conveying acceptance, even possessiveness, echoes Theseus' use of the same adjective during the opening scene: 'Come, my Hippolyta', and 'What cheer, my love?' The fact that Hippolyta (might well have) resisted the implications of that word during the opening scene makes her use of it now, immediately after the marriage ceremony, all the more telling. Perhaps equally telling is that the phrase 'my Theseus' establishes a correspondence between the first words an audience hears Hippolyta speak to the man who has just become her husband and the first words Titania speaks when she awakes from her sleep and finds herself reconciled with her husband: 'My Oberon, what visions have I seen' (IV.i.75).[11]

IV

Hippolyta's open silence occurs during the opening scene of a play in which Shakespeare calls attention to and celebrates his own success in using language to engender dramatic illusion. To solve the problem posed by the fact that Pyramus and Thisby must meet by moonlight, Bottom suggests they 'leave a casement of the great chamber window, where we play, open, and the moon may shine in at the casement' (III.i.48–50). Quince counters with a proposal to substitute figurative moonbeams for actual moonlight:

> Or else one must come in with a bush of thorns and a lantern, and say he comes to disfigure, or to present, the person of Moonshine.
>
> (ll.51–3)

Their laughable efforts highlight by contrast Shakespeare's success in coping with virtually the same problem. He deploys the resources of language in order to conjure up the illusionary darkness and moonlight in which much of *A Midsummer Night's Dream* takes place. We can better appreciate what Shakespeare achieves by means of words if we recall that most performances of the play in Shakespeare's time took place in daylight in an outdoor theatre. Those who watched those first performances imposed on the daylight that their eyes registered the fictional darkness and moonlight that Shakespeare's language imprinted upon their minds.[12] They saw 'not with the eyes, but with the mind' (I.i.234). By effectively using words to 'present' moonlight during the play, Shakespeare gives Theseus' description of how a poet uses language a validity that Theseus himself did not intend:

> And as imagination bodies forth
> The forms of things unknown, the poet's pen
> Turns them to shapes, and gives to airy nothing
> A local habitation and a name.
>
> (V.i.14–17)

Hippolyta's silence is open not because Shakespeare lacked the skill to give her words but because he did not exercise that skill, did not employ the power of his 'poet's pen' to give her silence precisely fixed meanings and effects. He did not use the words at his command to provide her silence with 'a local habitation and a name' – with specific 'shapes'. Until and unless her silence is given body during a performance, it remains one of those 'things unknown'. In effect, Shakespeare has assigned to those who perform *A Midsummer Night's Dream* the power to give Hippolyta's silence shape and local habitation. That power is not minor or peripheral, for the exercise of it determines the relationships among characters and the structural principle of the play. As the productions I have discussed illustrate, the exercise of that power can bring forth from Hippolyta's silence meanings and effects that differ, sometimes profoundly, yet remain compatible with the words that Shakespeare did pen.

Relinquishing the power to shape Hippolyta's silence entails risks. Like Quince, Bottom, and the others who rehearse and then perform the play of Pyramus and Thisby, actors and directors can, and have, and will run roughshod over the words a playwright puts down for them.[13] An open silence like Hippolyta's removes even the frail check that the dramatist's words impose upon their impulses and inclinations.

Balancing such risks are certain rewards. Because the words that came from Shakespeare's 'poet's pen' establish the existence of Hippolyta's silence but do not specify its meanings and effects, those who perform and produce the play must do more than enact Shakespeare's intentions. Lacking the words necessary to know what Shakespeare intended, they must use their skills to determine what the meanings and effects of her silence will be. They must enact intentions that are theirs, not Shakespeare's. As they do, *A Midsummer Night's Dream* becomes their play as well as his and acquires a vitality it would not otherwise have.

Hippolyta's silence, in its openness, also offers another benefit. It helps to endow *A Midsummer Night's Dream* with the capacity to change significantly while retaining identity and coherence – to remain itself yet be 'translated' not just from performance to performance and production to production but even from era to era across the centuries. To give but one example, *A Midsummer Night's Dream* can better and more revealingly accommodate and be adapted to the values and concerns brought to the fore by the feminist movement precisely because Hippolyta's silence allows for the possibility that she, like Hermia, does not submit to male authority. A version of the play that included words with which Hippolyta voiced her acceptance of Theseus' authority would not allow such a possibility. The freedom and flexibility generated by Hippolyta's silence increase the likelihood that, despite the changes in values and perceptions that come with time, *A Midsummer Night's Dream* will continue to find 'a local habitation' that will allow audiences better to understand themselves and their culture.

From Philip C. McGuire, *Speechless Dialect: Shakespeare's Open Silences* (Berkeley, CA, 1985), pp. 1–18

NOTES

[Around the middle of this century the formal analysis of theatrical performance began to diverge from traditional literary criticism, in ways that were signalled in universities by the emergence of departments of Theatre Arts or Theatre Studies, as distinct from departments of English. The nub of the differences between them was (and is) the status of the play-text: for those in Theatre Arts/Studies it is an embryo, mainly of interest for what it reveals of the theatrical conditions for which it was composed or for the uses to which it may be put in modern performance (performance itself being the proper object of study, not the text, drama being a live medium). For those in English departments, the play-text itself has traditionally been the site of meaning; performance is a secondary pleasure, which may or may not realise the meanings(s) of the text. Half a century later, however, these distinctions no longer hold water. Many of the forms of literary theory which have overtaken English studies in this time have displaced meaning both from the authors and texts and have vested it primarily in readers or their communities – or, to put it another way, in the vagaries of reading/performance rather than in any misplaced certainty of what authors 'intend' or texts incontrovertibly 'say'. To that extent, English studies and Theatre Studies have converged, rather than drifted further apart, since their first divorce. McGuire's essay, the first chapter in his book-length study, *Speechless Dialect: Shakespeare's Open Silences*, demonstrates this succinctly. Theatrical silences are analogous to all the deferred meanings, subtexts and against-the-grain readings of modern criticism. They challenge the act of interpretation itself. The version printed here has been very slightly altered by the author himself. Ed.]

1. For a perceptive discussion of the ambiguity of time and man's perception of it in this play, see James E. Robinson's article, 'The Ritual and Rhetoric of *A Midsummer Night's Dream*', *PMLA*, 83 (1968), 380–91.

2. This production was revived in 1962 and provided the basis for a 1969 film of the play that was designed for both British cinema and US television. Michael Mullin discusses the shift from stage to screen in 'Peter Hall's *A Midsummer Night's Dream*', *Educational Theatre Journal*, 28 (1975), 529–34. Jack J. Jorgens devotes a chapter of *Shakespeare on Film* (Bloomington, IN, 1977) to Hall's film, and he describes Hippolyta as 'domestic and dull, the director having obliterated all traces of her conflict with Theseus' (p. 54). I did not see either stage production, but I have studied the promptbooks of both and have seen the film several times.

3. Andrew Veitch, *Guardian* (London, Manchester), 8 July 1980, p. 9.

4. After opening in Stratford-upon-Avon in 1970, this production toured North America, was made part of the RSC's 1971–2 London repertoire, and began a one-year world tour in 1973. My comments are based on a performance I saw in London in August 1971, and on the promptbook for the world tour production, edited by Glen Loney and published as *Peter Brook's Production of William Shakespeare's* A Midsummer Night's Dream *for the Royal Shakespeare Company: The Complete and Authorised Action Edition* (Chicago, 1974). Loney observes: 'This version is perhaps the most definitive because it represents the refinements and simplifications which the production achieved in the Paris rehearsals for the tour and the later modifications introduced as the show travelled to such cities as Budapest, Helsinki, and Los Angeles. It is interesting to note that the production always moved in the direction of greater simplicity – rather than greater complexity – from its earliest moments at Stratford ... .The unnecessary and the extraneous did not survive, and they are not represented in this edition' (p. 3a).

5. In an interview published in Loney's edition, Alan Howard, who played Theseus and Oberon, says of Hippolyta: 'she apparently comes to this court and discovers that although he has said he is going to wed her in a *different* way, he appears to be making an extraordinarily barbaric judgement against another woman' (p. 42).

6. Egeus' response to this exercise of ducal authority is a silence that, like Hippolyta's during most of her time onstage in the first scene, is open. See Philip McGuire, 'Egeus and the Implications of Silence' in *Shakespeare and the Sense of Performance: Essays in the Tradition of Performance Criticism in Honor of Bernard Beckerman*, ed. Marvin and Ruth Thompson (Newark, DE and London, 1989), pp. 103–15.

7. For a discussion of the phenomenon of doubling, see Stephen Booth, 'Speculations on Doubling in Shakespeare's Plays', in Philip C. McGuire and David A. Samuelson (eds), *Shakespeare: The Theatrical Dimension* (New York, 1979), pp. 103–31. An expanded version of Booth's article was published as appendix 2 of his *King Lear, Macbeth, Indefinition, and Tragedy* (New Haven, CT, 1983), pp. 129–55.

8. This principle is akin to what C. L. Barber has called 'the saturnalian pattern', consisting of 'a basic movement which can be summarised in the formula, through release to clarification' (p. 4). His *Shakespeare's Festive Comedy: A Study of Dramatic Form and Its Relation to Social Custom* (Princeton, NJ, 1959) is a masterpiece to which I am deeply indebted. *A Midsummer Night's Dream* was the subject of three books between the mid-1960s and the mid-1970s: David P. Young, *Something of Great Constancy: The Art of* A Midsummer Night's

Dream (New Haven, CT, 1966); Stephen Fender, *Shakespeare*: A Midsummer Night's Dream (London, 1968); and T. Walter Herbert, *Oberon's Mazed World* (Baton Rouge, LA, 1977).

9. The shift from disorder to order can be sudden and total because there is a pattern to the confusion in which the characters are caught. In *The Court Masque* (Cambridge, 1927), Enid Welsford describes that pattern as a dance:

> The plot is a pattern, a figure, rather than a series of human events occasioned by character and passion, and this pattern, especially in the moonlight parts of the play, is the pattern of a dance ... .The appearance and disappearance and reappearance of the various lovers, the will-o'-the-wisp movement of the elusive Puck, form a kind of figured ballet. The lovers quarrel in a dance pattern: first, there are two men to one woman and the other woman alone, then a brief space of circular movement, each one pursuing and pursued, then a return to the first figure with the position of the women reversed, then a cross-movement, man quarrelling with man and woman with woman, and then, as a finale, a general setting to partners, including not only the lovers but fairies and royal personages as well.
>
> (pp. 331–2)

The pairings of the young lovers are constant because the love juice remains in Demetrius' eyes. That fact illustrates that the order that emerges toward the end of Act IV, like the disorder that preceded it, rests upon impulses and affections that are capable of changing swiftly, completely, and even randomly. In *A Midsummer Night's Dream*, order and disorder are not so much antitheses of one another as mirror images of one another. Discord is not extinguished by, but 'translated' into, concord.

10. The motif of women engaged in conflicts deserves specific mention. *A Midsummer Night's Dream* opens soon after a battle in which the Athenian army under Theseus has vanquished Hippolyta and her army of women. When the audience first sees Titania, she is engaged in a struggle that pits her and her attendants against Oberon and his. Oberon triumphs by using the love juice to bring Titania's sexual energies to such a pitch that she, doting on Bottom, no longer prizes the boy or the love that bound her to his mother. In victory Oberon reclaims Titania as his wife and takes the boy for himself. During Act III, Hermia and Helena come to the point where they are ready to fight one another. Each woman, in order to gain the man she wants, disregards the love and loyalty that since childhood have made them virtually one. 'So we grew together, / Like to a double cherry, seeming parted, / But yet a union in partition' (III.ii.208–10). Each subordinates

those ties to the desire for a different kind of intimacy and union, to the imperatives of sexual love. From a Freudian perspective, the women in the play can be said to grow up as each emerges from a state in which relationships with other women are valued to one in which relationships with men become paramount. One could also argue, however, that the motif of women who either cease to do battle with men or come to do battle with each other implies a vision, a fantasy, of male domination.

11. The harmony that Theseus and Hippolyta either have from the start or eventually establish is not, it must be stressed, synonymous with uniformity – with the obliteration of all differences. The two characters differ during the rest of Act V over a number of points – the truth of the lovers' 'story of the night' (l.23), the appropriateness of having the rude mechanicals perform, the role of an audience's imagination – but those differences are now (if they were not earlier) part of a larger harmony that makes concord of potential discord.

12. Shakespeare calls attention to this process by reversing it when Bottom, playing Pyramus, arrives at Ninus' tomb. Bottom describes the moonlight, in which the audience was to imagine Pyramus standing, by using words that in fact describe the sunlight actually illuminating the daytime performance of the play of Pyramus and Thisby and of *A Midsummer Night's Dream*:

> Sweet moon, I thank thee for thy sunny beams;
> I thank thee, moon, for shining now so bright;
> For, by thy gracious, golden, glittering gleams,
> I trust to take of truest Thisby sight.
> (V.i.265–8)

13. It is easy, tempting, and correct to say that 'Pyramus and Thisby', particularly Quince's delivery of the Prologue, is a classic example of performers abusing what a playwright has written. It is also true, however, that even though it is thoroughly botched, the rude mechanicals' performance of that play helps to make *A Midsummer Night's Dream* itself a success in performance.

7

Gaining a Father: the Role of Egeus in the Quarto and the Folio

BARBARA HODGDON

The role of Egeus in *A Midsummer Night's* is a tiny one. The character appears in only two scenes (I.i; IV.i) in all modern readers' texts. In both, he voices paternal authority and choice, complaining of his daughter Hermia's love for Lysander and asking that Theseus invoke the law of Athens to make her marry Demetrius or be put to death. Commentators on the play rarely accord him the status of a character: with unusual attentiveness, Granville-Barker notes the 'shrill rattle' of his I.i. speech.[1] Most regard him as a function, a blocking parent-figure crucial to the rapid exposition in the opening scene and a necessary dissenting presence in IV.i, repeating his objections and demands much like a broken recording. Once Theseus overbears his will and approves Hermia's marriage to Lysander, he disappears from the play. But only in the Quarto version.[2] In the Folio, his role continues into V.i., where his presence at first sustains and then resolves the conflicting points of view that set the play on its course. Egeus's absence in Q and his presence in F constitute a puzzle that deserves study. In what follows, I should like to examine the Folio variants surrounding his role in Act V, for they reveal dramatic possibilities that not only raise issues for readers and performers but also contribute to the current editorial controversy on multiple-text plays that offer different, perhaps characteristic, performance intentions.[3]

Briefly, the question concerns whether it is Philostrate (Q) or Egeus (F) who presents the brief of 'how many sports are ripe' to Theseus, describes the Pyramus and Thisbe play, tells Theseus that the play is about to begin, and remains onstage until Theseus concludes the evening's entertainment and directs a general exit. Usual editorial policy honours Egeus's presence more in the breach than the observance, confining any mention of him to footnotes or to discussions of textual authority. Almost unanimously, editors use the Quarto as a copy-text, adopting its ascription of Egeus's role in V.i to Philostrate. Defences range from Malone's comment that the lines are 'rightly given to Philostrate, who appears in the first scene as master of the revels to Theseus, and is there sent out on a similar errand' to Greg's conjecture that the actor who played Philostrate in I.i had been required for another part and that the bookkeeper transferred his part in V.i. to Egeus.[4] And Harold F. Brooks, the New Arden editor, states that the substitution of Egeus for Philostrate is 'a change Shakespeare cannot have wished for, though he might acquiesce in it as an expedient'.[5] Brooks masks only slightly the subjectivity of equating Shakespeare's wishes with his own; I would counter his argument by noting that rejections of the Folio variants as theatrical expediency are themselves speculative.

Alone among editors, and in accord with his general policy for the *New Variorum*, Furness uses the Folio as his copy-text. His comments on the Egeus–Philostrate matter are worth considering:

> In no scene throughout the play, except in the very last, are Philostrate and Egeus on the stage at the same time, so that down to this last scene one actor could perform the two parts, and this practice of 'doubling' must have been frequent enough in a company as small as at The Globe. In the last scene, however, it is the duty of Philostrate to provide the entertainment, and Egeus too has to be present. There can be no 'doubling' now, and one of the two characters must be omitted. Of course it is the unimportant Philostrate who is stricken out; Egeus remains, and becomes the Master of the Revels and provides the entertainment. In texts to be used only by readers any change whatever is needless, but in a text to be used by actors the prefixes to the speeches must be changed, and '*Phil.*' must be erased and '*Egeus*' substituted.[6]

Several things are pertinent here. First, Furness suggests the possibility of doubling Egeus and Philostrate initially, yet he fails to note that only four to six lines separate Philostrate's exit from Egeus's entrance in I.i., hardly time enough to exit, effect some change in appearance that will distinguish the two characters, and re-enter.[7] On this basis alone, the doubling theory as an explanation for the Folio variants can be questioned; my discussion of Act V will confirm its ineptness.[8] More significant in terms of my argument is that Furness affirms both Q (a readers' text) and F (a theatrical text). Implicitly, he acknowledges two entirely different perceptual experiences, two ways of reading. Each, of course, like the reconstructed texts on which they are based, is both subjective and speculative. With this in mind, let me now suggest how the Folio's performance instructions or signals in Act V generate a series of opportunities that alter, and enrich, the play.

The initial variant, the stage directions opening Act V, yields, at first, little apparent difference.[9]

> *Enter Theseus, Hippolyta, and Philostrate.*
> (First Quarto, G3, 20)
> *Enter Theseus, Hippolyta, Egeus and his Lords.*
> (Folio, 1790 s.d.; V.i. s.d.)

In the Quarto, Philostrate's appearance here echoes his presence in I.i.; this alone signals a strong return to beginnings, reinforcing the sense of a framing action, and might well be considered useful simply because of that. Yet neither Q nor F mentions Philostrate in the stage direction for I.i., which reads '*Enter Theseus, Hippolyta, with others*'.[10] Only Theseus's order to Philostrate lets us know he is included in that scene. The Folio, by directing the presence of Egeus *and his Lords* in V.i., more precisely echoes the 'with others' of the I.i. stage direction, reproducing the initial public situation. But F also signals a distinct change. Rather than interrupting the occasion, as he does in I.i., Egeus is from the outset integrated within it, if only as a silent onlooker. But this is only a slight rearrangement of pattern, as yet unremarkable. The overall impression of both texts is that Theseus and Hippolyta are not alone but are accompanied by a person or persons who remain silent for thirty-eight lines. And the dominant focus rests on the speakers, Theseus and Hippolyta, not on the listeners.

This time, it is the lovers, not Egeus, who interrupt Theseus and Hippolyta.[11] And after welcoming them, Theseus enquires about possible entertainments and calls for Philostrate (Q) or for Egeus (F). At first view, the majority opinion – that the answering lines should be assigned to Philostrate – seems reasonable enough. No bibliographical complexity surrounds the moment: *who* speaks the lines seems indeed less significant than that they are spoken at all. And a *Dream* without Egeus's presence here is obviously satisfyingly readable as well as playable. Yet that presence alters significantly both readerly and spectatorly perceptions of these moments and does so particularly if one considers a second Folio variant. Also dismissed by editors, the variant assigns the reading of the items in the brief to Lysander and the comment on them to Theseus, thus dividing between two speakers the lines ascribed, in Q, only to Theseus.[12] Here is the entire passage:

> **Theseus**   Come now, what masques, what dances shall we have
> To wear away this long age of three hours,
> Between our after-supper, and bedtime?
> Where is our usual manager of mirth?
> What revels are in hand? Is there no play,
> To ease the anguish of a torturing hour?
> Call Egeus.
> **Egeus**   Here, mighty Theseus.
> **Theseus**   Say, what abridgement have you for this evening?
> What masque, what music? How shall we beguile
> The lazy time, if not with some delight?
> **Egeus**   There is a brief how many sports are ripe:
> Make choice of which your highness will see first.
> **Lysander**   The battle with the Centaurs to be sung
> By an Athenian eunuch to the harp.
> **Theseus**   We'll none of that. That have I told my Love
> In glory of my kinsman Hercules.
> **Lysander**   The riot of the tipsy Bacchanals,
> Tearing the Thracian singer, in their rage?
> **Theseus**   That is an old device, and it was played
> When I from Thebes came last a Conqueror.
> **Lysander**   The thrice three Muses, mourning for the death
> Of learning, late deceased in beggary.
> **Theseus**   That is some Satire keen and critical,
> Not sorting with a nuptial ceremony.
> **Lysander**   A tedious brief Scene of young Pyramus,
> And his love Thisbe; very tragical mirth.
> **Theseus**   Merry and tragical? Tedious and brief?
> That is, hot ice, and wondrous strange snow.
> How shall we find the concord of this discord?
> (Folio, 1827–57; V.i. 32–60)

That Theseus asks for 'our usual manager of mirth' is the major reason editors give for assigning the speeches here to Philostrate, not Egeus. But, since Theseus asks four questions in rapid succession, all of which have to do with the evening's entertainment, it is most unlikely that an audience will pick up on only one and thus question Philostrate's absence. Even if they do, the inconsistency is of a kind Shakespeare is all too famous for elsewhere.

As Egeus answers Theseus's call and offers the brief of 'sports' Lysander reads out the titles, Theseus responding to each. This suggests that Lysander and Egeus are fairly close to one another and, perhaps, that Theseus stands somewhat apart. Either Lysander is reading over Egeus's shoulder or he takes, or snatches, the paper from Egeus. Whichever, the Folio text clearly gives Lysander an action to play, one which can show either that Lysander now has Egeus's approval or that – if he takes the brief (as he has taken Egeus's daughter) – he uses this opportunity to deny Egeus's voice and to assert his own – a kind of revenge for Egeus's initial denial of this suit as well as for cutting off his IV.i. explanation of how he and Hermia happen to be in the wood (Folio, 1671–9). Either possibility recalls the tensions and accusations both at the play's opening and in IV.i. and, lightly, either heals or continues them.

Breaking up the reading of the brief and the commentary also offers opportunities to deepen further connections with earlier moments. Theseus's responses to the first two offerings stress his kinship to Hercules and his triumphant return from Thebes. The third reminds us of the unsuitability of satire at a wedding. The last time Hercules was mentioned, Hippolyta is recalling being with him and hearing 'the hounds of Sparta; ... I never heard / So musical a discord, such sweet thunder' (IV.i.113, 116–17). At that point, Theseus seems anxious to prove that his hounds are every bit as fine as those of Hercules and Cadmus: in fact, he describes their qualities in detail in the next seven and a half lines (IV.i.119–23), glancing at the 'kinship' he again refers to in the Act V moments. Theseus's initial comments seem dismissive, as though he is half-listening, perhaps absorbed with Hippolyta. But his response to hearing of the Pyramus and Thisbe play differs markedly: it reveals direct and immediate interest, questioning further rather than stepping back to ignore the offering. And his final question, 'How shall we find the concord of this discord?', picks up Hippolyta's earlier phrase, 'so musical a discord'. The Folio text reinforces and points the moment, especially if Theseus now moves toward Egeus, his attention shifted, as the subsequent exchange between the two suggests.

As Egeus describes the play, his responses to it, and the players, Theseus resolves to hear it. Here, Folio and Quarto agree, giving the demurral to Philostrate:

> Phil   No, my noble Lord,
> It is not for you. I have heard it over,
> And it is nothing, nothing in the world;
> Unless you can find sport in their intents,
> Extremely stretched, and conned with cruel pain,
> To do you service.
> Theseus   I will hear that play,
> For never anything can be amiss
> When simpleness and duty tender it.
> Go bring them in, and take your places, Ladies.
>   (Folio, 1874–81; V.i. 76–84)

This ascription provides the only Folio evidence that both Egeus and Philostrate are present here – evidence that editors seize on to further argue the carelessness and imprecision of F. But, although the presence of both Egeus and Philostrate is playable, it seems more reasonable to assume, with Furness, that, while other speech-prefixes were changed, this one was accidentally overlooked, and to offer a possible explanation in terms of an inadvertent failure to correct Q2 copy.[13] Philostrate's status, after all, is nearly as marginal in Q as in F. Neither text notes his entrance at the play's beginning; he is simply an 'other'. In Q, Theseus names him three times, perhaps a means of supporting the Athenian world of the play. Mute until Act V, there he speaks eight lines. The Folio reduces three namings to two and eight lines to five. The alteration validates and stresses Egeus's presence, providing a formal, structural means of satisfying the demands of both narrative and occasion. Here, F also points, by giving to Egeus the 'review' of the play, to his willingness to indulge in laughter – a sign of his conversion. What is a wedding celebration without a joyful father?

Overall, the Folio variants introduce a livelier, more dynamic rhythm of interchange at this point. Before the lovers' entrance, Theseus has just completed a sustained speech of some length; several more – Egeus's description of the play, Theseus's rebuttal to Hippolyta's protest at seeing the play, Quince's two Prologues – are to follow. If Theseus both reads and comments on the brief, as in Q, his voice and presence alone dominate the moments. The Folio text also reveals Theseus's control but, in addition, generates a sense of widened community and carries forward an impression of complex interrelationships between characters as well as between scenes, tightening the play's fabric.

Because both Q and F direct only an '*Exeunt*' at the end of Theseus's epilogue-like speech following the Bergomask dance (Folio, 2152, s.d.; V.i.360, s.d.), the final variant affecting Egeus is not a variant at all but a conjecture about the ordering of an exit. In this, it parallels the necessity to order an exit, for performance, in a play such as *The Merchant of Venice*, in which the final exit is left similarly 'free' in both QI and F. And there, as here, the planning of that exit charges our final impression of the play, offering a retrospective patterning of the action. Is Antonio left onstage alone as the paired lovers exit? Or is the last image of Portia and Bassanio, Antonio having just cleared the stage after signalling farewell to his friend? Or do we see Jessica, her head bowed, as we hear the *kaddish*?[14]

Like *The Merchant of Venice*, *A Midsummer Night's Dream's* '*Exeunt*' contains multiple possibilities. But only the Folio text, with Egeus's presence in this last scene, suggests particularly resonant opportunities. It makes sense, given their station, that Theseus and Hippolyta exit first. Egeus can, of course, follow his Duke directly, leaving the four lovers to exit together, in pairs. But since Hermia and Lysander's love has provided a pivot for the play's action, it also makes sense to delay their exit, prefacing it with that of Helena and Demetrius. And if Egeus remains on the stage with his daughter and her husband, a further opportunity exists. Hermia can turn back from her exit with Lysander to embrace her father, and Lysander, following, can return to shake his hand, thus completely healing the initial rupture. Then the two can exit, leaving Egeus alone momentarily on the stage. Or the pair can simply exit, permitting Egeus's presence to register his singleness and isolation before he is replaced by Puck, speaking his darkening reminders of night and death before reassuring us that 'Not a mouse / Shall disturb this hallowed house'. Either of these final opportunities suggested by the Folio text links the ending of *Dream* to those of comedies such as *As You Like*, *Much Ado About Nothing*, *Twelfth Night*, and *The Merchant of Venice* where one character – consistently a male – remains uncoupled, providing a hint of loneliness or dissent that plays against the others' joy. Of course these reconstructions are all conjectural. But the Folio not only creates such possibilities; it actually enforces them. Egeus, if he is present, must exit *somehow*, and any form of exit will have meaning, suggesting either communion or isolation.

In summary, the Folio variants in Act V shape a sense of familial and community harmony that extends and strengthens the possibilities suggested in the Quarto. That particular theatrical circumstances lie behind these variants certainly seems probable, but to read them as 'a further subtraction from the authority of the Folio text' and to ascribe them to a bookkeeper or to a 'rather fussy but incompetent editor' seem unwarranted judgements.[15] My own view is that the variants I have noted complicate and enrich the performance possibilities for *A Midsummer Night's Dream*. They illuminate character, quicken rhythms of action and reaction, suggest a firmer resolution of discord, and deepen retrospective connections within the play. The other Folio variants – the most significant of which are added stage directions – need to be examined thoroughly and placed within a full bibliographical context before arriving at further conclusions. But this present study, in connection with other recent work on multiple-text plays, adds support to the theory that the Folio text reveals the influence, not of a compositor, an editor, or a bookkeeper, but of Shakespeare's own revising mind.

From *Review of English Studies*, 37 (1986), 534–42.

NOTES

[It is no accident that Barbara Hodgdon's essay came out within a year of the *Oxford Shakespeare: The Complete Works*, general editors Stanley Wells and Gary Taylor (Oxford, 1986), the most radical edition of Shakespeare this century. It is not that she was necessarily in sympathy with all the editorial principles behind that edition (though it did 'restore' Egeus to Act V of *A Midsummer Night's Dream*, in defiance of most modern practice). The key link is a shared questioning of the Shakespearean text we have inherited, a scepticism about some of the commonest assumptions about Shakespeare as a writer and a man of the theatre. Most editorial practice since the eighteenth century has aimed to produce the 'best' Shakespearean text possible, which has usually meant opting – where there is a choice – for the most 'readable' of the early versions as the basis for an edition, augmenting it where appropriate with variants and additions from other early texts, and revising the whole to make good the supposed deficiencies of early editors and printers. The result of this can be to produce a modern 'composite' Shakespeare which does not correspond with any actual version of the play as it was known to his contemporaries. Wells and Taylor determined to cut across all that: 'we have devoted our efforts to recovering and presenting texts of Shakespeare's plays as they were acted in the London playhouses which stood at the centre of his professional life' (General Introduction, p. xxxix). While not denying that some of the more 'readerly' of the early texts might represent versions of what Shakespeare actually wrote, they focused single-mindedly on the plays as early modern theatrical scripts. The text earlier editorial practices most traduced was *King Lear*, which exists in two markedly different early versions, the 1608 quarto and the 1623 folio. In the early 1980s, the practice of conflating these for modern editions was widely challenged, for example in Steven Urkowitz, *Shakespeare's Revision of 'King Lear'* (Princeton, NJ, 1980) and Gary Taylor and Michael Warren (eds), *The Division of The Kingdoms: Shakespeare's Two Versions of 'King Lear'* (Oxford, 1984). Wells and Taylor responded by printing both versions in the *Oxford Shakespeare*. They did not accord any other play this special treatment, but Barbara Hodgdon's essay demonstrates just how significant the differences between the early versions of *A Midsummer Night's Dream* also are. The quarto is undoubtedly a more 'readerly' text, the folio a more theatrical one. But the differences go beyond the medium, redefining – however ambiguously – questions of ducal and patriarchal authority. Ed.]

1. Harley Granville-Barker, 'Preface to *A Midsummer Night's Dream*', in *More Prefaces to Shakespeare*, ed. Edward M. Moore (Princeton, NJ, 1974), p. 112.

2. Since Q2 clearly derives from Q1 without independent authority, Q1 and Q2 count, as evidence, as one text.

3. See the following selective list of studies. For the *King Lear* controversy: Peter W. M. Blayney, *The Texts of 'King Lear' and Their Origins*: vol. 1, *Nicholas Okes and the First Quarto* (Cambridge, 1982); Keith Brown, 'Chimeras Dire? An Analysis of the "Conflated" *Lear* Text', *Cahiers E*, 20 (1981), 71–82; Thomas Clayton, 'Old Light on the Text of *King Lear*', *Modern Philology*, 68 (1980–1), 347–67; P. W. K. Stone, *The Textual History of 'King Lear'* (London, 1980); Gary Taylor, 'The War in *King Lear*', *Shakespeare Survey*, 33 (1980), 27–34; Gary Taylor and Michael Warren, *The Division of the Kingdoms: Shakespeare's Two Versions of 'King Lear'* (Oxford, 1984); Steven Urkowitz, *Shakespeare's Revision of 'King Lear'* (Princeton, NJ, 1980); Michael J. Warren, 'Quarto and Folio *King Lear* and the Interpretation of Albany and Edgar', in *Shakespeare: Pattern of Excelling Nature*, ed. David Bevington and Jay L. Halio (Newark, DE, 1978), pp. 95–107. For other plays: Gary Taylor, '*Troilus and Cressida*: Bibliography, Performance, and Interpretation',

Shakespeare Studies, 15 (1982), 99–136; Stanley Wells and Gary Taylor, *Modernising Shakespeare's Spelling, with Three Studies in the Text of 'Henry V'* (Oxford, 1979).

4. *The Plays and Poems of William Shakespeare*, ed. Edmond Malone (London, 1821). W. W. Greg, *The Shakespeare First Folio: Its Bibliographical and Textual History* (Oxford, 1955), p. 243. So also in the Cambridge, Yale, Pelican, Signet, Riverside, Craig-Bevington, and New Penguin editions.

5. *A Midsummer Night's Dream*, ed. Harold F. Brooks (London, New Arden, 1979), p. xxxii.

6. *The New Variorum 'A Midsummer Night's Dream'*, ed. H. H. Furness, 8th edn (Philadelphia, 1923), pp. xiv–xv.

7. As in Brooks, New Arden edn, p. xxxii n. 1. But see David Bevington, who notes a series of quick changes in various Tudor plays. Much, he concludes, depends on the nature of the two roles (*From Mankind to Marlowe* [Cambridge, MA, 1962], p. 91).

8. Although contemporary practice often doubles some roles in *Dream*, in examining both reviews and prompt-books (at the Shakespeare Centre Library, Stratford-upon-Avon) from 1897 through 1981, nowhere do I find a record of doubling Egeus and Philostrate. I would agree with Stanley Wells, the New Penguin editor, who comments that it seems desirable to keep the two roles distinct, for the only quality drawing them together is that both serve functional roles (*A Midsummer Night's Dream* [Harmondsworth, 1967], p. 156).

9. Quotations from the Folio are taken from *The Norton Facsimile: The First Folio of Shakespeare*, ed. Charlton Hinman (New York, 1968), cited as 'Folio'. Quotations from the First Quarto are taken from *Shakespeare's Plays in Quarto*, ed. Michael J. B. Allen and Kenneth Muir (Berkeley, CA, 1981) and are given with reference to signatures in that volume. Through line numbers from the facsimile, and modern act, scene, and line numbers from the Arden *A Midsummer Night's Dream* are given. In all quotations, spelling and typography have been normalised according to modern conventions.

10. Quarto A2, I; Folio I.i s.d.

11. Each conversation Theseus and Hippolyta share reveals some tension, however slight, between them; each is interrupted by more public demands at a point where they might be supposed to continue talking and/or, perhaps, to reach toward a further shared intimacy. See I.i. 19; IV.i. 126; V.i. 27.

12. Granville-Barker remarks: 'Lysander's reading of the brief, leaving Theseus the comments only, might be worth trying' (Granville-Barker, p. 134).

13. See Furness, *New Variorum*, p. xv. I am indebted to Gary Taylor not only for suggesting that the failure to correct Q2 copy may account for the speech-prefix here but also for reading and commenting on the entire manuscript.

14. The BBC-television production (1981) gave us Antonio alone, in a moment recalling the play's opening. John Barton's RSC production at The Other Place (1977) showed us Portia and Bassanio, seated slightly apart. In Jonathan Miller's National Theatre production (1972) starring Laurence Olivier, Jessica remained on stage alone after the others had gone, listening to the *kaddish*.

15. New Arden edn, p. xxxii; Greg, *First Folio*, p. 246.

8

Bottom's Up: Festive Theory

ANNABEL PATTERSON

> Even though chronology places regularity above permanence, it cannot prevent heterogeneous, conspicuous fragments from remaining within it. To have combined recognition of a quality with the measurement of the quantity was the work of the calendar in which the places of recollection are left blank, as it were, in the form of holidays.
>
> (Walter Benjamin: *On Some Motifs in Baudelaire*)

On 29 September, Michaelmas Day, 1662, Samuel Pepys recorded in his diary a characteristically guilty moment:

> This day my oaths for drinking of wine and going to plays are out, and so I do resolve to take a liberty to-day, and then to fall to them again. To the King's Theatre, where we saw 'Midsummer's Night's Dream,' which I had never seen before, nor shall ever again, for it is the most insipid ridiculous play that ever I saw in my life. I saw, I confess, some good dancing and some handsome women, and which was all my pleasure.[1]

The psychological conflicts for which Pepys's diary is famous have in this instance an ideological quotient – the conflict between the Restoration court's support of the stage and the Puritan principles he had incorporated[2] – a conflict which descends, obviously, from the Elizabethan theatre's relation to governmental allowance and control. And lest we should doubt that this conflict, in Pepys, was serious, we should take note of his 'Observations' at the New Year, 1662: 'This I take to be as bad a juncture as ever I observed.

172

The King and his new Queen minding their pleasure at Hampton Court. All people discontented; some that the King do not gratify them enough; and the others, Fanatiques of all sorts, that the King do take away their liberty of conscience' (3:208). The moral embarrassment in which Pepys finds himself is especially signified by the contradictory function of 'liberty' in these two entries, the Nonconformist liberty of conscience threatened by the Act of Uniformity dialectically opposed to the festival liberty that Pepys resolves to allow himself (one of many such suspensions of his private rules) for Michaelmas Day.

Pepys's critical reaction also speaks to the theatre history of *A Midsummer Night's Dream*, which already, one can tell from his mention of 'good dancing', had succumbed to operatic or balletic impulses. These impulses dominated all productions from 1692, when it was rewritten as a spectacular opera with music by Henry Purcell, through 1914, when Harley Granville-Barker produced the uncut text 'in a world of poetic and dramatic rather than scenic illusion'.[3] For over two centuries, then, the play that Shakespeare wrote was rendered invisible by conspicuous display; and its most striking metadramatic feature, the concluding amateur theatricals of Bottom the weaver and his colleagues, lost both its structural and social force. In 1692 'Pyramus and Thisbe' was moved to the middle of the performance, and in 1816 the Covent Garden performance had as its grand finale a pageant of 'Triumphs of Theseus'. The result was a performance whose last word, in the year after Waterloo, was the extravagant celebration of monarchical and military power.

The *Dream* has also tempted literary critics to subordinate Bottom and his colleagues, or to neutralise the impact of the play-within-the-play. The temptation is posed by the speech of Theseus that both summarises the erotic experiences of the young Athenians on midsummer night, and serves as the aristocratic prologue to the artisan's playlet:

> More strange than true. I never may believe
> These antique fables, nor these fairy toys.
> Lovers and madmen have such seething brains,
> Such shaping fantasies, that apprehend
> More than cool reason ever comprehends.
>
> The poet's eye, in a fine frenzy rolling,
> Doth glance from heaven to earth, from earth to heaven,

> And as imagination bodies forth
> The forms of things unknown, the poet's pen
> Turns them to shapes, and gives to airy nothing
> A local habitation and a name.
>
> (V.i.2–17)[4]

Like the stage history, the tradition of privileging this Thesean aesthetic as the locus of Shakespeare's intentions had the effect of making the *Dream* an 'airy nothing', unaccountable to social or political realism, while at the same time giving to Theseus an exegetical authority that his own behaviour scarcely justifies. And though this critical tradition has been roundly challenged, most notably by Jan Kott's counter-privileging of Bottom and his fellows[5] (the academic equivalent of Peter Brook's famous 1970 production) it probably retains its dominance in the classroom.

In fact, even as within this speech imaginative process requires the assistance of things known – bodies, names and local habitations – Shakespeare gave the *Dream* a 'local habitation' so historically specific that the play would make no sense (as Pepys discovered) when performed outside its own cultural environment. The evidence occurs in two passages, close neighbours to each other, in the second act, where the story of Oberon's quarrel with Titania over the changeling boy is told from its beginnings and given a new impetus. In planning his revenge on Titania for her refusal to give up the child into his retinue, Oberon describes to Puck where he may find the 'little western flower', that will be the instrument of her enchantment. Quite gratuitously in terms of plot or strategy, he explains the origins of the flower's erotic capacities as an instance of displaced energies:

> That very time I saw (but thou couldst not),
> Flying between the cold moon and the earth,
> Cupid all arm'd. A certain aim he took
> At a fair vestal, throned by the west,
> And loos'd his love-shaft smartly from his bow
> As it should pierce a hundred thousand hearts.
> But I might see young Cupid's fiery shaft
> Quench'd in the chaste beams of the watery moon;
> And the imperial votress passed on,
> In maiden meditation, fancy-free.
>
> (II.i.155–64)

Missing its target, the shaft strikes the flower, which is thereby transformed from milk-white to purple, from mere flower to

concept, 'love-in-idleness'. The erotic drive is displaced into the ter-
ritory of the symbolic, producing an excess of textual energy that
seems to require special attention. The original audiences would
certainly have recognised its galvanic source in the implied presence
of Elizabeth herself. As H. H. Furness remarked in 1895,

> That there is an allegory here has been noted from the days of Rowe,
> but how far it extended and what its limitations and its meanings
> have since then proved prolific themes. According to Rowe, it
> amounted to no more than a compliment to Queen Elizabeth, and
> this is the single point on which all critics since his day are agreed.[6]

Was it, however, so clearly a compliment? Increasingly as she
aged, the problems posed by Elizabeth's status as unmarried female
ruler were either finessed or exposed to critical scrutiny by the motif
of virginity as power. As the moon goddess, Diana, Cynthia or
Phoebe, she was celebrated as the Belphoebe of Spenser's *Faerie
Queene*, and the Cynthia of Ben Jonson's *Cynthia's Revels* and
Ralegh's *The Ocean's Love to Cynthia*, all texts of the 1590s when
Elizabeth was approaching or in her sixties.[7] And as *A Midsummer
Night's Dream* is in one sense a play about moonshine, the lunar
presence invoked in its lines is far from a positive force: 'O, me-
thinks, how slow/This old moon wanes!' cries Theseus, 'She lingers
my desires.'

Further, as the title of Spenser's poem indicates, the myths of the
classical moon-goddess also merged, for the unique moment of
Elizabeth's reign, with fairy legends of Titania and Oberon. Even in
Ovid's *Metamorphoses*, Titania was another name for Diana
(3:173); during a royal progress of 1591 the 'Fairy Queen' presented Elizabeth with a chaplet that she had received from
'Auberon, the Fairy King';[8] and after her death Thomas Dekker referred to Elizabeth as Titania in his *Whore of Babylon* (1607). This
alternative mythology also appears in the *Dream,* and with equally
problematic resonance. For Titania, far from remaining chastely
aloof, engages in a struggle for domestic power with Oberon that,
however we attribute the fault, has had a disastrous effect on the
environment.

Titania herself rehearses these natural disasters, in the other
passage of topical significance:

> The ox hath therefore stretch'd his yoke in vain,
> The ploughman lost his sweat, and the green corn
> Hath rotted ere his youth attain'd a beard;

The fold stands empty in the drowned field,
And crows are fatted with the murrion flock;
The-nine-men's-morris is fill'd up with mud,
And the quaint mazes in the wanton green
For lack of tread are undistinguishable.
(II.i.93–100)

And on the basis of this passage, and our knowledge that the one season in Shakespeare's career that was notorious for its bad weather and bad harvests was 1595–6, a consensus has developed for dating the *Dream* at some point in 1596. This dating alone might have generated speculation about the frontal presence of a group of artisans, whose amateur theatricals contribute the play's conclusion, if not its resolution. It was not until 1986, however, that Titania's lament and the artisanal presence were connected, by Theodore Leinwand, to the abortive Oxfordshire rising of November 1596, when Bartholomew Stere, a carpenter, and Richard Bradshawe, a miller, had planned an anti-enclosure riot of distinctly violent proportions.[9] Depositions concerning this event were still being heard in London by the Privy Council during January 1597; it was said that Stere's 'owtward pretense was to ... helpe the poore cominaltie that were readie to famish for want of corne, But intended to kill the gentlemen of that countrie ... affirming that the Commons, long sithens in Spaine did rise and kill all the gentlemen in Spaine, and sithens that time have lyved merrily there.'[10] The handful of leaders were all artisans; and although the rising literally came to nothing (the leaders could find no followers), the Privy Council took the matter extremely seriously.

To write seriously about comedy can unfortunately give the impression that one has no sense of humour. Yet it is not implausible to see an allusion to a time of hardship not only in Titania's speech, but also in the name of one of Shakespeare's artisan actors, Robin Starveling. Titania's speech, with its invocation of natural rhythms and cosmic distress, invites large and complex notions of drama's relation to festivity and ritual action, traditionally connected with the seasonal cycle and the socialisation of fertility; but Starveling's name and artisanal status reminds us that harvest cycles have social and economic correlatives. Their intersection in Shakespeare's play needs to be warily described, not least because certain theorists of popular culture, especially in France, have emphasised how easy it was for festival or carnival events to get out of control and become riots, or, conversely, as in the notorious Carnival at Romans, to serve as the pretext for organised class warfare.[11]

It cannot now be erased from our consciousness that when Shakespeare committed himself to write *A Midsummer Night's Dream* his environment was, if anything, even more disturbed than it had been in 1591–2. Nor do we need to posit his knowledge of the puny Oxfordshire rising, late in 1596. According to Brian Manning, there were at least thirteen disturbances in 1595 alone in London and suburbs, of which twelve took place between 6 and 29 June,[12] that is to say, in that same Midsummer season that the Privy Council had seen as part of the problem in 1592. Of these, one was initiated by a silk-weaver who reproached the mayor for misgovernment, and was rescued from confinement in Bedlam by the intervention of the crowd. Another, on 29 June, involved 1,000 rioters, a mixture of artisans and apprentices (including silk-weavers), took several days to suppress, and concluded, on 24 July, with the execution of five persons.[13] A pamphlet published to explain the severity of the punishment insisted that the insurgents were precisely not to be excused by the concept that carnival behaviour had gotten out of hand:

> But it may (by some) be here objected, sedition and rebellion are unfit tearmes to be used in the case I am now to handle: for the Prentises of London had no seditious purpose, no intention of open rebellion. Truely I perswade me, a headlong wilfulnes continued by a custome of abused libertie, gave first fyre to this unadvised flame: but he that shall dout, that a most trecherous resolution, and dangerous purpose followed, shall make question at a most apparent truthe ... [14]

On 5 November 1595, the Stationers' Register listed *The poor man's Complaint*, and on 23 August 1596, *Sundrye newe and artificiall Remedies against famyne ... uppon the occasion of this present Dearthe*. Well before November 1596, then, when Stere staged his sequel to these events Shakespeare would have seen the social and cultural signs of unusual, economic distress; and he might even have noticed how frequently weavers were featured in the more public and violent protests. As Buchanan Sharp observed,

> Most of the symptoms of social distress are to be found in the words and actions of artisans in general and clothmakers in particular; ... they made the loudest complaints about food prices and unemployment by means of riot, attempted insurrections, and frequent peti-

tions to local justices and to the Privy Council ... it was to their complaints above all that the authorities listened and responded in the formulation of policy.[15]

All this being said, and all the more clearly for its admission, Shakespeare's play evidently staged its own resistance to social pessimism, and especially, perhaps, to the argument that festival liberty leads to violence. Shakespeare did not, however, close his eyes to the social scene. By invoking the dangerous Midsummer season in his title, by featuring a group of artisans as his comic protagonists, by making their leader a weaver, by allowing class consciousness to surface, as we shall see, in their relations with their courtly patrons, and especially in the repeated fears expressed by the artisans that violence is feared from them ('Write me a prologue, and let the prologue seem to say we will do no harm with our swords' [III.i.15-17]), he faced his society squarely; and instead of the slippage from carnival to force, he offered it a genuinely festive proposition. Bartholomew Stere's assertion that rebellion was the only route to 'a meryer world'[16] is countered (whether before or after its utterance) by Shakespeare's promise that 'Robin shall restore amends'. The *Dream*, therefore, seems to have aspired to the role of legitimate mediation that, in *Henry* VI, *Part 2*, only an aristocratic counsellor was authorised to perform.

Of all the comedies, this one offers the most powerful invitation to explain it by some theory of festive practices. The question is, which branch of festive theory? There are three main branches to which the *Dream* has hitherto been tied, directly or implicitly. All have support from some part of the text, but none by itself can explain the whole. Indeed, they tend partially to contradict each other, or perhaps to repeat a contest that was actually occurring in Shakespeare's day. The first is based on Shakespeare's allusion to Elizabeth's lunar presence in Oberon's speech, which, as in Rowe's theory of compliment, has been used to argue that she must have been present in the original audience: and this assumption, combined with the fact that *within* the play a marriage is celebrated, has produced an 'occasionalist' argument: that the *Dream* was itself written to celebrate an aristocratic wedding.[17] This occasionalist theory relies, primarily, on the *Dream's* opening and closing emphasis on a season of 'merriment' ordered by Theseus, in order to change the tone of his courtship of Hippolyta from conquest to celebration, and on his goodnight speech after the artisans' play is ended:

> ... Sweet friends, to bed,
> A fortnight hold we this solemnity,
> In nightly revels and new jollity.
>   (V.i.369–72)

Despite the difficulty that critics experience in finding an appropriate marital occasion during 1595–6, and an uneasy recognition that the play seems rather to *problematise* than celebrate marriage, it is somewhat alarming to see how readily this hypothesis has been absorbed as fact into texts designed for students; Sylvan Barnet, in the Signet edition, for example, states categorically that the *Dream* 'was undoubtedly intended as a dramatic epithalamium to celebrate the marriage of some aristocrat' (p. xxv). And the occasionalist premise also associates the reader with the courtly circle around Theseus, and therefore with the Thesean aesthetic. Yet this framing festive plot actually represents a strategy by which popular drama was increasingly brought, involuntarily, under court control. By identifying Philostrate (in the list of Dramatis Personae) as 'Master of the Revels' to Theseus, the Folio text of the *Dream* alludes to an office created by Elizabeth in 1581 as an instrument for ensuring high quality in her own entertainment, for initiating the recentralisation of the theatre under court patronage, and for keeping it under surveillance.[18] Although the office did not become as influential under Elizabeth as later under James, and the theatre in the 1590s continued to be alternatively tolerated and regulated by local authorities, with the Privy Council and the Lord Chamberlain intervening as little or as much as court policy dictated, its very title designates a much smaller, more tightly supervised and essentially courtly concept of dramatic entertainment than Shakespeare's theatre generally assumes. Rather, Shakespeare's own situation as a member of the Chamberlain's company would situate him somewhere *between* the court and amateur popular theatricals, with the occasional 'command performance' bringing him closer to Bottom and his colleagues than to those, frequently themselves aristocrats, who created the royal entertainments. The artisanal hope of being 'made men', with 'sixpence a day' for life, is a parodic version of that discontinuous patronage relation; but the play speaks more to its uneasiness than to its rewards, as well as to Shakespeare's self-consciousness about how the popular theatrical impulse was in danger of being appropriated to hegemonic ends.

The second branch of festive theory refers not to courtly revels but to popular rituals, and assumes that the play was motivated less by the social needs of the Elizabethan court than by instincts and behaviour usually interrogated by anthropologists. When C. L. Barber published his ground-breaking *Shakespeare's Festive Comedy* in 1959,[19] he connected Shakespeare with a large and today still expanding intellectual movement that includes the work of Durkheim, Van Gennep and Victor Turner. Barber's innovation was to set Shakespeare's early comedies in the socio-historical context of English popular games, entertainments and the rituals accompanying Easter, May, Whitsun, Midsummer, or Christmas holidays, or the harvest home. Some of these festive occasions, like the annual excursions from rural parishes to bring in the May, which Robert Herrick's gorgeous *Corinna's Going a Maying* and Phillip Stubbes' virulent *Anatomie of Abuses* both, though from opposite points of view, represent as an excuse for feminine defloration, were vestiges of ancient pagan fertility rites. In the *Dream*, Theseus assumes that the four young lovers whom he has found asleep in the forest 'rose up early to observe/The rite of May' (IV.i.135–6). Others, like the lord of Misrule festivities primarily associated with the twelve days of Christmas, were secularised versions of the religious Feast of Fools, which enacted the Christian inversions of exalting the low and humbling the proud. In *Twelfth Night*, this temporary misrule is epitomised in the name of Olivia's 'allowed fool', Feste, and in Feste's antithesis to Malvolio the puritan, who would unduly narrow the space permitted to fooling in a courtly household and so becomes its victim. But misrule was also adapted to and merged with the country feasts and improvised in taverns, a social fact that Shakespeare explores in *Henry IV*. Morris dances, too, like May Day rituals with their phallic Maypoles, were genetically connected to fertility rites, as well as to the legends of Robin Hood with their theme of social outlawry. The morris, as a mixture of sexual energy and political subversion, was extremely interesting not only to Puritan writers like Stubbes but also to Elizabethan and Jacobean dramatists. While Titania's reference to the 'nine men's morris ... filled up with mud' is a pun (within a lament for infertility) that overrides an alternative etymology,[20] Shakespeare alludes to the transgressive aspects of the morris in *Henry VI, Part 2*, where Jack Cade is described by Richard of York, who plans to exploit his energies, as capering 'like a wild Morisco, Shaking the bloody darts as he his bells' (III.i.346–66). In *Henry V* the Dauphin, assuming that Henry is still in his tavern phase, mocks the English preparations for war as a 'Whitsun morris dance' (II.iv.25); and Hamlet compares his dead father to the morris-dancer's hobby-horse, 'whose epitaph is "For O, for O, the hobby-horse is forgot" (III.ii.140–1); his mother's disloyalty and the failure to commemorate his father participates in the broader betrayal of drama's roots and his country's ancient customs.[21] These instances carry important valences, national, cultural and political, which seem to privilege the past and the primitive even as they are registered as such.

In Barber's view, however, all of these festive or folk elements in Shakespeare's plays were part of a cultural migration in which the archaic and amateur forms of dramatic representation and ritual were absorbed by the mature national theatre. Claiming that saturnalian impulse, 'when directly expressed, ran head on into official prohibition', Barber concluded that the transfer of festive impulses to the theatre was an enforced 'shift from symbolic *action* towards *symbolic* action' (p. 57).

> Shakespeare's theatre was taking over on a professional and everyday basis functions which until his time had largely been performed by amateurs on holiday. And he wrote at a moment when the educated part of society was modifying a ceremonial, ritualistic conception of human life to create a historical, psychological conception. His drama, indeed, was an important agency in this transformation: ... In making drama out of rituals of state, Shakespeare makes clear their meaning as social and psychological conflict, as history. So too with the rituals of pleasure, of misrule, as against rule: his comedy presents holiday magic as imagination, games as expressive gestures.
>
> (p. 15)

This is the move that aestheticises; that seeks to distinguish between 'art' and 'life', between literary and non-literary texts; and that therefore, in its invocation of the unexaminable (Thesean) term, 'imagination', begs the very questions that cultural historians must attempt to answer. Barber's strongest message was that both the archaic festivals and their Elizabethan echoes functioned to reaffirm, through reconciliatory symbolic action, the hierarchical structure of society.

If Barber represents the idealist version derived from social history, its equivalent in anthropology is found in the work of

Victor Turner, himself much influenced, however, by Barber. In a late work, *From Ritual to Theatre*,[22] Turner admitted that his own thinking had been shaped by 'early exposure to theatre', specifically *The Tempest*, which Turner had seen as a child of five. In *The Ritual Process* (1969), Turner developed his theory of *communitas*, or the individual's sense of belonging, voluntarily, to a larger, cohesive and harmonious social group, on the idealist model of ritual action inherited from Durkheim and Van Gennep. Thus Turner argued initially that 'cognitively, nothing underlines regularity so well as absurdity or paradox. Emotionally, nothing satisfies as much as extravagant or temporarily permitted illicit behaviour.' This regulatory motive accounts for the fact, he thought, that inversion rituals occur most often 'at fixed points in the annual cycle ... for structural regularity is here reflected in temporal order'.[23] However, in the later *Dramas, Fields, and Metaphors,* inversion rituals were seen rather as motivated by some natural disaster or 'public, overt breach or deliberate non-fulfilment of some crucial norm', which requires remedial intervention rather than regulatory confirmation.[24] And communitas was reconceived as running *counter* to the stratified and rule-governed conception of society, in the space that Turner called *liminality*, in which social distinctions are temporarily suspended. In liminal situations, the lower social strata become privileged, and bodily parts and biological referents, conceived as the source of regenerative energy, are revalued; hence the ritual use of animal disguises, masks and gestures. An exchange takes place, Turner argued, between the normative or ideological poles of social meaning, which dictate attitudes to parents, children, elders and rulers, and the physiological poles or facts of life (birth, death, sexuality) which the norms exist to regulate; and in this exchange 'the biological referents are ennobled and the normative referents are charged with emotional significance' (p. 55), which renders them once again acceptable.

By proposing this ritual exchange between rules and energies as demanded by natural disasters or unusual breaches in social relations, Turner's model seems more promising than Barber's for interrogating the most ritual components of the *Dream*, the breach between Oberon and Titania that has resulted in crop failure and disrupted the natural cycle, and the manner in which that breach will be healed. But even in its late form Turner's festive theory remains idealist, in the sense that the purpose of festive rituals is, in the last analysis, reconciliation, getting the social rhythms running smoothly once more.

There is, of course, an alternative possibility: that popular festival forms and inversion rituals were actually subversive in intent and function all along. This position is represented in Shakespeare studies by Robert Weimann, and more generally by Mikhail Bakhtin's study of Rabelais, preceded as it was by a social history of carnival forms. Weimann's magisterial study established the possibility of a class-conscious analysis of popular traditions, and, by extending the inquiry to the tragedies, discovered the levelling implications of Shakespeare's fools, clowns and grave-diggers.[25] Bakhtin, to whom Victor Turner acknowledged a debt, provided our most powerful explanation of carnival's emphasis on the material grotesque, or the 'lower bodily stratum', belly, buttocks and genitals. This movement of festive impulse downwards, or degradation, Bakhtin argued, was intended as social fertilisation: 'to bury, to sow, and to kill simultaneously, in order to bring forth something more and better ... Grotesque realism knows no other level; it is the fruitful earth and the womb. It is always conceiving.'[26] But he also insisted that fertilisation was essentially a social myth of populist self-definition and incorporation:

> We repeat: the body and bodily life have here a cosmic and at the same time an all-people's character; this is not the body and its physiology in the modern sense of these words, because it is not individualised. The material bodily principle is contained not in the biological individual, not in the bourgeois ego, but in the people, a people who are continually growing and renewed ... the collective ancestral body of all the people.
>
> (p. 19)

Yet, though both of these influential studies assume a Marxist theory of history, neither finally provided a radical solution to the old polarities that have plagued aesthetic debates since their first beginnings: high versus low culture, mind versus body, consciousness versus material practice. Weimann's book was as deeply influenced by Barber as by Marx, producing in effect a version of the Thesean aesthetic, by which the festive and ritual elements that Shakespeare recorded were seen as the raw material for a new formal synthesis of the natural with the conventional, of primitive with learned humanist materials; and Shakespeare himself, working at a transitional moment when social change made visible the very concept of archaism, appears as the genius at the end of the evolutionary trail. Leaning on the modern preference for a disinterested art, Weimann praised 'Shakespeare's universal vision of experience' as 'more comprehensive and more vital ... in ... its scepticism and its freedom', than either of the traditions it drew from (p. 251); and even his own insights into the subversiveness of topsy-turveydom were constrained by the conviction that class consciousness was not fully available as a category of thought in Shakespeare's time. The echoes of folk misrule in the plays were, he thought, 'playfully rebellious gestures', and 'the contradictions between the popular tradition and the culture of the ruling classes were to some extent synthesised with the needs and aspirations of the New Monarchy and were overshadowed by an overwhelming sense of national pride and unity' (pp. 24–5).

Bakhtin could equally be charged (and indeed has been) with universalism, for insufficiently specifying the historical vectors of carnival events.[27] For while he situated Rabelais in a 'history of laughter' from the middle ages to the nineteenth century, with occasional references to Marxist historiography, Bakhtin explicitly rejected Veselovsky's nineteenth-century theory of clowning as a populist defence against feudal values: 'No doubt,' wrote Bakhtin, 'laughter was in part an external defensive form of truth':

> It was legalised, it enjoyed privileges, it liberated, to a certain extent, from censorship, oppression, and from the stake. But ... laughter is essentially not an external but an interior form of truth ... Laughter liberates not only from exterior censorship but first of all from the great interior censor; it liberates from the fear that developed in man during thousands of years; fear of the sacred, of prohibitions, of the past, of power ... The seriousness of fear and suffering in their religious, social, political, and ideological forms could not but be impressive. The consciousness of freedom, on the other hand, could be only limited and utopian.
>
> (pp. 94–5)

'It would therefore be a mistake,' Bakhtin concluded, to presume that festive and carnival forms expressed 'a critical and clearly defined oppositon' (p. 95).

In what follows, I propose to create a gargantuan mingle-mangle of the strongest and boldest suggestions that these different festive theories proffer, while pushing them beyond their own aesthetic or procedural inhibitions. I rely for conceptual support on Shakespeare himself, who within the text of *A Midsummer Night's Dream* seems to have recognised much of the thinking I have just described and the conflicting interests it represents (then and now); and, by making the different versions of festive theory modify and correct each other, produced in the end a more capacious proposal. Within the aristocratic premise of 'revels', for instance, certain surprises are introduced. Theseus's selection of the 'tragical mirth' of the artisans' play is carefully articulated as a rejection of learned, humanist entertainments:

> 'The battle of the Centaurs, to be sung
> By an Athenian eunuch to the harp.'
> We'll none of that;
> 'The riot of the tipsy Bacchanals,
> Tearing the Thracian singer in their rage.'
> That is an old device;
> 'The thrice three Muses mourning for the death
> Of Learning, late deceas'd in beggary'?
> That is some satire, keen and critical,
> Not sorting with a nuptial ceremony.
> (V.i.44–55)

What does sort with a nuptial ceremony, apparently, includes the ribald: the by-play on Wall's 'stones' (a vulgarism for testicles) 'chink' and 'hole', through which Pyramus and Thisbe try to make physical contact. 'My cherry lips,' complains Thisbe to Wall, who is of course a man, 'have often kiss'd thy stones,/Thy stones with lime and hair knit up in thee' (V.i.190–1). It is noteworthy that neither the Quarto nor the Folio text authorises the stage direction '*Wall holds up his fingers*', a bowdlerising intervention added by Edward Capell in 1767 and now a standard feature of modern editions, running counter to the text's bawdry, and discouraging a producer from having Pyramus and Thisbe bend to reach each other through the open legs of Snout the tinker.[28] Yet this interpretation, and the kind of laughter it would provoke, would have 'sorted' well with the sexual ambience of Renaissance wedding festivities, as well as with their archaic precedents in bedding rituals; 'in which,' remarked George Puttenham in his *Arte of English Poesie* (1580), 'if there were any wanton or lascivious matter more then ordinarie which they called *Ficenina licentia* it was borne withal for that time because of the matter no lesse requiring.'[29] Even the main festive plot, therefore, requires the *Dream's* audience, then and now, to consider the relationship between broad sexual humour and the social construction of the audience; for by making his courtiers enjoy this 'palpable gross' entertainment Shakespeare precludes the argument that his obscenity was really beneath him, designed only for those convenient receptacles of critical discards, the 'groundlings'. In Bakhtin's terms, the boundary between courtly and popular entertainment is broached by the material grotesque, by the laughter that drives the festive imagination downwards to the lower bodily stratum.

On the other hand, the festive plot that most attracted Barber's attention, the May game that takes the four young lovers into the forest, cannot be explained merely in Barber's terms, as one of those archaic fertility rituals absorbed and contained by the transforming imagination; not, at any rate, unless that imagination is as defined by Theseus. It is, after all, only Theseus who, finding them asleep after the confusions of identity and erotic attraction are resolved, assumes 'they rose up early to observe/The rite of May' (IV.i.131–2), whereas in fact the motive for the transgressive excursion was escape from parental and patriarchal oppression. Barber's account of the magical doings in the forest underestimates the severity not of the 'sharp Athenian law' (I.i.162) by which marital arrangements were based on dynastic as opposed to erotic imperatives, but of Shakespeare's treatment of it; a law administered by Theseus, and manifestly intended to be felt by the audience as unjust, while reminding them of its correlative in Elizabethan England. At the very least, then, we need for this part of the *Dream* a festive theory that, like Victor Turner's, admits the political or ideological dimension of festive actions, some sense of the norms of 'respect for elders' and 'obedience to political authorities' that ritual will again render acceptable. But if we look to Turner for a model for the way this plot is handled we shall still be disappointed. There is no exchange between rules and energies in this tale of adolescent silliness, underlined by the very ease with which the young people's emotions are rearranged. Even Shakespeare's calendrical vagueness (is it May or Midsummer?) which evidently worried Barber,[30] is naughtily incompatible with Turner's original theory that the festival calendar mimics and hence reinforces social order. The callowness of the young escapees, moreover, remains when the parental and societal inhibitions have been finessed away, not by a genuine reconciliation, but by magical legerdemain. It expresses itself in their mockery of the very play that speaks to what their own predicament was, and what its ending might have been. When Bottom leaps up to 'assure' his courtly audience that 'the wall is down that parted their fathers', and that burials are therefore unnecessary (V.i.337–8), he marks, as they themselves are incapable of doing, the sociological seriousness that their own festive plot implied. Once again, the courtly and the popular seem to change places; and it only adds to the complexity of the exchange that the artisans do *not* present an entertainment with its roots in folk tradition; rather, they struggle to give the courtiers what they might be supposed to admire, an Ovidian legend in the high rhetorical and hence self-parodying mode.

But more transgressive still is the third festive plot – Titania's quarrel with Oberon over the changeling boy, which results in disastrous weather and crop failure, and which can only be resolved by the most extreme example of status inversion and misrule that Shakespeare's canon contains, the infatuation of the Queen of Fairies with a common artisan who is also, temporarily, an ass. This is the plot, also, that Louis Montrose has marvellously related to psychoanalytic conceptions of gender and power in Elizabeth's reign, and, under the aegis of Theseus's phrase for imaginative work, 'Shaping Fantasies', suggested that within the fantasy of Titania's liaison with Bottom lies 'a discourse of anxious misogyny' precipitated by the myth of the Virgin Queen and the pressures it exerted on male sensibilities.[31] Montrose put vital pressure on aspects of the play that Barber's benign thesis overlooked – the dark pre-history of Theseus as betrayer of women, the repressed myth of Amazonian independence that Hippolyta represents, the harshness of Theseus's treatment of Hermia (even during his own festive season), Titania's elegiac account of her friendship with the changeling boy's mother, who died in childbirth, even the subjects of the rejected entertainments, with their allusions to eunuchs and Centaurs, rape and dismemberment.

While Montrose's approach is true to the *Dream's* mixture of light and dark, and subtle in its handling of the Elizabethan semiotics of gender, his psychoanalytic reading does not give Shakespeare his due. It implies that these darker resonances in the play rose up from its author's and the national (male) unconscious, as distinct from being part of a conscious analytic project. Assuming that the *Dream* in its conclusion both 'reaffirms essential elements of a patriarchal ideology', and 'calls that reaffirmation in question', Montrose determines that those contradictory projects occur 'irrespective of authorial intention' (p. 74). And Montrose's psychoanalytic theory also distracts attention from the socioeconomic component in the episode that he reads as the male's revenge – the amazing suggestion not only that a queen could be made by magic to mate with a male from the bottom stratum of society – as well as from the fact that its results are positive. For thanks to Bottom the weaver, the crisis in the natural cycle and the agricultural economy is resolved, albeit by restoring male authority. In Montrose's essay, Titania's liaison with Bottom is related not to festive inversions, but rather to the dream of Simon Forman, professional physician and amateur drama critic, who fantasised that the queen had made herself sexually available to him; and it is only a detail, over which Montrose does not pause, that his dream rival for the queen's affections is 'a weaver, a tall man with a reddish beard, distract of his wits' (p. 62). In *both* dreams, fortuitously, Forman's and Shakespeare's, there is staged a contest for significance, for exegetical control, between critic and weaver, high and low culture. But in Shakespeare's *Dream*, the weaver (who is also a dreamer) wins.

Let us now return to Turner's proposal that rituals of status inversion or revitalisation frequently make use of animal masks, and imagine with new eyes what the Elizabethan audience might have seen when Bottom appears on the stage with an ass's head replacing his own. Weimann had noted 'the surprising consistency of the ass' head motif from the *mimus* down to *A Midsummer Night's Dream*' (p. 50); but he assumed that it, like the calf's hide which the Elizabethan fool still wore in the Mummer's Play, the coxcomb, antlers, horns, and foxtail, was merely 'the survival of some kind of mimetic magic, which, after having lost its ritual function, became alienated from its original purpose and hence misunderstood as a comic attribute' (p. 31). But in the *Dream*, the ass's head distinguishes itself from comic props and animal masks in general, and becomes part of a complex structural pun, by which the ritual exchange between rules and energies does after all take place, and the lower bodily parts are, as in Turner's theory, ennobled. Bottom is not only the bottom of the social hierarchy as the play represents it, but also the 'bottom' of the body when seated, literally the social ass or arse. It is typical of the *Oxford English Dictionary*'s conservativism that it does not sanction this meaning of the word in Shakespeare's day, with the result that generations of editors have been satisfied with 'bottom' as a technical term for the bobbin in weaving. Yet as Frankie Rubinstein observes in her dictionary of Shakespeare's sexual puns, Shakespeare and his contemporaries took for granted that *ass*, as the vulgar, dialectical spelling of *arse*, was the meeting point of a powerful set of linked concepts: 'Shakespeare ... used "ass" to pun on the ass that gets beaten with a stick and the arse that gets thumped sexually, the ass that bears a burden and the arse that bears or carries in intercourse.'[32] And she cites in analogy the Fool's rebuke to Lear that speaks to a male humiliation by the female, paternal by filial: 'When thy clovest thy crown i' th' middle, and gav'st away both parts, thou bor'st [barest] thine ass on thy back o'er the dirt: thou hadst little wit in thy bald crown when thou gav'st thy golden one away ... thou gav'st them the rod, and putt'st down thine own breeches's' (I.iv.167–71, 180–1). Here exposed bodily parts, top and bottom, crown and arse, unite in a political allegory of status inversion and corporal punishment. And in the 1640s, John Milton made the same set of meanings converge in a metaphorical beating of one of his opponents: 'I may chance not fail to endorse him on the backside of posterity, not a golden, but a brazen Asse';[33] thereby including in the multiple pun, for good measure, *The Golden Ass* of Longinus.

In the *Dream*, the structural pun on *ass* is anticipated by Puck's gratuitous 'bottom' humour, his account of pretending to be a stool that removes itself from under the buttocks of 'the wisest aunt telling the saddest tale' being an early warning signal of popular fundamentalism:

> Then slip I from her bum, down topples she,
> And 'tailor' cries ...
>
> (II.i.51–4)

Here the play on *tale/tail(er)* is one of the puns that Howard Bloch, himself influenced by Bakhtin, explored in his rule-breaking study of the French medieval fabliaux.[34] Bloch argued that these jokes are ultimately metacritical and serve to theorise the jongleur's profession. The Old French homophony between *con* (cunt) and *conte* (tale) 'or, in English, the tail and the tale ... signifies the closeness of physical and linguistic longings'; postmodernist theory fuses 'the desire so often expressed in sexual terms on the level of theme and the desire for the story itself' (p. 109). But because Bottom is also an ass, the structural pun in the *Dream* has a still more complex resonance, one that requires precisely those social categories from which Bloch's deconstructive work, regrettably, would liberate popular obscenity.

In the great medieval encyclopaedia of Bartholomaeus Anglicus, translated in 1582 by Stephen Batman as *Batman upon*

Bartholome, the ass is defined as a creature in whom coalesce the meaning-systems implied by Shakespeare's puns: 'The Asse is called Asinus, and hath that name of Sedendo, as it were a beast to sit upon ... and is a simple beast and a slow, and therefore soone overcome & subject to mannes service' (XIX:419). The theme of servitude symbolised by the ass was, of course, rendered fully allegorical by Apuleius, whose episode of Lucius's period of slavery in the bakery has been recognised as 'the only passage in the whole of ancient literature which realistically ... examines the conditions of slave-exploitation on which the culture of the ancient world rested'.[35] And Bakhtin, who claimed that the ass is 'one of the most ancient and lasting symbols of the material bodily lower stratum, which at the same time degrades and regenerates', connected *The Golden Ass* with the 'feast of the ass' which commemorates the Flight to Egypt, and also with the legends of St Francis of Assisi.[36]

As visual pun and emblem, therefore, Bottom stands at the fulcrum of Shakespeare's analysis of the festive impulse in human social structures. Is he merely a comic figure, the appropriate butt of Thesean critical mockery, and his liaison with Titania the worst humiliation an upstart queen could suffer? Or does his (im)proper name, in symbolic alliance with his ass's head, invoke rather an enquiry into the way in which the lower social orders, as well as the 'lower bodily stratum', function, and suggest that the service they perform and the energies they contain, are usually undervalued? Hinting as to how this question might be answered, Shakespeare included a brilliant gloss on the multiple pun that is Bottom, keying his festive theory into the most impeccable source of ideology available to him. At the moment of his transformation back into manhood, Bottom implicates his own ritual naming in the central act of interpretation that the *Dream* demands:

> Man is but an ass if he go about to expound this dream. Methought I was – there is no man can tell what. Methought I was – and methought I had – but man is but a patched fool if he will offer to say what methought I had. The eye of man hath not heard, the ear of man hath not seen, man's hand is not able to taste, his tongue to conceive, nor his heart to report, what my dream was. I will get Peter Quince to write a ballad of this dream: It shall be called 'Bottom's Dream', because it hath no bottom.
>
> (IV.i.205–15)

It has long been recognised that this passage contains an allusion to I Corinthians 2:9 ('Eye hath not seen, nor ear heard, neither have entered into the heart of man, the things which God hath prepared for them that love him'). But so quick have most commentators been to denigrate Bottom that they focus only on his jumbling of the biblical text, rather than on its context of profound spiritual levelling. Even Weimann, who connected it to his theme of popular topsy-turveydom (p. 40), does not pursue the biblical context to its logical conclusion, in I Corinthians 12:14–15, where the metaphor of the body is developed more fully in terms of a Christian communitas:

> If the whole body were an eye, where would be the hearing? If the whole body were an ear, where would be the sense of smell? But as it is, God arranged the organs in the body, each one of them, as he chose. If all were a single organ, where would the body be? As it is, ... the parts of the body which seem to be weaker are indispensable, and those parts of the body we invest with greater honour, and our unpresentable parts are treated with greater modesty, which our more presentable parts do not require. But God has so adjusted the body, giving the greater honour to the inferior part, that there may be no discord in the body, but that the members may have the same care for one another.

In the *Dream* which has no bottom because Bottom dreamed it, the 'unpresentable parts' of the social body are invested with greater honour by their momentary affinity with a utopian vision that Bottom wisely decides he is incapable of putting into words, at least into words in their normal order. Shakespeare's warning to the audience is unmistakable; prudent readers, especially those who are themselves unprivileged, will resist the pressure to interpret the vision. Yet its inarticulate message remains: a revaluation of those 'unpresentable' members of society, normally mocked as fools and burdened like asses, whose energies the social system relies on.

But how far did this social criticism intend to go? How much are we really to make of the artisans' fears of frightening the ladies, and the constant need to break the dramatic illusion lest the courtly audience think that their mimic swords are drawn in earnest? What is to be made of the prologue actually written for the playlet, that 'tangled chain [of being]; nothing impaired, but all disordered' (V.i.124–5) which, as Leinwand observed, 'teeters back and forth between deference and offensiveness',[37] creating in its *double enten-dres* the very sociopolitical apprehensions that the artisans most wished to avoid? And what was the London theatrical ambience in 1595–6? In September 1595 the Mayor wrote to the Privy Council 'Toutching the putting doune of the plaies at the Theatre & Bankside which is a great cause of disorder in the Citie', and specifically proposed a connection between this and the 'late stirr & mutinous attempt of those few apprentices and other servantes, who wee doubt not driew their infection from these & like places'.[38] This record connects with the Privy Council's embargo in 1592, as also with the memory of that 'Play at Windham' that had actually, if the historians of Kett's uprising were to be believed, served as the occasion for a major social upheaval. Yet in 1595–6, if *A Midsummer Night's Dream* is to be believed, Shakespeare was willing to argue, with Montaigne, that there could be 'honest exercises of recreation', that plays acted 'in the presence of the magistrates themselves' might actually promote 'common societie and loving friendship'. The *Dream* imagines a festive spirit deeper and more generous than the courtly revels that seemed, in the 1590s, to be appropriating plays and actors; an idea of social play that could cross class boundaries without obscuring them, and by those crossings imagine the social body whole again; and a transgressive, carnival spirit daring enough to register social criticism, while holding off the phantom of 'the Play at Windham', the dramatic scene of violent social protest. It would not be until after *King Lear* (Shakespeare's darkest experiment in role-reversal and carnival exposure), and not until after the Midlands Rising (the country's gravest social crisis since 1549) that Shakespeare was forced to admit that the popular voice had grievances that the popular theatre could no longer express comedically. In 1595–6, it only 're-hearse[d] most obscenely and courageously' (I.ii.100–1) for that later, more demanding project.

There is, however, one qualification to this otherwise genial thesis. In 1549, we remember, the worst of the grievances listed by the ventriloquist was the rebels' sense that their case was the subject of mockery: 'their miserable condition, is *a laughing stocke to most proud and insolent men. Which thing ... grieveth them so sore, and inflicteth such a staine of evill report: as nothing is more grievous for them to remember, nor more injust to suffer.*'[39] Economic deprivation and physical hardships, in other words, are deemed less oppressive than the mockery that makes of those same sufferings a 'laughing stocke'. In relation to the *Dream*, this part of the story is potent. When Bottom and his fellows are mocked by the aristocratic audience, the audience outside the *Dream* has the opportunity to consider whether or not to laugh themselves, which sort of festive spirit to select for their own enjoyment. If laughter is necessary to mediate social tensions, Shakespeare's festive theory seems to argue, then let it be a laughter as far removed as possible from the red-hot iron of social condescension.

From Annabel Patterson, *Shakespeare and the Popular Voice* (Oxford, 1989), pp. 52–70.

NOTES

[Annabel Patterson's essay is a chapter in her book, *Shakespeare and the Popular Voice*. Its relationship to festive theory needs no further elucidation beyond the very detailed discussion it contains itself. The essay, however, should also be seen as forming part of a wider attack on the view of Shakespeare as anti-democratic, a supporter of Elizabethan social hierarchy and the institutions that held it together, and so contemptuous of the lower orders which it was the function of those institutions to keep in their place. Part of Patterson's book is devoted to demonstrating that this view of Shakespeare was largely an anti-Jacobin myth constructed in the nineteenth century. But it has undoubtedly been given new impetus by one strand of recent historicist thinking, which has emphasised the extent to which Elizabethan theatre may have been geared to the tastes and expectations of the more privileged members of society who (it has been argued) formed a disproportionate and unrepresentative majority of the audience. (On the argument over Shakespeare's audience, see Ann Jennalie Cook, *The Privileged Playgoers of Shakespeare's London, 1576–1642* [Princeton, NJ, 1981], Martin Butler, *Theatre and Crisis 1632–1642* [Cambridge, 1984], Appendix II, 'Shakespeare's unprivileged playgoers, 1576–1642', pp. 293–306, and Andrew Gurr, *Playgoing in Shakespeare's London* [Cambridge, 1987].) That argument in turn tends to emphasise the theatres' close dependence on the court for their very survival, as against the suggestion that they spoke of and to a broad spectrum of popular culture. The whole of Patterson's book is dedicated to rebutting that approach, applying strategies which allow 'the popular voice' to speak through the Shakespearean text, irrespective of its institutional placement. Hence her determination in this essay to cut through the tendency of many theorists to see the festive or the carnivalesque as ultimately *conservative* phenomena, their topsy-turveydom finally reinforcing the natural-seeming order to which society ultimately returns, indeed possibly being provoked or licensed by those in authority precisely to that end. Richard Wilson mischievously describes Patterson's book as 'predicated on her vision of the Bard as a Jeffersonian democrat' (*Will Power: Essays on Shakespearean Authority* [London and Detroit, 1993], p. 17), but it is testimony to the many – often conflicting – voices which modern criticism finds in the Shakespearean text. Ed.]

1. *The Diary of Samuel Pepys*, ed. Robert Latham and William Matthews, 11 vols (Berkeley and Los Angeles, 1979), 3:208.

2. Although Pepys's editors conclude that by 1660 he was 'clearly an Anglican by habit and sentiment' (*Diary*, 1:xviii), he was educated first at Huntingdon grammar school (of which Oliver Cromwell was an alumnus) and subsequently, following the path of John Milton, at St Paul's School and at Puritan Cambridge. One of his cousins, Richard Pepys, became Cromwell's Lord Chief Justice of Ireland; and Pepys himself recorded in his *Diary*, for 1 November 1660, his embarrassment when one of his old school-fellows 'did remember that I was a great roundhead when I was a boy' (1:280).

3. See R. A. Foakes (ed.), *A Midsummer Night's Dream* (Cambridge, 1984), pp. 12–17.

4. References are to the New Arden edition: *A Midsummer Night's Dream*, ed. Harold Brooks (London, 1979).

5. Jan Kott, *The Bottom Translation* (Evanston, IL, 1987), pp. 29–68.

6. H. H. Furness (ed.), *A Midsommer Nights Dreame*, New Variorum Edition (1895, repr. New York, 1966), p. 75. How prolific were the efforts of the old historical allegorisers can be seen from the seventeen pages of annotation that Furness had to provide for this single passage.

7. See also Louis Montrose, '"Shaping Fantasies": Figurations of Gender and Power in Elizabethan Culture', *Representations*, 1:2 (1983), p. 80, on the 'last most extravagant phase' of the cult of virginity. Montrose mentions the 'sacred Temple of the Virgins Vestal' that was featured in the 1590 Accession Day pageant. [Reprinted in this volume. Ed.]

8. See ibid. p. 80, citing John Nichols, *Progresses and Public Processions of Queen Elizabeth*, 3 vols (1823; rep. New York, 1966), 118–19.

9. Theodore Leinwand, '"I believe we must leave the killing out": Deference and Accommodation in *A Midsummer Night's Dream*, *Renaissance Papers* (1986), 17–21.

10. *Calender of State Papers Domestic*, 1603–10, vol. 28, art. 64, p. 373 (misplaced and misdated). For accounts of the Oxfordshire rising, see Buchanan Sharp, *In Contempt of all Authority: Rural Artisans and Riot in the West of England, 1586–1660* (Berkeley, CA, 1980),

pp. 39–40; John Walter, 'A "Rising of the People"? The Oxfordshire Rising of 1596', *Past and Present*, 107 (1985), 90–143.

11. See Yves-Marie Bercé, *Fête et Révolte: Des mentalités populaires du XVIe au XVIIIe siècle* (Paris, 1976), especially pp. 55–92, 'Les Fêtes changées en Révolte'. The fullest description of the Roman happening is by Le Roy Ladurie, *Carnival in Romans*, trans. Mary Feeney (New York, 1979). Reversing Bercé's thesis, François Laroque argued, in relation to *Henry VI, Part 2*, that Jack Cade's *Jacquerie* turned into a carnival. See 'Shakespeare et la fête populaire: le carnaval sanglant de Jack Cade', in *Reforme, Humanisme et Renaissance*, 11 (1979), 126–30.

12. Brian Manning, *Village Revolts: Social Protest and Popular Disturbances in England, 1509–1640* (Oxford, 1988), p. 208.

13. Brian Manning, *Village Revolts*, pp. 209–10. Apparently here too, reversing the situation in 1592, one of the authorities sided with the insurgents; in this instance it was Sir Michael Blount, lieutenant of the Tower, who resisted Mayor John Spencer's attempts to restore order, and who was later accused of conspiring to support the Earl of Hertford's claim to the throne.

14. *A Students Lamentation that hath sometime been in London an Apprentice, for the rebellious tumults lately in the Cities hapning: for which five suffred death on Thursday the 24, of July last. Obedientia servi Corona* (London, 1595), B1r. Significantly, this pamphlet cannot help connecting the apprentice riot to 'peasant ideology': 'Of Jacke Straw, Will Daw, Wat Tiler, Tom Miller, Hob Carter and a number more such seditious inferiour ringleaders ... what wrongs forsooth they went about to right: but when they had got head, what wrong did they not count right?' (B2v–3r).

15. Buchanan Sharp, *In contempt of all Authority*, p. 31. See also p. 37, for the indictment of a weaver for seditious words in November 1596. The plight of the weavers in 1595 was protested by Thomas Deloney in a published letter. See Frances Consitt, *The London Weavers Company* (Oxford, 1933), pp. 312–16. I owe this reference to Arthur Kinney.

16. See John Walter, 'A "Rising of the People"? The Oxfordshire Rising of 1596', *Past and Present*, 107 (1985), 90–143.

17. See for instance, John W. Draper, 'The Queen Makes a Match and Shakespeare a Comedy', *Yearbook of English Studies*, 2 (1972), 61–7; Steven May, 'A *Midsummer Night's Dream* and the Carey–Berkeley Wedding', *Renaissance Papers* (1983), 43–52; and, for a non-marital occasion, Edith Rickert, 'Political Propaganda and Satire in *A Midsummer Night's Dream*', *Modern Philology*, 21 (1923), 43–52, who connected the play to an entertainment given for the queen by

Edward Seymour, earl of Hertford, and hence to the problem of the earl's secret marriage to Lady Katherine Grey, whose child, declared illegitimate by the angry queen, was, Rickert thought, obliquely represented by the changeling boy.

18. On the office of the Master of the Revels, see Virginia Gildersleeve, *Government Regulation of the Elizabethan Drama* (1908, repr. Westport, CT, 1975).

19. C. L. Barber, *Shakespeare's Festive Comedy: A Study of Dramatic Form and its Relation to Social Custom* (Princeton, NJ, 1959).

20. Compare Edmond Malone, *The Plays and Poems of William Shakespeare*, 10 vols (London, 1790), 2:464: 'Some, however, have thought that the "the nine men's morris" here means the ground marked out for a morris dance performed by nine persons.'

21. On the hobby-horse, compare Malone, 9:307: 'Amongst the country may-games there was a hobby-horse, which, when the puritanical humour of those times opposed and discredited these games, was brought by the poets and ballad-makers as an instance for the ridiculous zeal of the sectaries.'

22. Victor Turner, *From Ritual to Theatre* (New York, 1982), p. 9.

23. Victor Turner, *The Ritual Process: Structure and Antistructure* (Chicago, 1969), p. 176.

24, Victor Turner, *Dramas, Fields and Metaphors: Symbolic Actions in Human Society* (Ithaca, NY, 1974), p. 35.

25. Robert Weimann, *Shakespeare and the Popular Tradition in the Theater*, ed. Robert Schwartz (Baltimore, MD, 1978, 1987).

26. Mikhail Bakhtin, *Rabelais and his World*, tr. Helene Islowsky (Boston, 1968, Bloomington, IN, 1984), p. 21.

27. See Peter Stallybrass and Allon White, *The Politics and Poetics of Transgression* (London, 1986), pp. 12–22.

28. For an extended defence of this as an intended staging, see Thomas Clayton, '"Fie What a Question's That If Thou Wert Near a Lewd Interpreter": The Wall Scene in *A Midsummer Night's Dream*', *Shakespeare Studies*, 7 (1974), 101–23.

29. George Puttenham, *The Arte of English Poesie* (London, 1589), p. 43.

30. Barber, *Shakespeare's Festive Comedy*, p. 120: 'Shakespeare does not make himself accountable for exact chronological inferences.'

31. Louis Adrian Montrose, '*Shaping Fantasies*'.

32. Frankie Rubinstein, *A Dictionary of Shakespeare's Sexual Puns and their Significance* (London, 1984), p. 17.

33. John Milton, *Colasterion*, in *Complete Prose Works*, ed. D. M. Wolfe et al. (New Haven, CT, 1953–82) 2:2:57.

34. See R. Howard Bloch, *The Scandal of the Fabliaux* (Chicago and London, 1986): 'In the counting of the vagina and the anus, we recognise the accounting of the poet who plays upon the homophone *con* [cunt] and *conte* [tale] ... The debate between adjacent body parts is, at bottom, that of the jongleur who, in addressing his audience makes *cons* and *culs* speak' (p. 106).

35. See Jack Lindsay, tr., *The Golden Ass* (Bloomington and London, 1932), p. 22; and for an extension of Shakespeare's interest in Apuleius, J. J. M. Tobin, *Shakespeare's Favorite Novel* (Lanham, MD, 1984), especially pp. 32–40.

36. Bakhtin, *Rabelais and his World*, p. 78.

37. Leinwand, 'Deference and Accommodation', p. 22.

38. E. K. Chambers, *The Elizabethan Stage*, 4 vols (Oxford, 1923), 4:318.

39. Alexander Neville, *Norfolkes Furies, or a View of Ketts Campe: Necessary for the Malecontents Of our Time, for their instruction, or terror, and profitable for every good Subject*, tr. R[ichard] W[oods], (London, 1615), B2r (italics added).

9

The Kindly Ones: The Death of the Author in Shakespearean Athens

RICHARD WILSON

Whenever Karl Marx contemplated British politics he was reminded of *A Midsummer Night's Dream*, and when he considered Britain's token opposition he thought of the bathetic mew of Snug the Joiner. Victorian parliamentarians who imagined themselves as earth-shakers, he joked, were like Shakespeare's craven craftsman, unconvincingly acting out the rage of the British lion; while the thunder of a *Times* editorial was a charade to which the only poss-ible response was Demetrius's ironic applause for Snug's fox-like valour: 'Well roar'd lion!' The secret of British compromise, Marx deduced, was contained in the discretion with which the workers and nobles defer for each other in Shakespearean Athens; and if modern France had gone from revolutionary tragedy to constitu-tional comedy, this was because Napoleon III had learned from Duke Theseus to manage politics 'as a masquerade in which grand costumes, words, and postures serve only as masks,' and the Paris mob played its part 'as Nick Bottom plays that of the lion,' *sotto voce* and roaring 'as gently as any sucking dove' (I.ii.87). After 1848, Marx considered, conservative rule throughout Europe was 'like the lamentable comedy of Pyramus and Thisbe performed by Bottom and his friends': a pitiful burlesque. History repeats itself the second time as farce in a parliamentary system, he inferred, because sovereignty and subversion are both neutralised in the synthesis that is predicted in Shakespeare's play: 'It is like the lion in *A Midsummer Night's Dream*, who calls out: "I am a lion!" and then whispers "I am not a lion, but only Snug". Thus every extreme is at one time the lion of contradiction, at another the Snug of mediation.'[1] Representing bloody tragedy as a comic game, therefore, parliament tames the revolution; and if Shakespeare remained, as Eleanor Marx reported, her father's Bible, that was in part because of the uncanny way in which the plot of *A Midsummer Night's Dream* seemed to him to premonitor this historic reversal.

The lion who did not dare to roar was an Aesopian figure, according to Marx, for the British culture of consensus. He noticed, that is to say, that the headpiece worn by Snug has metadramatic significance in Shakespeare's comedy, like the face of the choric actor in Greek tragedy which carried the caption, 'I advance behind my mask'. For the Duke who commands a performance of 'very tragical mirth' from the 'Hard-handed men that work in Athens ... Which never labour'd in their minds till now' (V.i.57,72–3), is, indeed, the prototypical Shakespearean prince: in his wisdom that power requires circuses and that far from being set against authority, theatricality is, in Stephen Greenblatt's words, 'one of power's essential modes'.[2] As Thomas Nashe explained when the aldermen objected to playhouses in 1592, the English monarchy could learn from what the actor told Augustus, the 'patron of all witty sports', when 'there happened a great fray in Rome about a player ... Whereupon the Emperor ... called the player before him, and asked why a man of his quality durst presume to make a quarrel about nothing. He smilingly replied: "It is good for thee, O Caesar, that the people's heads are troubled with brawls about our light matters; for otherwise they would look into thee and thy matters."'[3] In an essay on the Stuart fashion for classical plays, Martin Butler confirms that what drew dramatists to the ancient world was precisely the seriousness with which rulers took the 'airy nothing' of theatre (V.i.16) when legendary 'Roscius was an actor in Rome' (*Hamlet*, II.ii.389); so it is significant that Shakespeare's *Dream* has been connected with a wedding on 19 February 1596 in the family of the official most identified with such patronage, the Lord Chamberlain, Lord Hunsdon.[4] For the antics of Julius Caesar, who makes 'the tag-rag people ... clap and hiss him ... as they use to do the players in the theatre' (*Julius Caesar*, I.ii.255–8), are prefigured by this Duke of Athens when he likewise plots with his Master of Revels to legitimate the violence of his empire with triumphal games:

> Go Philostrate,
> Stir up the Athenian youth to merriments;
> Awake the pert and nimble spirit of mirth;
> Turn melancholy forth to funerals;
> The pale companion is not for our pomp.
> Hippolyta, I woo'd thee with my sword,
> And won thee doing thee injuries;
> But I will wed thee in another key,
> Will pomp, with triumph, and with revelling
>   (I.i.12–19)

Though Bacon scorned such 'masques and triumphs' as 'but toys,'[5] a shift in humanist thinking on public entertainment is detectable in Montaigne, who admired Demosthenes for avoiding 'all magnificence' in 'parades of athletes and festivals', yet recognised the awesome power of the amphitheatre, 'where you could seat a hundred thousand men', under a system where 'authority depended (in appearance at least) on the will of the people'.[6] The marble O of the ancient circus might provide panoptic discipline for a modern town, as the professors of Vicenza demonstrated when they built their semi-globular *Teatro Olimpico* in 1584. Likewise, it was Olympic Greece which in 1612 inspired Midland landowners to sponsor their Cotswold Games as an antidote to peasant revolt. And Theseus, who despite impatience with 'antique fables' and 'fairy toys' (V.i.3), revives the defunct Midsummer custom of gadding through the 'quaint mazes in the wanton green' (II.i.99), seems to personify this neoclassical strategy, with his Platonist scheme to 'find the concord' in the discord of his subjects through the 'music' of race meetings and the office of his 'usual manager of mirth' (IV.i.105; V.i.60). His marriage to the Amazonian Queen would literally provide a key of pomp and circumstance with which to harmonise family, church and royalty when set to Mendelssohn's march; but in the meantime it would offer a programme for the manufacture of consensus by monarchs such as James I, whose *Book of Sports* and triumphal entry into London inaugurated a true 'theatre state'. Yet if this Duke is exemplary for Shakespeare's later rulers in commemorating his wedding with an amnesty to 'overbear' the 'ancient privilege of Athens' and pardon sexual crimes (I.i.41; IV.178), their duplicity in the taverns of Eastcheap and brothels of Vienna casts suspicion on his motive when he likewise despatches an *agent provocateur* downtown to 'stir up' the delinquent to misrule. For Shakespeare's Athens has an underworld like London's, we infer, and magistrates who have devised the blueprint for a metropolitan police.

'Turn melancholy forth to funerals': there is no place in this Athens for a Don John, Jacques, or Malvolio, and the banishment of the malcontent that closes later comedies here initiates the plot. Yet ever since Jan Kott exposed a diabolical underside to Shakespeare's *Dream*, with its 'slimy, hairy, sticky creatures' that arouse 'violent aversion,'[7] critics have interpreted this tactic as a psychological repression, and it has become a commonplace that 'if death is officially absent from our play ... indications of its proximity abound'.[8] Thus, Louis Montrose traces a cycle of sexual violence throughout the text emanating from its Ovidian sources and patriarchal dread of female power;[9] and René Girard sees a scapegoat ritual in which blood sacrifice is deflected by Puck from its intended victims, the feuding boys, Demetrius and Lysander.[10] This anthropological criticism merges with an old historicism which has long speculated that the play is an allegorical mirror to reflect the crisis of the 1590s, and that Titania's report on the ruined harvest refers specifically, as the Arden editor deduced, to the calamitous dearth of 1595–7 (II.i.88–114).[11] What these readings share is a belief that the play is structured according to the looking glass logic of an actual dream, and that the method in its madness is the metonymic dream-work decoded by that Freudian analyst, Mercutio, when he observes how lovers always dream of kisses; courtiers, curtsies; lawyers, fees; and soldiers, 'cutting foreign throats' (*Romeo and Juliet*, I.iv.70–88). Whatever the critic, then, there is respect for Hippolyta's intuition that 'all the story of the night told over ... More witnesseth than fancy's images' (V.i.23–5); and a sense that this 'talking cure' abreacts desires and anxieties which shadow the play in fantasies of rape and murder, and fears of those 'jaws of darkness' that gape in 'Sickness, war, or death' (I.i.142–8). Exiled at the start, the 'pale companion' returns by night, to haunt those 'cross-ways' where the hanged are buried with the unconscious of the text (III.ii.383).

'What a dream was here! ... Methought a serpent ate my heart away' (II.ii.148): like that 'green and gilded snake' that coils about the sleeping Oliver in *As You Like It* (IV.iii.109), Hermia's nightmare belongs to a pastoralism that insists on the coincidence of desire and death: *Et in Arcadia Ego*. And from the instant when the Duke sentences her 'Either to die the death, or to abjure for ever the society of men' for loving Lysander (I.i.65–6), *A Midsummer Night's Dream* stages the tension of the condemned, suspended between a verdict and reprieve. Under the sign of the scaffold, then, this solstice is passed in 'fog, as black as Acheron', the river of Hades, conjured by the 'king of shadows', Oberon (III.ii.347–56). What many critics perceive, however, is that the threat of death to which the lovers subject themselves by their desires is sublimated in the *Lamentable Comedy and Most Cruel Death of Pyramus and Thisbe* presented by the mechanicals, which travesties both Ovid's tragic story and the *Liebestod* of *Romeo and Juliet*. There the Bacchic blood which dyed the mulberry a lurid 'deep dark purple colour' in Golding's *Metamorphoses* is dissolved into the narcotic 'juice' of that 'little western flower ... now purple with love's wound', which seems, when Puck lays it 'on sleeping eyelids', to emblematise the toxicity of Shakespeare's own Aesculapian art (II.i.166–70). Metonymy and condensation, rather than metaphor and displacement, govern this author's dreaming, we observe, which functions not as an antidote but as a poison. Moreover, Girard further notices a sinister similarity between the three alternative dramas offered for performance to Theseus, which all involve 'something that vainly attempts to force its way' into the *Dream*, but is 'everywhere on the periphery, marginal, excluded, yet unmistakably present': namely, the brutal scapegoating of a poet:

> [Reads] 'The battle with the Centaurs, to be sung
> By an Athenian eunuch to the harp'?
> We'll none of that; that I have told my love,
> In glory of my kinsman Hercules.
> [Reads] 'The riot of the tipsy Baccanals,
> Tearing the Thracian singer in their rage'?
> That is an old device, and it was play'd
> When I from Thebes came last a conqueror.
> [Reads] 'The thrice three Muses mourning for the death
> Of learning, late deceas'd in beggary'?
> That is some satire, keen and critical,
> Not sorting with a nuptial ceremony.
>
> (V.i.44–55)

Emasculation, dismemberment, oblivion: in all three tragedies, Girard comments, 'a poet happens to be the victim. In the first he is castrated; in the second, lynched. In the third, he dies alone, abandoned by all. This last is the modern way of doing things.'[12] From the Greek castrato and the martyred Orpheus, to the destitute genius in a garret, whom scholars identify as Robert Greene, snuffed out by poverty in 1592, Philostrate's repertoire flatters his prince with the progress of censorship from mutilation of the body to enlightened neglect. Shakespeare would revert to the savage spectacle of the violent death of the author in *Julius Caesar*, when the poet Cinna meets the fate of Orpheus at the hands of the Thracian women, as the mob shouts to 'Tear him to pieces ... Tear him for his bad verse!' (III.iii.28–30). Later in the same play, however, we also observe the modern practice, when another Poet is mocked by the subjects of his satire for the 'vileness' of his 'cynic rhyme' (IV.iii.132); and in Athens it seems there is doubt about which form of censorship applies. The Duke runs a line through *The Death of Learning* with the wariness of one who knows how 'the poet's pen ... gives to airy nothing / A local habitation and a name' (V.i.15–17), but defends the suppression on aesthetic grounds. In a patronage system, we see, literary criticism is superseding torture as the more subtle means of cultural control; yet the first concern of Peter Quince when his actors receive their parts is that he will suffer like Orpheus if their performance similarly makes 'the ladies ... shriek: and that were enough to hang us all'. Francis Flute's fear of sharing the embarrassment of the Athenian eunuch, when he is effeminised as Thisbe, testifies to the same panic about a catastrophic loss of voice; and the rendition of *Pyramus and Thisbe* stutters on Nick Bottom's solemn confirmation that 'if you should fright the ladies out of their wits, they would have no more discretion but to hang us' (I.ii.70–6). Evidently the Maenads still menace this Renaissance court.

'That would hang us, every mother's son': the players' anxiety about how 'the Duchess and the ladies' will respond (ll.70–3) is given weight by official reaction in 1597 to the play called *The Isle of Dogs*, when the actors and the part-author, Ben Jonson, were imprisoned in the Marshalsea for performing 'very seditious and slanderous matter'.[13] None of the text survives, but the title implies an Aesopian fable such as that which doomed the last Englishman executed for seditious libel, William Collingbourne, hanged in 1484 'for making a foolish rhyme' about Richard III and his ministers, Catesby, Ratcliffe and Lovell, which ran: 'The Cat, the Rat, and Lovell the Dog / Do rule all England, under a Hog.' According to the poet, the meaning of this doggerel 'was so plain, that every fool perceived it'; and Annabel Patterson comments that his mistake had indeed been to breach a tacit compromise between English authors and authority, whereby each knew 'how far a writer could address contemporary issues' in code, 'so that nobody would be *required* to make an example of him'.[14] Likewise, John Stubbs had the hand cut off which penned an over-explicit squib on the Queen in 1579; but the compact was also liable to be broken by the state, as was shown in 1633, when William Prynne lost his ears for libelling the King, despite his plea that he 'had no ill intention ... but may be ill interpreted'. Quince's worries belong to the period between these verdicts analysed by Richard Dutton, when government insecurity led to a nervy inconsistency towards topical material, such as the deposition of Richard II played on the eve of Essex's rebellion in 1601, as the Queen noted, '40 times in open streets and houses'. Though no Elizabethan actors were hanged or mutilated for libel, as Philip Finkelpearl points out, they were right to be apprehensive about such a system, which might one day tolerate them and the next haul them before the judges, as Shakespeare's colleagues were on that occasion.[15] For even this most 'puzzling incident of non-censorship'[16] revealed the Damoclean justice under which theatre functioned.

If critics are polarised between those who stress the reluctance of the censors, and others, such as Jonathan Dollimore, who insist that 'dramatists *were* imprisoned and harassed by the State for staging plays',[17] this divide is a measure, Dutton argues, of the Janus-face of Renaissance theatrical authority; and it is an ambiguity that troubles Shakespeare's text. For when Bottom demands to know 'What is Pyramus? A lover, or a tyrant?' he raises doubts about how to represent power to the powerful and whether the Duke will prove 'condoling' like a lover or imitate his cousin 'Ercles' ... tyrants' vein' (I.ii.19–36). It had been as Hercules that Caesar notoriously took to the boards, and 'carried away with the violence' of the role, slew an actor 'dead at his feet, and after swung him (as the poet said) about his head'; so Bottom's 'humour' to play the tyrant and 'make all split' (l.25) is tempting fate. The 1598 Vagrancy Act would indeed ordain penalties of whipping and death for unlicensed playing; and Quince's eagerness to modulate his actors' frenzy reflects a genuine attempt to forestall such confusion of reality with fiction. Though critics are right, then, to view these scenes as indicative of 'how the play speaks to itself, in a surreptitious voice', of its conditions of production, they underestimate the dangers in 'the unforeseeable consequences ... of getting the ladies over-excited'.[18] Like *Julius Caesar*, *A Midsummer Night's Dream* is a play about poetry and power, and how they read each other, and the trap Quince is so desperate to avoid is precisely the hermeneutic circle which had made ancient theatre so lethal, when stage-struck Caesars projected themselves into the parts of tyrants, regardless of the stock disclaimer that if the characters portrayed put anyone 'in remembrance of things past, / Or things intended, 'tis not in us to help it'.[19] In 1605 Chapman, Jonson and Marston would risk having 'their ears cut and noses' for offending the King in *Eastward Ho!*;[20] but Quince knows the best apology for actors before an audience whose intentions are so hard to read is a Delphic periphrasis:

> If we offend, it is with our good will.
> That you should think, we come not to offend,
> But with good will. To show our simple skill,
> That is the true beginning of our end.
> Consider then, we come but in despite.
> We do not come, as minding to content you,
> Our true intent is.
>
> (V.i.108–14)

Shakespeare's *Dream* is 'contaminated', Montrose writes, by the legends of Theseus's tyranny, which it recycles to engender further 'violence, fear and betrayal ... for it shapes the fantasies by which it is shaped, begets that by which it is begotten.'[21] There can be no escape, for this New Historicist reading, from the violence of representation; but what such paranoia misses is a deeper *anxiety* of representation, and the dream-like process the play rehearses whereby nightmare scenarios are revised. For the classical canon is constantly edited in Shakespeare's comedy, which proceeds through a series of rejected scripts. Seneca's *Hercules*, Euripides' *Bacchae*, above all, Ovid's *Metamorphoses*, are all evaded during the action as potential endings of a plot that seems, instead of impasse, to seek a way out of the textual labyrinth, as Theseus led the young from that 'wood of Crete' (IV.i.112), and its human monster, in a different myth. Rather than shaping struggle, culture is here the thing which struggle shapes, and the most typical cultural act is the redaction the players undertake when Bottom objects that 'There are things in this comedy of Pyramus and Thisbe that will never please,' and Tom Snout agrees that since 'the ladies cannot abide' to see a sword, 'we must leave the killing out, when all is said and done'. Bottom's solution, to 'put them out of fear' with a prologue 'to say we will do no harm with our swords,' would appear, in fact, to have extra-dramatic status as a statement of authorial intention to dilute Ovidian blood (III.i.8–21). Likewise, the rewriting to entreat the Ladies 'not to fear, not to tremble' at the Lion, on the under-standing that he is 'no such thing' but 'a man, as other men are,' (ll.40–3) seems designed so as not to 'let Aesop fable' on this summer's night (*3 Henry VI*, V.v.25). Thus, far from perpetuating a cycle of violence, the disingenuousness of this author is to deny his own affectivity, with a contract that stakes everything not on sharing, but on renouncing power, as Bottom bargains with the Ladies: 'my life for yours!' (l.40).

What is an author? An author, Foucault observes, is not, as we imagine, the origin of meaning, but rather, 'the principle by which, in our culture, one limits, chooses, and impedes the circulation of fiction ... a figure for our fear of the proliferation of meaning.' Books and discourses began to have authors, Foucault explains, 'to the extent that authors became subject to punishment.' Renaissance writing was therefore fraught with risk; but from the Shakespearean period, according to this account, a penal system of censorship gave way to an authorial system of ownership, as texts which previously circulated anonymously were validated only when endowed with names. Henceforth the censor could relax to the degree that authors took upon their own heads responsibility for their words, allowing us 'to ask of each fictional text: From where does it come, who wrote it, when, under what circumstances, or with what design?'[22] It is this responsibility which seems to be staged in the *Dream*, when Quince translates the fable into his own iambic pentameter, composes Pyramus's prologue and Lion's apology, interpolates Moonshine and Wall, cuts the warring parents, and writes '"Bottom's Dream" ... to be sung in the latter end of the play' (IV.i.212–16). Unlike King Claudius, then, Theseus does not need to ask his Master of Revels, 'Have you heard the argument? Is there no offence in it?' (*Hamlet*, III.ii.227–8), because the author has censored himself and followed the advice of James I, to 'beware of writing anything on the commonwealth or such subjects, except metaphorically,' since these matters were 'too grave for a Poet to mell in'.[23] For the effect of his revision is to render management re-dundant when the Master hears his mirth, and to reduce his source, as the minister says, to an innocuous 'nothing, nothing in the world' (V.i.77–8). The privileges of an author begin, we see, at the point when literature retreats from 'the world' of referentiality into the empty 'nothing' of its own aesthetic void:

> All for your delight,
> We are not here. That you should here repent you,
> The actors are at hand; and by their show,
> You shall know all, that you are like to know.
>
> (V.i.114–17)

If Shakespeare avoided the pains of authorship through such self-effacement, this was by a design we must distinguish, as Leah Marcus remarks, from innocence of intention; and sweet Quince, whose 'small Latin' is such an obstacle to his love of Ovid, can indeed be seen as a 'humble alter ego' of the author whose own Ovidian style earned him his reputation as 'honey-tongued'.[24] So, if this carpenter who so rapidly writes, casts, costumes, equips, revises, rehearses, and stages his play by royal command, is Shakespeare's self-portrait, then the *Dream* can be compared to pictures of the artist in his studio, such as *Las Meninas (The Waiting Women)* by Velazquez, which is another representation where representation 'undertakes to represent itself', in Foucault's words, 'in all its elements, with its images, the eyes to which it is offered, the faces it makes visible, the gestures that called it into being.'[25] For in this portrait the Baroque painter depicted himself working in a similar *métier*, beside the ladies and dwarfs of the court, who pass judgement on his canvas, as he gazes out of the frame to a place hypothetically occupied by his models, who are dimly reflected, peering from a mirror at the back, as the King and Queen, positioned where we, the spectators, in fact stand. 'The entire picture is looking out at a scene for which it is itself a scene';[26] so, like the *Dream*, this is a work that describes a moment when art cuts itself free from the world to which it refers, but is obliged by its terms of production to restore that world as compliment to a prince. For if the mirror functions in the painting like the play within the play, both presuppose that they depend on one who cannot be presented, because of occupying, paradoxically, the centre stage. In each, this ghostly figure is the patron on whom everything depends; for Shakespeare, 'the imperial votress', Queen Elizabeth, who passes by in the realm of anecdote, unseen except as a pale reflection (II.i.163), putative spectator of a play that hinges, as Montrose remarks, not 'upon her presence or intervention, but, on the contrary, her absence, her exclusion'.[27]

Quince calculates that 'to bring moonlight into a chamber' is one of theatre's 'hard things', and can only be done through a glass darkly, as Bottom suggests throwing the shutters of 'the great chamber window, where we play, open; and the moon may shine in at the casement' (III.i.45–54). So, if this moon who spies through windows as she pretends a 'maiden meditation, fancy-free' (II.i.164), is, as editors presume, a refraction of Elizabeth in her guise as Diana, the technical problem of presenting moonshine seems metonymic of the difficulty of representing power on the Renaissance stage. As they quiz the almanac to find whether 'the moon doth shine that night we play', the actors acknowledge the queen of the night as a presiding genius, but Robin Starveling's effort 'to disfigure ... the person of Moonshine' with 'a bush of thorns and a lantern' is ludicrous as an illusion of majesty. Any literal attempt to 'find out moonshine' is bound to be frustrated (III.i.48–57); and this is lucky, because the moon is throughout invested with ominous repressive powers. She is the 'fruitless moon' (I.i.73), 'the cold moon' (II.i.156), 'the wat'ry moon' (II.i.162), 'the wand'ring moon' (IV.i.98), the 'governess of floods' whose frigid emotions cause disaster, as, 'Pale in her anger [she] washes all the air, / That rheumatic diseases do abound. / And thorough this distemperature we see / The seasons alter' (II.i.103–7). Above all, this moon is old and tired, her days numbered from the start: 'but O, methinks, how slow / This old moon wanes! She lingers my desires, / Like to a stepdame or a dowager / Long withering out a young man's revenue' (I.i.3–6). The whole community waits upon this dying heiress, longing for 'the next new moon', whose masculine succession, 'like to a silver bow, / New bent in heaven', will bring mercy to his subjects and marriage to the court (I.i.83;9); but the impudence of this image of the haggard crone with her hoard of jewels makes it improbable that Gloriana was present in that 'great chamber' in Blackfriars when the Dream was first performed.

Editors notice a discrepancy in Shakespeare's plot, which promises that 'four happy days bring in / Another moon' and 'the night of our solemnities' (I.i.2–11), but which accelerates to the wedding next day. Moreover, since Oberon and Titania are 'ill met by moonlight' on their way to 'moonlight revels', and Quince rehearses 'by moonlight', the old moon is still in the sky on Midsummer night, and is again seen, by Puck, after midnight at the end of the second day (II.i.60,141; I.ii.95; V.i.358). Neither new moon nor the moonless night preceding it comes as expected in *A Midsummer Night's Dream*, which closes with the 'horned moon' still 'withering out' her end (ll.232–5). If this moon is like the mirror in the painting, then, and reveals a face of power that cannot be presented on stage, Shakespeare's almanac must tabulate the uncertain political conjunction it records, which the critics maintain was that of the hungry summer of 1595, when 'the ox stretch'd his yoke in vain, / The ploughman lost his sweat, and the green corn … rotted ere his youth attain'd a beard' (II.i.93–5). 'The husbandman perceiveth that the new moon maketh plants and creatures fruitful,' recorded Reginald Scot in 1584, 'but decaying in the wane,' and that 'One born in the spring of the moon shall be healthy; in the time of the wane, when the moon is utterly decayed, the child cannot live.' Mention of the lunar cycle is a reminder, therefore, of the belief that, as governess of menstruation and tides, a waning moon brought blood, tears, sterility and death, so that, as John Aubrey warned, 'it is not good to undertake any business at the last period of her revolution.'[28] 'Swear not by the moon, th'inconstant moon,' Juliet had cautioned Romeo, 'That monthly changes in her circled orb' (*Romeo and Juliet*, II.ii.109–10); and the aged moon of Shakespeare's *Dream* does resemble the worn-out face that looked down in 1595 on a world of 'pacts and sects' whose greatness ebbed with hers (*King Lear*, V.iii.18–19).

In the autumn of her *annus horribilis*, when Shakespeare began his play about dreams and divinations, the Queen was not expected to live long; but the author superstitiously avoided looking for the new moon through the window of his text. Likewise, custom counselled caution when he gestured at the declining planet, since it was reckoned 'unlucky to point at the moon', lest you became her prisoner, like the Man in the Moon.[29] When the moon climbs on stage, framed by the play within the play, the smoking candle Moonshine swings in his lantern comes as near to satire, then, as any action dared. 'All I have to say,' mumbles Starveling, 'is, to tell you that the lantern is the moon; I the Man i'th'Moon; this thorn-bush my thorn-bush; and this dog my dog' (V.i.247–9); and if his pantomime seems nonsensical, this is because it parodies the symbols of masques with which Elizabeth was regaled. 'If we had thought so much would have been said of us,' she rasped after one such charade on November 17, where Essex acted out his love, 'we would not have come down tonight', and so went back to bed.[30] With the Man in the Moon, however, the players circumvented the taboo on royal allusion, since this most 'ancient and popular superstition' tells of a 'poor man which stole a bundle of thorns' for firewood, and was punished by being 'set into the moon, there for to abide for ever'. 'The face of the man in the moon', according to folklore, 'is the face of a man who went hedging';[31] so, Starveling is living up to his name when he mimes one of the most militant rites of social protest: breaking of fences, trespass, and theft of wood. No wonder the Duke quips that 'the man should be put in the lantern', for this was the custom that gave a name to the radicalism of 'the plain people of London' who would call themselves the Levellers.[32] Or that the courtier should so relish the gallows humour when he condemns the actors: 'Why, all these should be in the lantern' (ll.237–50). The shadow that crosses the moon at this joke is that of a noose, for the dictionary reminds us that in Tudor slang to be 'in the lantern' meant to be hanged from the post.

'Marry, if he that writ it had ... hang'd himself ... it would have been a fine tragedy' (ll.343–6): Theseus's verdict gives the last twist to a chillingly self-reflexive game in which Shakespeare tempts judgement. For his moon is like the artist's mirror in reflecting not only his play, but the absent presence beyond, where Elizabeth's 'small light' was 'already in snuff' as Starveling's candle guttered 'in the wane' (ll.240–4). At the end Puck will carefully sweep such 'wasted brands' away; but at this moment the superstitious might read the future in 'the dead and drowsy fire' (ll.360–78); as a London servant foretold the Queen's eclipse and a new king from her kitchen fire in 1595. On June 6 this prophecy was proclaimed at Mansion House by a weaver who made 'hard speeches' against the government and predicted a land of plenty when Elizabeth died. Assuming him to be mad, the Mayor committed him to Bedlam, from where he was rescued, however, by a mob of apprentices, who began to realise his dream by erecting a gibbet outside the Mayor's door and raiding the market stalls for butter and fish. And when the organisers of this price fixing were arrested, citizens attacked the prison and set them free. Altogether, there were a dozen riots in London during the Midsummer season preceding Shakespeare's play, an outburst of fury against food shortage historians describe as the 'most dangerous urban uprising' between the accession of the Tudors and the Civil War.[33] The climax came on June 29, when a thousand artisans fought the militia on Tower Hill, cheered by troops from the Tower, whose Governor was subsequently discovered to have plotted to install the Earl of Hertford as king.[34] So strong were the Earl's expectations of succession that the Governor was never tried; but on July 4 martial law was declared, and under its terms six craftsmen were drawn on hurdles through the streets and hanged. Shakespeare's Midsummer tableau, with the starving tailor as the Man hanging from the gallows in the sky, seems, in the circumstances, a mute paraphrase of the 'moonshine' of the Queen's Peace.

Peter Quince, joiner; Nick Bottom, weaver; Francis Flute, bellows mender; Tom Snout, tinker; Snug, joiner; Robin Starveling, tailor: the cast list of the lamentable comedy played in Athens reads, in the light of the Midsummer nightmare of 1595, like the indictment of a conspiracy trial. And it is easy to imagine what a prosecutor would make of the activities of this 'crew of patches [and] rude mechanicals, / That work for bread upon [the city's] stalls,' who plot to trespass 'in the palace wood, a mile without the town, by moonlight,' under cover of a seasonal mumming traditionally acted under 'the Duke's oak' (I.ii.94–102; III.ii.9–10). Once met, these masterless men assign themselves aliases, disguise themselves with masks, false beards, and women's clothes, and debate whether to 'leave the killing out' or 'do harm' with their swords, before they depute one of their number to 'enter into the brake' deep in the park wearing animal skin, and on a given 'cue', 'steal' from the estate as much 'provender' of cereals, meat, and liquor as he can (III.i.71; IV.i.199,31), while the others keep up a riotous noise of rough music on 'the tongs and the bones' (l.29). Questioned by magistrates, the main offender justifies his crimes with a 'ballad' in which he claims to have been under the orders of the Queen of the Fairies, who had promised him the Land of Cockaigne (l.213). The ringleader's defence, that he had been incited to misrule by a high official, will cut no ice against such self-incriminating evidence; for in fact this case is one that will recur at assizes in late medieval and early modern England, when two opposing concepts of justice clash, as they do in London in 1595, and the old calendar customs that sanctioned lawlessness run up against new rules of property and profit. In particular, it will be at Midsummer and the feast of Corpus Christi that the Whitsun game of free-for-all, with its rites of trepass and disguise, will carry its player into violent conflict with authority; such as that which occurred in Kent on Midsummer Night 1451, when:

> William Cheeseman, yeoman; Tom Crudd, husbandman; John Jope, yeoman; Jack Nash, sadler; Dick Peek, butcher; Will Stone, labourer; with others unknown, in riotous manner and arrayed for war with breastplates, halberds, bows and arrows ... and covered with long

beards and painted on their faces with black charcoal, calling themselves the servants of the Queen of the Fairies, intending that their
names should not be known, broke into the park of Humphrey,
Duke of Buckingham, at Penshurst and chased, killed and took away
from the said park 10 bucks and 72 does belonging to the said Duke,
against the King's Peace and the statute of parks lately issued.[35]

Like the gang who cut down hedges in Windsor Park in 1607
under pretext of Shrovetide football, the Penshurst fairies were
acting a hallowed scenario of resistance. 'And these are not fairies?'
asks the victim of one such riot, Sir John Falstaff, after he has been
mugged under Herne's Oak, 'I was three or four times in the
thought they were not fairies.' In *1 Henry IV* the outlaw knight had
himself posed as one of 'Diana's foresters ... minions of the moon'
(I.ii.25), for Shakespeare knew that English fairies were likely to be
footballers of towns like Windsor, where the Fairy Queen would
turn out, as she does in *The Merry Wives*, to be a citizen 'Finely
attired in a robe of white' (IV.iv.70; V.v.121–2). Fairyland had been
secured by Jack Cade's rebels in 1450, when they too dubbed their
hero 'Queen of the Fairies'.[36] So, when Bottom is 'translated' to the
'fairy kingdom' in the Duke's park (III.i.114; II.i.144), he treads a
well-known maze into the world of popular politics, where hunger
is sure to be relieved. For fairies were agents of folk justice, according to Keith Thomas, and appeals to their Queen were recalls to
collective values.[37] Theologians even imagined them Catholics, as
Richard Corbet fancied: 'since of late, Elizabeth, / And after, James,
came in, / They never danced on any heath, / As when the time hath
been. / By which we note the Fairies were of the old profession, /
Their songs were Ave Maries, / Their dances were procession.'[38] But
if Queen Mab was as Marian as Mercutio also hints, her moral
economy was that of the real little people: peasants and craftsmen.
Thus, Ben Jonson saw her as 'She, that pinches country wenches / If
they rub not clean their benches, / And with sharper nails remembers, / When they rake not up the embers'; and Thomas notes that
fairy law was retributive if not propitiated: 'They might reward
benefactors, but if neglected would avenge', for fairies were both
good and evil.[39] In the *Dream* this dualism of punishment and
reward is fought out in the nocturnal war between Oberon and
Titania, but it is focused in Puck, the 'merry wanderer' who tram-
ples 'over park and over pale' (II.i.4,43) unless correctly pacified,
he:

That frights the maidens of the villagery,
Skim milk, and sometimes labour in the quern,
And bootless make the breathless housewife churn,
And sometimes make the drink to bear no barm,
Mislead night-wanderers, laughing at their harm.
Those that Hobgoblin call you, and sweet Puck,
You do their work, and they shall have good luck.

(ll.34–41)

'Those that Hobgoblin call' him, or 'sweet Puck', or 'that shrewd and knavish sprite / Call'd Robin Goodfellow' (ll.33–4), know what's in a name, for 'Modo he is called, and Mahu', philologists note, since his name is legion who can never be named: Old Nick, Satan, the Devil, who is also, sometimes, Oberon. 'The Prince Darkness is a gentleman', we believe (*King Lear*, III.iv.140), as long as he is respectfully addressed, for what matters is *how* he is spoken to. Thus, Carlo Ginzburg has described the folk religion of north-east Italy in the 1590s as premised on 'night battles' for control of the crops, which were fought by 'wanderers' who called the powers of darkness by a name they gave themselves: the *benandanti*, or 'goodfellows'.[40] The logic of this homeopathic magic is, of course, that of the *pharmakon* – the poison that cures – which Derrida sees as language's repression of its Other; so it is no coincidence that Shakespeare's Fairies have optimistic names from folk pharmacy: Cobweb, Moth and Mustardseed; or, as we might say, penicillin. Sweet Puck, who administers the purple juice, is thus truly the spirit of this play, as his nicknames enact its tactics of appeasement. By literally reducing him to a diminutive, *A Midsummer Night's Dream* placates the Evil Eye with the most apotropaic of devices, euphemism: the a figure, as Goethe defined it, 'by which we reject what we fear', not by expulsion but by inoculation.[41] And since two of his kinder names are Hermes and Mercury, it is apt that Robin is the messenger of a plot that depends, as Quince says, on such 'translation' (III.i.112). For what is deliberately lost in translation by Shakespeare's metamorphosis of Ovid is the Bacchic violence of both myth and history. So, where Collingbourne had been 'hanged, cut down, and had his bowels ripped out of his belly and cast into the fire',[42] this author adopts a mask of meek 'simplicity', like Quince, to pay his 'poor duty' (V.i.101–5) to 'They that have power to hurt and will do none' (*Sonnet 94*) if properly addressed:

> *Approach, ye Furies fell!*
> *O Fates, come, come!*
> *Cut thread and thrum:*
> *Quail, crush, conclude, and quell.*
> (V.i.273–6)

Bottom had promised to 'tear a passion to tatters' as Hercules (*Hamlet*, III.ii.10), and now his histrionics remind us that as well as the founding of the Olympic Games, one Herculean feat had been to rescue Theseus from Hades by making the Furies drunk.[43] So, if Hecate and the Erinnyes do figure England's Queen and court in the eyes of Shakespeare's players, Quince's bombast seems an epitome of that self-irony which functions, according to Pierre Bourdieu, with every linguistic offering, but never more abjectly than in the anxiety of the *petit bourgeois* towards their products, 'which pushes them into paroxysms on formal occasions, or utterances of artificial confidence'.[44] Theseus observes just such 'hyper-correction' when clerks 'shiver and look pale, / Make periods in the midst of sentences' and 'Throttle their practis'd accent in their fears'; and he knows it is through this 'modesty of fearful duty' that his own power is 'misrecognised' (in Bourdieu's terms) as an anodyne 'symbolic violence' (V.i.93–101). These Athenians already grasp the poststructuralist theory, then, that censorship is best exercised as 'a euphemisation imposed on the producers of symbolic goods ... which condemns the dominated either to silence or shocking outspokenness'. For by reducing the Angry Ones to helpless mirth, Shakespeare's mechanicals allow them 'to take what they mistake' (l.90), and so invoke the 'gentle, unrecognised violence of debts and gifts'. Overt censorship was never as complete, since now 'the agent is censored once and for all'.[45] Thus, as Puck reminds us at the end, this play functions as an exorcism, and what it exorcises by occlusion is the violence of its own origin under the gaze of She who can never be directly faced: 'triple Hecate' (l.374), the three-formed goddess who is the moon in heaven, the witch of hell, and – as Gloriana – both at once on earth.

'Behold her silver visage in the watery glass' (I.i.112): despite the danger of divining with mirror and moon, Shakespeare at last reflects the image of his Queen. For Pyramus's call to the 'Sisters Three' to judge him identifies the Ladies before whom the action has been played (l.323); and the Amazons, Maenads, and Queens are all implicated in the verdict of these Fates and Furies by the sentences they too pass on the artisan, artist, and art. For Ginzburg's *benandanti*, the night judges were a 'wild hunt' of witches, who were pacified with oblations, like those left in Shakespeare's Athens, of food and drink; and for Frazer's Greeks, they were souls of the dead, to be appeased with a mock marriage and murder, like Bottom's, of a man in animal skin.[46] As Girard remarks, Shakespeare is a comparativist in anthropology,[47] and what he compares are ancient and modern rites to propitiate the powers that be. So, though the Epilogue frets whether the actors will 'have unearned luck … to 'scape the serpent's tongue' that menaced Hermia (ll.419–20), these Furies are soon defanged, for are they not indeed the Eumenides, whose very name – The Kindly Ones – was given them in Athens? Hippolyta speaks for them all when she admits, 'I pity the man' (l.279), and Medusa's face dissolves in smiles. With such sweet sorrow does royalty secure consent, for its frightening Ladies are all 'good fellows' when the *Dream* forgets the violence that it dreamt. So, unlike Orpheus, whose song 'drew savage beasts against their kind', but was ended by '*Bacchus* drunken rout' when 'they murdered him, that never till that hour did utter words in vain',[48] this author will be applauded when his Lion brings forth sweetness to turn death into a figure of speech: 'And the Duke had not given him sixpence a day for playing, I'll be hang'd' (IV.ii.21). The fable he 'preferred' (l.37) prompted his tact, being spun out in Ovid to cheat the Bacchae of prey; but Shakespeare knew better than his idol, who died exiled by Augustus for indiscretion, the importance of deflecting tragedy with 'witty sport':

> If we shadows have offended,
> Think but this, and all is mended,
> That you have but slumbered here,
> While these visions did appear.
> And this weak and idle theme,
> No more yielding but a dream,
> (V.i.409–14)

'Fairies away!' (II.i.144): by collapsing his own meaning into the diminutiveness of an inaccessible aesthetic domain, this poet tamed the Furies into Fairies where Orpheus and Ovid failed, and ensured his troupe became 'but shadows' of reality (l.208), and not shades. As Marx appreciated, Shakespeare's dreaming played its part in the containment of civic violence which determined that, though

London suffered all the overpopulation, unemployment, inflation, and plague endemic in early modern cities, it did not experience the chronic urban conflict that raged elsewhere. The nightmare of the Tudor regime – that the weaver of Southwark would make cause with the 'heavy ploughman' of Kent (V.i.359), incited by some 'pale companion' of the elite – was prevented by a culture of rapprochement Shakespeare symbolised in his multiple converging plot; whilst the Crown learned from the rioting of 1595 that the secret of stability was, as he envisaged, satisfaction of London's appetite for 'good hay, sweet hay' (IV.i.33) through regular supply of corn. History suggests that the thing of greatest constancy that grew on Bankside from the story of the citizens' mad Midsummer night, was a network of 'barns and garners never empty' (*The Tempest*, IV.i.111), 'for laying up of wheat and service of the city', together with 'certain Ovens, in number ten, of which six be very large ... purposely made to bake out the bread corn of the said garners, for relief of the poor citizens, when need should require.'[49] It was by such management that the paradoxical outcome of the famine of the 1590s was, as *A Midsummer Night's Dream* had foreseen, not the overthrow but the strengthening of municipal order, since, though Shakespeare's England 'was not capable of eliminating dearth, it was capable of interpreting and resisting the phenomenon to preserve itself. Society emerged from the crisis with its values and authority reinforced, for dearth highlighted the one and enhanced the legitimacy of the other.'[50]

It had been Orpheus and his surrogates, according to Ovid and Frazer, who were ploughed into the ground to restore the crops;[51] and in the Greece of the *Dream* the death of the author serves an equivalent symbolic effacement: 'No epilogue, I pray you; for your play needs no excuse ... when the players are all dead, there need none to be blamed' (V.i.341–3). Bottom's ballad to 'expound' the story of the night will never now be told; for, given rope to hang himself, its author submits instead to an aesthetic closure. Yet, 'How he terrifies me', wrote Rilke of Shakespeare's actual Epilogues, 'This man who draws the wire into his head, and hangs himself / Beside the other puppets, and henceforth / Begs mercy of the play.'[52] Theseus speaks of English monarchy, when he comments on such self-erasure: 'The kinder we, to give them thanks for nothing' (l.89). The Kindly Ones knew the Bard's 'tongue-tied' silence constituted their 'welcome' (ll.100–5), and they rewarded him with the preferment of which he dreamt. The poet returned the kindness, avoiding, even when saluting their Garter investiture, or when the Queen died, writing his sovereign's or her successor's name. Thus, England's Ovid kept faith with what Frazer calls a 'debt to the savage': the taboo hedging kings with divinity by punishing mention of them, and even causing their names to be thrown on tablets into the sea.[53] No wonder the dynasty shook his hand when he promised to 'restore amends' and weave a vapid 'nothing' about their names and habitations (V.i.424). For while the London 'lion roars' and the Irish 'wolf behowls the moon', his Fairies' last treat will be to bless the 'palace with sweet peace' to ensure the 'owner of it blest, / Ever shall in safety rest' (V.i.403–6). Thus, by euphemising its own absent present, Shakespeare's mirror of allusion repelled its history back with a curse of 'Evil to him who evil thinks'. For it was this royal motto, with the oldest of precautions, which gave the author a poetics of circumspection to turn the Evil Eye upon itself:

> To Windsor chimneys shalt thou leap,
> Where fires thou findest unrack'd and hearths unswept ...
> Search Windsor Castle, elves, within and out,
> Strew good luck, ouphes, on every sacred room,
> That it may stand till the perpetual doom ...
> And *Honi soit qui mal y pense* write
> In emerald tufts, flowers purple, blue and white.
> (*The Merry Wives of Windsor*, V.v.43–70)

'Backed by our supreme authority, / He'll command a large majority': the endorsement of Britain's leadership by W. S. Gilbert's Queen of the Fairies expressed a fundamental truth about the Shakespearean constitution Marx described.[54] And for generations Shakespeare's 'fairy charactery' (l.73) did seem to guard the House of Windsor, until in another horrible year of another *fin-de-siècle* we were at last reminded that neither play nor palace can escape the 'drowsy fire' of history that smoulders where 'the wasted brands do glow', when on 30 September 1992 the castle was consumed by flames from a 'glimmering light' which servants left 'behind the door' (V.i.361–78), and 'Everything happened in a few moments, as if for centuries those ancient pages had been yearning for arson and were rejoicing in the sudden satisfaction of their immemorial thirst.'[55]

From *Essays and Studies*, 46 (1993), 1–24

NOTES

[Richard Wilson's essay first appeared in a special issue of *Essays and Studies*, edited by Nigel Smith, which was devoted to the theme of censorship. It is reproduced here with a few revisions by the author, and some trimming of the notes by the editor. Wilson approaches the topic, not in relation to the formal processes of the licensing and regulation of Elizabethan drama (though these are directly reflected in *A Midsummer Night's Dream* by Philostrate, Theseus' Master of the Revels – the court official who, throughout Shakespeare's career, was the censor of plays). He is more concerned with the forms of self-censorship imposed on writers in early modern England, caught between the older patronage model of authority and the emerging pressures of a capitalist economy – and trapped in a class system in which the upper and lower echelons mutually deferred to one another, as they have largely continued to do ever since. Peter Quince, the harassed artisan/playwright, ever anxious not to offend, may be a joke in the play but he is also a revealing self-portrait of the author. The essay may be seen as part of Wilson's wider engagement with the place of Shakespeare in English culture, most particularly in his book, *Will Power: Essays on Shakespearean Authority* (London and Detroit, 1993), where he observes how 'Authority and authorship combine in the words of this glover's son to usurp the breath of kings, yet his language never loses the mark of its production: "subdued / To what it works in, like the dyer's hand" (Sonnet 111)' (Preface, p. ix). The essay opens, revealingly, with a reference to Karl Marx, and might broadly be described as Marxist in its emphases; but it is a Marxism inflected by Michael Foucault's critique of Marxism as an analytic tool (particularly in matters of power and authority), and also by an appreciation of how New Historicists and cultural materialists had opened up the old Marxist terms of reference in the 1980s. (On which, see Wilson's Introduction to *New Historicism and Renaissance Drama*, ed. Richard Wilson and Richard Dutton [Longman, 1992], pp. 1–32.) It might properly, therefore, be described as post-Marxist. Ed.]

1. Quoted in S. S. Prawer, *Karl Marx and World Literature* (Oxford, 1976), pp. 58, 168, 179, 242, 244, 246. All quotations from Shakespeare are from the Arden editions.

2. S. Greenblatt, 'Invisible Bullets: Renaissance Authority and its Subversion, *Henry IV and Henry V*', in R. Wilson and R. Dutton (eds), *New Historicism and Renaissance Drama* (London, 1992), p. 98.

3. T. Nashe, 'Pierce Penniless', in *The Unfortunate Traveller and other works*, ed. J. B. Steane (Harmondsworth, 1972), p. 115: 'A Player's Witty Answer to Augustus'.

4. M. Butler, 'Romans in Britain: *The Roman Actor* and the Early Stuart Classical Play', in D. Howard (ed.), *Philip Massinger: A Critical Reassessment* (Cambridge, 1985), pp. 139–70. The association of *A Midsummer Night's Dream* with the wedding of Elizabeth, daughter of Sir George Carey and granddaughter of Henry, Lord Hunsdon, and Thomas, son of Lord Berkeley, was proposed by Peter Alexander in *Shakespeare's Life and Art* (London, 1939), p. 105; supported by Harold Brooks in the Arden edition of the play (London, 1979), pp. lvi–lvii, and is now generally accepted. For Hunsdon's defence of the players, see R. Dutton, *Mastering the Revels: The Regulation and Censorship of English Renaissance Drama* (London, 1991), pp. 105–6.

5. F. Bacon, 'Of Masques and Triumphs', in *Essays*, ed. M. J. Hawkins (London, 1973), p. 115.

6. M. Montaigne, 'On coaches', in *The Complete Essays*, tr. M. A. Screech (London, 1991), pp. 1021, pp. 1024–6.

7. J. Kott, 'Titania and the Ass's Head', in *Shakespeare Our Contemporary* (London, 1965), p. 182.

8. R. Girard, 'Sweet Puck! Sacrificial Resolution in *A Midsummer Night's Dream*', in *A Theatre of Envy: William Shakespeare* (Oxford, 1991), p. 239.

9. L. Montrose, '*A Midsummer Night's Dream* and the Shaping Fantasies of Elizabethan Culture', in R. Wilson and R. Dutton (eds), *New Historicism and Renaissance Drama* (London, 1992), pp. 109–30. [Reprinted in this volume in the original version, entitled '"Shaping Fantasies": Figurations of Gender and Power in Elizabethan Culture'. Ed.]

10. See Note 8.

11. H. F. Brooks (ed.), pp. xxxvi–xxxviii.

12. Ovid, *Metamorphoses*, trans. A. Golding (London 1567; repr. London, 1961), IV: 152, p. 85. Girard, *A Theatre of Envy*, p. 240.

13. C. H. Herford and P. Simpson, *Ben Jonson: Life and Works*, vol. 1 (Oxford, 1925), pp. 15–16.

14. For Collinbourne's case, see A. Patterson, *Censorship and Interpretation: The Conditions of Writing and Reading in Early Modern England* (Madison, WI, 1984), pp. 12–13. See Patterson also on the cases of Stubbs (pp. 25–6) and Prynne (p. 107).

15. See P. Ure (ed.), *Richard II: The Arden Shakespeare* (London, 1966), p. lix. For a review of conflicting theories concerning the *Richard II* incident, see Dutton, *Mastering the Revels*, ch. 6.

16. P. J. Finkelpearl, 'The Comedians' Liberty: Censorship of the Jacobean Stage Reconsidered', *English Literary Renaissance*, 16 (1986), 124; Patterson, *Censorship and Interpretation*, p. 17.

17. J. Dollimore, *Radical Tragedy: Religion, Ideology and Power in the Drama of Shakespeare and his Contemporaries*, rev. edn (Hemel Hempstead, 1989), p. 24.

18. J. H. Kavanagh, 'Shakespeare in ideology', in J. Drakakis (ed.), *Alternative Shakespeares* (London, 1985), pp. 154–5.

19. P. Massinger, *The Roman Actor*, I.iii.139–40, in P. Edwards and C. Gibson (eds), *The Plays and Poems of Philip Massinger* (Oxford, 1976), III, p. 33.

20. Herford and Simpson, *Ben Jonson: Life and Works*, vol. 1, p. 38.

21. L. Montrose, '*A Midsummer Night's Dream* and the Shaping Fantasies of Elizabethan Culture', pp. 121 and 130.

22. M. Foucault, 'What is an Author?', in P. Rabinow (ed.), *The Foucault Reader: An Introduction to Foucault's Thought* (Harmondsworth, 1984), pp. 109–18.

23. Quoted in Patterson, *Censorship and Interpretation*, p. 20.

24. L. Marcus, *Puzzling Shakespeare: Local Reading and its Discontents* (Berkeley, CA, 1988), pp. 40–1.

25. M. Foucault, *The Order of Things: An Archaeology of the Human Sciences*, trans. anon. (London, 1974), p. 16. In the background of Velazquez' picture there is also a mysterious 'pale companion', who stands, framed in the door, giving the lie to the mirrored illusion of the King and Queen.

26. Ibid., p. 14.

27. Montrose, '*A Midsummer Night's Dream*, and the Shaping Fantasies of Elizabethan Culture', p. 125.

28. R. Scot, *The Discovery of Witchcraft* (London, 1584), IX, ii and iii, and J. Aubrey, *Remains* (London, 1881), p. 85, quoted in I. Opie and M. Tatem (eds), *Oxford Dictionary of Superstitions* (Oxford, 1992), pp. 260 and 261.

29. Ibid., pp. 264 and 282–3.

30. G. B. Harrison, *The Life and Death of Robert Devereux, Earl of Essex* (London, 1937), p. 91.

31. J. Brand, *Observations on the Popular Antiquities of Great Britain* (London, 1849), III, p. 476; Opie and Tatem, *Dictionary of Superstitions*, p. 264.

32. Leveller pamphlet quoted in P. Burke, 'Popular Culture in Seventeenth Century London', in B. Reay (ed.), *Popular Culture in Seventeenth Century England* (London, 1988), p. 51.

33. Historic Manuscripts Commission, *Salisbury Papers*, V, 248–50; IX, p. 191; *Calendar of State Papers Domestic, 1595–7*, p. 82; BL. Lansdowne MS. 78, nos. 64–5 (ff. 159–61); R. Manning, *Village Revolts: Social Protest and Popular Disturbances in England, 1509–1640* (Oxford, 1988), p. 208. See also P. Williams, *The Tudor Regime* (London, 1979), pp. 329–30.

34. See R. Manning, 'The Prosecution of Sir Michael Blount, Lieutenant of the Tower of London, 1595', in *Bulletin of the Institute of Historical Research*, 57 (1984), 216–24.

35. F. R. J. Du Boulay (ed.), *Kent Records: Documents illustrative of medieval Kentish Society*, Kent Archaeological Society (Ashford, 1964), pp. 254–5.

36. R. Flenley, *Six Town Chronicles* (London, 1911), p. 127.

37. K. Thomas, *Religion and the Decline of Magic: Studies in Popular Beliefs in Sixteenth and Seventeenth Century England* (Harmondsworth, 1973), pp. 724–34.

38. R. Corbett, 'The Fairies' Farewell', lines 29–36, in *Poems of Richard Corbett*, ed. J. A. W. Bennett and H. R. Trevor Roper (Oxford, 1955), pp. 49–52.

39. Thomas, *Religion and the Decline of Magic*, pp. 728 and 730–1.

40. C. Ginzburg, *The Night Battles: Witchcraft and Agrarian Cults in the Sixteenth and Seventeenth Centuries*, trans. J. and A. Tedeschi (London, 1983).

41. Quoted in K. Burke, *The Philosophy of Literary Form: Studies in Symbolic Action* (rev. edn New York, 1957), p. 46.

42. R. Fabyan, *The New Chronicles of England and France*, ed. H. Ellis (London, 1811), p. 672, quoted in V. J. Scattergood, *Politics and Poetry in the Fifteenth Century* (London, 1971), p. 21.

43. R. Graves, *The Greek Myths* (Harmondsworth, 1955), vol. 1, pp. 224–5.

44. P. Bourdieu, *Language and Symbolic Power*, trans. G. Raymond & M. Adamson (London, 1992), pp. 82–3.

45. Ibid., pp. 137–8; P. Bourdieu, *The Logic of Practice*, trans. R. Nice (Cambridge, 1990), p. 127.

46. Ginzburg, *The Night Battles*, pp. 22–5 (and for the folk motif of the 'wild hunt' of the wandering dead, see pp. 42–50); J. Frazer, *The*

Golden Bough: V: Spirits of the Corn and of the Wild (London, 1912), p. 30.

47. Girard, *A Theatre of Envy*, p. 237.

48. Ovid, *Metamorphoses*, XI, 18, 41–2. In Golding Apollo 'Dispoints the Serpent of his bit' when it is about to feed on Orpheus's disembodied head (l.65).

49. J. Stow, 'Borough of Southwark', in *A Survey of London* (London, 1603; repr. Oxford, 1908), ed. C. L. Kingsford, p. 65.

50. J. Walter and K. Wrightson, 'Dearth and the Social Order in Early Modern England', in *Past and Present*, 71 (May 1976), 42.

51. Ovid, *Metamorphoses*, XI, 53; J. Frazer, *The Golden Bough: V*, pp. 16–34; *The Golden Bough: IV: Adonis, Attis, Osiris: Studies in the History of Oriental Religion* (London, 1907), pp. 330–4.

52. R. M. Rilke, 'The Spirit Ariel', in *Selected Poems of Rainer Maria Rilke*, trans. J. B. Leishmann (Harmondsworth, 1964), p. 74.

53. Frazer, *The Golden Bough: V*, pp. 357–9.

54. W. S. Gilbert, *Iolanthe* (1882), Act II.

55. U. Eco, *The Name of the Rose*, trans. W. Weaver (London, 1983), p. 483.

10

Or

TERENCE HAWKES

NEDAR

I can begin by unveiling some Shakespearean words never before
seen or heard:

> And last, forget not that I nurtured you
> Till, pouring forth your beauty, uncasked then
> For other palates' savour, you were drawn
> Down into new blood and, embodied thence,
> Sprang wondrous free beyond your parent's power.

The lines are to be spoken by one of the characters in *A
Midsummer Night's Dream*. Let me introduce Nedar.

Nedar is one of Helena's parents. The name is not English, certainly not quintessentially so in the way that the non-Greek names in
the play such as Bottom, Snug, or Peter Quince obviously aim to be.
But the name Nedar does not occur in the Ancient Greek world
either, and so can scarcely claim derivation from the play's world of
Athens. Ovid calls Helen (of Troy) 'Tyndar's daughter', a reference
to King Tyndareos of Sparta, and T. Walter Herbert hears an echo of
that in Nedar's name – though the matter is complicated by the story
which nominates Zeus (disguised as a swan) as her genuine father.[1]

If Greekness at that more exalted level suggests fertile ground,
then we might note that Zeus's Helen certainly haunts this play's
Helena in the form of glancing references. Demetrius, waking with
the love-juice in his eyes, perceives the formerly scorned Helena
anew as 'O Helen, goddess, nymph, perfect, divine!' (III.ii.137) – a
description which annoys the recipient, since she takes it for a joke.

223

Later, Thesus's denunciation of imaginative excess complains of the lover who 'Sees Helen's beauty in a brow of Egypt' (V.i.11), and in the performance of *Pyramus and Thisbe,* Thisbe offers to be 'trusty' 'like Helen, till the Fates me kill' (V.i.195) – presumably intending to refer to Hero. But these references, whatever else they signal, offer no link with Nedar. Perhaps they serve merely to reinforce the point that the play's gawky, 'painted maypole' (III.ii.296) is hardly Helen of Troy.

Until now, Nedar has had no lines to utter in the play. But if that silence, like all silences, speaks, its topic must be ownership. For Nedar's name is only ever presented in the possessive mode: its two formulations in the play are first, Lysander's assertion that

> Demetrius, I'll avouch it to his head,
> Made love to Nedar's daughter, Helena
>   (I.i.106–7)

and second, Egeus's recognition that

> My lord, this is my daughter here asleep,
> And this Lysander; this Demetrius is,
> This Helena, old Nedar's Helena.
>   (IV.i.127–9)

In the play's terms this mode seems wholly appropriate and it apparently accords with the filial ambience of an Athens in which daughters are more or less wholly owned, as property, by their fathers, to be disposed of according to their will. Egeus, Hermia's father, makes this perfectly clear. Hermia's 'obedience' is legally 'due' to him, and he begs 'the ancient privilege of Athens' that 'As she is mine, I may dispose of her' (I.i.37–41). Indeed, the relation is exactly one of property:

> she is mine, and all my right of her
> I do estate unto Demetrius.
>   (I.i.97–8)

Theseus, recently successful in a war against the matriarchal society of the Amazons (Plutarch records that he eventually married an Amazon named Hyppolita, which concluded the war), confirms this absolute right in no uncertain terms, and in the process tells us a good deal about how daughters are regarded in his newly victorious patriarchy:

What say you, Hermia? Be advis'd, fair maid.
To you your father should be as a god:
One that compos'd your beauties, yea, and one
To whom you are but as a form in wax
By him imprinted, and within his power
To leave the figure, or disfigure it.

(I.i.46–51)

That appalling metaphor – no less so if 'disfigure' means to change rather than wound – gives the full weight of the paternal power at stake in this kind of property relationship. Mothers clearly have no part in it.[2] And when Peter Quince later uses the word in what is presumably a malapropism,

> one must come in with a bush of thorns and a lantern, and say he comes to disfigure or to present the person of Moonshine.

(III.i.55ff)

– it casually disgorges its subtext, speaking of the forcible manipulation of physical appearance and so generating the same slight *frisson* of horror despite – or maybe because of – its overtly comic context. The only right any daughter retained in this society was – again a sort of 'property' right – her 'virgin patent' (I.i.80).

OLDER WOMEN

If they have considered Nedar at all, most readers of the play will have done so on the basis of a major assumption, that the name refers to Helena's father. However, the lines I have composed, Hamlet-like, above, obviously challenge that. They do so because the grounds for assuming Nedar's maleness – if any – are dubious. The nearest version of the name in Ancient Greece exists as 'Neda', the name of a river, and, presumably before that, of a nymph associated – interestingly enough – with Zeus. In that form, 'Neda' is of course female. An 'old Neda' could easily be Helena's mother.

Surprisingly perhaps, for a play so taken up with youth, love, procreation and marriage, *A Midsummer Night's Dream* seems haunted by the shadowy images of older women. The play begins with Theseus complaining, like an impetuous legatee, of

how slow
This old moon wanes! She lingers my desires,

Like to a step-dame or a dowager
Long withering out a young man's revenue.
(I.i.3–6).

Of course, 'dowagers', older women who possess 'endowments' or sums of 'revenue', can be benign creatures. Lysander's elopement with Hermia will be facilitated by such a 'widow aunt',

a dowager
Of great revenue, and she hath no child –
From Athens is her house remote seven leagues –
And she respects me as her only son.
(I.i.157–60)

But these women are largely invisible, excluded from the main action and firmly exiled to its borders. I am not here drawing on those 'silences' in the play whose very existence is mocked by Richard Levin, in which the text is said actively to 'repress' or 'conceal' a feminine or maternal 'subtext', conflicting with and contradicting the imperatives of its patriarchal world.[3] The 'hidden mother' that Coppélia Kahn aims to retrieve in King Lear is perhaps suppressed in that play in a way that Nedar is not in this.[4] A personage called Nedar is not 'hidden', but overtly referred to twice in the text of A Midsummer Night's Dream.

Lysander's 'widow aunt', crucially important to the plot, has a similar claim to existence, even though she never appears on the stage. And she inhabits the same shadow zone as Thisbe's mother (a part assigned to Robin Starveling, the tailor, in Pyramus and Thisbe [I.ii.55] who also never appears. The 'votaress' of Titania's order, the mother of the disputed changeling, whose 'swimming gait' in pregnancy is so strikingly reported (II.i.130–4) dwells there too.

Of course, there are male absentees announced by the text: Pyramus's father (to be played by Tom Snout), Thisbe's father (a part claimed by Peter Quince), the Indian Boy demanded by both Oberon and Titania. But these are outweighed by a growing and finally tumultuous crowd of older women who gradually accumulate on the play's margins: the 'breathless housewives', the gossips, the 'wisest aunt, telling the saddest tale'(II.i.37ff.) all routinely tricked by Puck, the 'ladies or Fair Ladies' (III.i.38) congenitally afraid of swords and lions, confronted by Bottom and Snug, and the 'mothers' with whom the ambitious 'mother's sons' of the mechanicals consistently assert their filiation (I.ii.73 and III.i.69). All this takes place in the shadow of what Louis Adrian Montrose calls the 'pervasive cultural presence' of the ageing Queen Elizabeth, who functions as 'a condition of the play's imaginative possibility' and might even have been physically present as part of its first audience.[5]

If Nedar can thus reasonably claim a place amongst the play's host of banished older women, that perhaps draws attention to her curious name's final, seductive dimension. As an uncomplicated anagram of 'Arden', a Hellenised version of something essentially English, it effortlessly mingles aspects of the play's two worlds. And in the presence of a text committed to giving to airy nothing 'a local habitation and a name', we might remember that Arden was, of course, the family name of Shakespeare's mother.

ONE MORE TIME

The definition of what a mother is or may be forms a crucial concern for all cultures, none more so than the Elizabethan.[6] Montrose suggests that the period saw a concerted Protestant effort to appropriate the Virgin Mary's maternal symbolism and make it part of the mystique of the Virgin Queen. At the time of *A Midsummer Night's Dream*, Elizabeth was clearly an old woman. But in terms of the symbols with which ideologies work, her situation was massively paradoxical. Obviously mortal, she wore the monarchical mantle of immortality. Ageing, and so evidently subject to change, she embodied, as an emblem of monarchy, that notion of continuing sameness and political permanence asserted by her father's motto: *Eadem Semper*. For reasons of state a virgin, she was also that state's 'mother'.[7] In fact, within a very few years she would be replaced by a monarch the basis of whose authority was his opposite claim to be *parens patriae*, the father of his country.[8]

A Midsummer Night's Dream might be expected at least to engage with such paradoxes. Yet in respect of the obviously important issue of maternity, the play seems specifically to marginalise, if not exclude, the nurturing, vessel-like relationship of mother to child, which traditionally tempers the inseminating, constitutive and 'imprinting' role of the father. If Nedar is Helena's mother, her silence is eloquent in its reinforcement of Montrose's point that 'Hermia and Helena have no mothers; they have only fathers'.[9] In other words, in the immediate context in which the plot unfolds, the fundamental mother–daughter relationship which we might presume to have been the basis of the defeated Amazonian matri- archy over which Theseus triumphed before the play began, has been wholly suppressed by the time of his support of Egeus's claims. Whatever else the play has on offer, it is certainly not the delights or consolations of motherhood.

Indeed what is odd about Nedar – and what constitutes the basis for most readings' suppression even of the name – is that the char- acter seems superfluous. As a parent, Nedar appears merely repeti- tive of a principle fully and powerfully presented elsewhere, perhaps in Egeus. The barely mentioned Nedar, in short, seems almost an excrescence, the merest adjunct, virtually redundant, surplus to re- quirements, a left-over perhaps from another version of the play, a nervous repetitive textual tic that could easily be removed and no one would notice. If Nedar had been given words to say, no doubt some editor would long ago have recommended their excision.

On that basis, excision waits in the wings for quite a lot of *A Midsummer Night's Dream*. For in its general style, the same sort of apparently gratuitous repetition that Nedar seems to represent, that promiscuous proliferation of additional ways of putting things, turns out to be a feature of the text which apparently cries out for pruning. Modern critics and editors, avid for unity of intention, purpose and meaning in these matters, persistently reach for their secateurs.

And yet the truth is that a repetitive mode invests the whole play, almost to an extent that seems to insist on repetition as one of its central concerns. Even at the end, it seems barely able to reach a conclusion, but splutters out with a succession of more or less con- ventional endings, one after the other. The main plot of *A Midsummer Night's Dream* ends after all with Act IV. Act V seems to some degree 'added' on in order to allow for the performance of another play. But even the emphatically signalled end of *Pyramus and Thisbe* ('Adieu, adieu, adieu' [V.i.334] is followed by Bottom's surprising 'starting up' to address the audience (V.i.337). Then comes a Bergomask dance (V.i.348), preferred to an 'epilogue' from the mechanicals; then the exit of Theseus, Hippolyta, the lovers and the Court (V.i.356); then Puck's ritual sweeping of the stage with a broom (V.i.357–76); then the sudden entry of Oberon, Titania and 'all their Train' (V.i.377); then the song 'Now, until the break of day/Through this house each fairy stray ...' (V.i.387); and then

Puck's final address to the audience, which is of course not final at
all, since it would be followed by the reappearance of the whole
cast to receive the audience's applause (V.i.409–22).

The same 'spluttering' that marks the ending permeates the
action of the play from the start. It offers to move forward pur-
posefully enough:

> Now, fair Hippolyta, our nuptial hour
> Draws on apace; four happy days bring in
> Another moon
>
> (I.i.1–3)

but Theseus goes quickly on to his complaint about the new moon
being 'lingered' by an old moon. The course of the true love it describes may never run smooth, but neither does its exposition.
Theseus began by wooing Hippolyta with his sword: now he will
wed her in 'another key'. But, immediately after the order has been
given to 'stir up the Athenian youth to merriments' (I.i.12) in celebration of love's fruitfulness, Egeus enters, proposing to put his
daughter to death unless a quite different set of nuptials takes place
in accordance with his wish. And the lovers' later 'visions' and 'revisions' of each other are no less characteristic instances of the same
stopping, starting, alternating and hiccuping mode.

Confusion generated by this process seems to soak through to the
individual words of the text and to take its toll of the way these are
read. A good example occurs with the multiple illustrations of his
argument layered into Theseus's famous rationalist analysis of the
lovers' story at the beginning of Act V:

> Lovers and madmen have such seething brains,
> Such shaping fantasies, that apprehend
> More than cool reason ever comprehends.
> The lunatic, the lover, and the poet
> Are of imagination all compact:
> One sees more devils than vast hell can hold;
> That is the madman: the lover, all as frantic,
> Sees Helen's beauty in a brow of Egypt:
> The poet's eye, in a fine frenzy rolling,
> Doth glance from heaven to earth, from earth to heaven;
> And as imagination bodies forth
> The form of things unknown, the poet's pen
> Turns them to shapes, and gives to airy nothing
> A local habitation and a name.

> Such tricks hath strong imagination,
> That if it would but apprehend some joy,
> It comprehends some bringer of that joy:
> Or, in the night, imagining some fear,
> How easy is a bush suppos'd a bear!
>
> (V.i.4–22)

The last two lines have often proved too much for some twentieth century critics who have proposed cutting what they see as a final, exasperating repetition.[10] Dover Wilson quotes R. G. White's comment 'Would Shakespeare, after thus reaching the climax of his thought, fall a-twaddling about bushes and bears?' and he notes the 'loss of dignity' in the rhythm caused by these lines, which he concludes must therefore have been interpolated.[11] E. K. Chambers, editing the play for the Warwick Shakespeare, concludes that 'These lines are rather bald after what they follow' and suggests that they are perhaps a survival from an earlier version of the play.[12] But David Young notes that the shift from blank verse to couplet which they embody is 'very characteristic of the play'.[13]

A plausible-sounding process of revision has been put forward in explanation of these repetitive features, and Dover Wilson has suggested that the two lines in question here are 'so poor' partly for this reason. Indeed, he cites the whole passage as a 'very beautiful' example of how the irregular verse-lining of this passage in the original Quarto can give us clues to the history of dramatic texts.[14]

But something is surely very wrong here. Far from being a mere superfluous addition to the speech, the lines

> Or, in the night imagining some fear,
> How easy is a bush suppos'd a bear!

could be said genuinely to further its argument. Theseus is making the case that in those of 'strong imagination', the activity of 'apprehension', involving the imaginative generation of an emotion, leads almost immediately to its 'comprehension' by means of concrete actualisation in the material world. This, he then claims, applies equally well to the two opposed spheres of joy on the one hand and fear on the other.

The word which is causing the trouble is one whose implications take us to the centre of the play: 'or'. As Theseus uses it here, 'or' links two polarities whilst maintaining the difference between them. The scholars who wish to excise it, however, are reading it lulled by the play's overriding repetitive rhythms, as if it invoked mere sameness. In short, they are reading 'or' as if it were 'and'.

In fact, 'and' could be said to be the opposite of 'or'. 'And' certainly proposes repetition, more of the same. But 'or' has a more disturbing function. It introduces alternatives, realignments, different possibilities, unconsidered consequences, surprising subsequence; it signals a worrying, revisionary and subversive current which sets itself against the progressive course announced by Theseus, committed to pushing forward, apace. If 'and' in general terms indicates 'the same', 'or' implies difference. Why should the larger rhythms of the play almost drown it out?

The first moments of *A Midsummer Night's Dream* are indeed peppered with 'or's and the complications and hesitancies they announce. Hermia is to be disposed of 'either to this gentleman/Or to her death' (I.i.43–4). Her father has the power to 'leave' her figure 'or disfigure it' (l.51). She must decide 'either to die the death, or to abjure/For ever the society of men' (ll. 65–6), fit her fancies to her father's will 'Or else the law of Athens yields you up ... To death, or to a vow of single life' (ll. 119–21). Even the recursive figures of stichomythia rings with 'or's undermining of the straight path of true love:

> Lysander   The course of true love never did run smooth;
>   But either it was different in blood –
> Hernia   O cross! too high to be enthrall'd to low.
> Lysander   Or else misgraffed in respect of years –
> Hernia   O spite! too old to be engag'd to young.
> Lysander   Or else it stood upon the choice of friends –
> Hernia   O hell! to choose love by another's eyes.
> Lysander   Or, if there were a sympathy in choice
>   War, death, or sickness did lay siege to it
>
>   (I.i.134ff.)

Overtly, *A Midsummer Night's Dream* seems set on the celebration of unending repetition. It focuses not only on marriage and the continuing generation of children through which the society constantly renews itself, but also on the endless and endlessly fruitful cycle of the seasons which ensures that the festival of Midsummer Night comes around year after year. To compare medieval, or early modern culture with our own, an old historical perspective suggests, is to compare a circle with a straight line. A culture whose central mode is repetitive, whose circular and cyclical commitment to kingship, Christianity, orality and seasonal rotation involves it in the ceaseless generation of 'the same', contrasts sharply with that post-industrial way of life whose straightforward linear mode, inseparable from democracy, enlightenment, literacy and factory production, we inherit. Committed as it is to sameness, where ours is committed to change, such a culture might be said to be proposing an endless 'and'. *Eadem Semper* indeed.

But it might also be said that in tandem with the 'and' motif of permanent recurrence, *A Midsummer Night's Dream* also covertly offers to engage with an opposite mode represented by the word 'or'. It is one in which repetition – presupposing though it does sameness, absence either of change or difference – ironically also generates the conditions in which change must occur. To return to the older women which the play seems bent on excluding, this suggests that we might probe beyond the notion that they simply indicate the degree and extent to which women are excluded and degraded in a patriarchal society. Perhaps a deeper level of exclusion also operates, one which gives some reason for the first.

In a society committed to the preservation of things as they are, ageing, particularly the ageing of women, and specifically the ageing of a woman monarch, points to an ineluctable, opposite and feared principle of irrevocable change. The process of growing older, of becoming inevitably barren, will always challenge and even contradict the endlessly repetitive, permanently fruitful modes indicated by the eternal return of Midsummer and the constant reproduction, through children, of human society. A play which banishes older women to its margins is banishing those in whom the linear processes of life have brought about what we still crudely stigmatise as an unpalatable 'change'. In the modern word 'menopause' there lingers the notion that far from being an acceptable and organic inheritance of women, the 'change' introduces an inappropriate hiatus and final cessation of the 'natural' monthly cycle for which women were properly and permanently designed.[15] By this, a 'menopausal' woman can still only be defined negatively. Far from embodying a positive stage of development, she apparently turns into a creature in whom a fundamental process has permanently paused. The Elizabethan vocabulary contains no word that adequately describes this changed condition. In its own way, perhaps *A Midsummer Night's Dream* is offering its reiterated 'and' as a bulwark against an unavoidable 'or' of literally unspeakable enormity. And if the play hints that this is partly what we may 'mean by' it, it turns into a cruel enough celebration for a wedding.

SAME DIFFERENCE

That might serve to remind us once more that the new world order constructed by Theseus has a disturbing commitment to a complex notion of 'disfiguring'. It extends from the threatened violence with which Hermia is confronted, to the gentler spectacle of actors who 'disfigure' themselves by dressing up as Walls, Moons and Lions, a process which in one case leads to a grotesque 'translation' from one species to another. In fact, a motif of disfiguring, translating change is all-pervasive. It could even be said that *A Midsummer Night's Dream* invests wholesale in metamorphosis to the extent that the change it most powerfully chronicles is one to which the art of drama particularly lends itself: the repeated metamorphosis of spectators into participants. This happens on and off the stage. Oberon both observes and participates in the interrelationships of the lovers. He acts as 'audience' to as well as participant in Titania's duping. Theseus, Hippolyta and their court constitute a famously participating audience for the performance of *Pyramus and Thisbe*, and Puck has, of course, been first a spectator of and then a participant in the rehearsals for that play: 'I'll be an auditor;/An actor too perhaps, if I see cause' (III.i.75–6). Finally, when, at the end of *A Midsummer Night's Dream* itself, Puck addresses its larger audience in the theatre,

> So, goodnight unto you all.
> Give me your hands, if we be friends,
> And Robin shall restore amends.
> (V.i.422–4)

the applause which now enters the play's actual content, completes and confirms those spectators' transformation into participants and aptly concludes the play.

It is therefore entirely appropriate that, at the height of the action, Helena should recall and foreground an idyllic, change-free 'sameness' which once seemed able to contain and resolve all the differences in the world:

> We, Hermia, like two artificial gods,
> Have with our needles created both one flower,
> Both on one sampler, sitting on one cushion,
> Both warbling of one song, both in one key,
> As if our hands, our sides, voices and minds,

> Had been incorporate. So we grew together,
> Like to a double cherry, seeming parted,
> But yet an union in partition,
> Two lovely berries moulded on one stem;
> So, with two seeming bodies, but one heart;
> (III.ii.203–12)

But that state is now over and 'all forgot' (ll.201–2). Change and distinction reign, differences and particularities abound, men can and do choose between Helena and Hermia and their relationship is utterly altered as a result. In this sense, the process of 'disfiguring' or radical, revisionary change constitutes a major dimension of the play and for that reason most commentators have rightly seen Ovid's *Metamorphoses* as a considerable influence upon it.

But the mechanism of change in the *Metamorphoses* is a far from simple matter. For not only do Ovid's stories chronicle physical changes on a massive scale, they also in their telling embody a structural principle of change through an extensive use of the rhetorical mode of *digressio*. As a result, these are not straightforward narratives. Repetition, recapitulation, hesitation, circularity, starting and restarting, the embedding of stories within stories, a wholesale refusal of simple linear progression, these are as much the characteristics of the *Metamorphoses*, as they are of an older, pre-Socratic and pre-literate world at large, to which Ovid had access.[16] Moreover, the stories are not new, but collected and recycled from a wide range of sources. Marshall McLuhan has made the case that the process of multifarious 'disfigurement' which the stories recount, finds itself echoed in the kind of narration which realises them, and the circulating, repetitive mode in which it takes place.

As a result, a major paradox emerges: repetition, or the generation of more of the same, itself becomes the basis for change and the construction of difference. 'Ovid is the re-teller of tales. It is the re-telling that is the metamorphosis.' In McLuhan's view, this derives from a broader principle, whereby the cessation of some activity, followed by its repetition, actually serves to bring change about: 'the technique of metamorphosis is quite simply that of the *arrest*, the interval, whether of space or time or rhythm. It is this that causes the change or metamorphosis. So, even a replay in football acts as a metamorphosis.'[17]

McLuhan saw Ovid as an unrecognised but deeply significant influence on the writings of post-Symbolist artists such as Joyce, Eliot and Pound, one which partly manifested itself in the characteristic Symbolist interest in the disruption of linear sequence and the suppression of 'connectives'.[18] The halting of sequence, and the 'double-take' or repetition which that brings about, has the effect of making us aware of our usual dependence on linearity and sequential progression. This awareness produces (even constitutes) change because it generates a new and disconcerting awareness of our present environment and of its otherwise unnoticed effects upon us. From the Romantics on, repetition, recuperation, appears as the crucial mode of an art whose aim is to sensitise its audience to its environment, and thus effect a revolutionary change in awareness and response. For Wordsworth, the basis of a poetry appropriate to such a purpose was to be its expression of emotion *recollected* in tranquillity. Far from acting as a bulwark against 'or', the repetitive, recycling, revisionary activity represented by 'and' helps to produce it.

In *A Midsummer Night's Dream*, a similar Ovidean principle seems to operate at the play's heart. Its halting, disruptive and repetitive mode has been noticed. And as the plot unfolds, change seems to spring from the very stratagems designed to maintain sameness, to the dismay of those caught up in the process. The very idea of filial generation, for example, whereby a father 'imprints' a 'form in wax', deals in an evident sense of repetition through the metaphor of 'reproduction', and its links with 'printing' and 'reprinting'.[19] Yet, as Egeus discovers, the notion that parents can thus safely 'repeat' themselves in their children runs full tilt into its opposite when the children seek to undertake liaisons in the world beyond the family. In fact, a central paradox emerges whereby the process of filiation, committed to an 'imprinting' repetition of the same, inevitably leads on to a social process of affiliation, through marriage in this case, which must, willy-nilly, be committed to difference.[20]

THE NAMING OF PARTS

A calculated feature of the complex of paradoxes inhabiting the *Metamorphoses* is that its chronicle of fundamental change from same to different (initially even from Chaos to Order, from Golden Age to Silver, Bronze and Iron) as well as its multifarious exercises in digression, proceeds by means of what it serenely claims to be an 'unbroken thread' of verse. Its commitment to continuity, to going on unchangingly linking story of change to story of change, continually 'replaying' its theme of radical alteration, constitutes a final and unifying structural feature. Here the distinction between 'and' and 'or' is playfully elided to justify the final paradoxical claim made by the author that, as a result of the complex manoeuvres of chronicling change, he will remain always the same. The repetitions of 'and' may normally and inevitably result in 'or' but in his case, the reverse will happen. 'Or' will lead to 'and'. The stories he tells of change will ensure that he remains the same forever, achieving a kind of personal immortality: ' ... my name will be imperishable ... If there be any truth in poets' prophecies, I shall live to all eternity, immortalised by fame'.[21]

In an Elizabethan context, Ovid's pretensions seem at first sight to have some validity, and the poet's claim that 'my name will be imperishable' invites confirmation. Names seem obvious bulwarks against fundamental metamorphosis because they appear to deal, in this play at least, in the unchanging essences of their bearers. That is, they frequently invoke an ancient principle whereby 'name' reflects 'nature' which Harry Levin has aptly dubbed 'psychological onomatopoeia'.[22]

In a play which focuses a good deal of attention on the nuts and bolts of its own art, the rehearsals of *Pyramus and Thisbe* rank amongst the most memorable moments. In fact, *A Midsummer Night's Dream*'s emphasis on 'playing' and on witnessing and giving audience in the broadest sense seems to acquire a palpable social bearing largely as a result of the complex connection between the fictions of drama and the nature of social reality so acutely probed by the mechanicals in those scenes. Their naïve and heavy-handed manipulation of established dramatic conventions serves, in effect, to make manifest the complex nature of the relationship between performer and audience, player and part, that drama brings about in any community. This, surely, is the serious point animating Bottom's famous injunction about naming:

> Nay, you must name his name, and half his face must be seen through the lion's neck; and he must himself speak through, saying thus, or to the same defect: 'Ladies', or 'Fair ladies, I would wish you,' or 'I would request you,' or 'I would entreat you, not to fear, not to tremble: my life for yours! If you think I come hither as a lion, it were pity of my life. No, I am no such thing; I am a man, as other men are': and there, indeed, let him name his name, and tell them plainly he is Snug the joiner.
>
> (III.i.35ff.)

The essence of that relationship lies less in its capacity to afford entertainment or distraction from material social reality, than in the reverse: its capacity to confirm and reinforce the complexities of the social fabric. For to be 'a man as other men are' involves, in this setting, commitment to a *social* role over and above one's temporary, liberating carnival or festival role in a play. And it is this continuing social role, that, in an oral community, finally imprints itself upon its bearer in the form of a name. Naming that name reinforces that role daily, branding its bearer on the tongue. One is plainly and manifestly understood to be Snug the Joiner, Bottom the Weaver, Quince the Carpenter, Snout the Tinker, Starveling the Tailor, or one is nothing, and the pages of names such as Joiner, Weaver, Carpenter, Tinker and Taylor, to say nothing of Wheelwright, Hunter or Smith still to be found in the telephone directories of modern Britain testify to the ubiquity of the practice.

Commitment to and involvement in an oral community is of course signalled and confirmed directly by the use of trade names in this fashion. In the cyclical structures characteristic of such societies, names and nature, speech and way of life, personal identity and social identity develop intricate links that the culture seeks to nourish and conserve. John of Gaunt's embodiment of the same ancient principle – he is Gaunt by name and gaunt by nature – proves memorably emblematic of a whole way of life under threat in *Richard II*.

That one's inherited and unchanging social role, imprinted in the utterance of one's very name, provides the solid basis for any temporary carnivalesque abandonment of that role, must be a first principle of a society whose way of life is fundamentally oral in mode. Everyone must know, by means of talking and listening, face to face, exactly who everyone else 'really' is. The temporary abandonment of that quotidian identity should not diminish, indeed it ought to strengthen, reinforce, even guarantee that social role.

The rehearsals for *Pyramus and Thisbe* make exactly this point and in these terms. The names of the characters are stressed from the beginning. The 'scroll of every man's name' (I.ii.4) is presented, followed by the reading out of the 'names of the actors' and their trades in a careful ritual which covers the whole cast:

> Quince   Answer as I call you. Nick Bottom, the weaver?
> Bottom   Ready. Name what part I am for, and proceed.
>   ...
> Quince   Francis Flute, the bellows-mender?
> Flute   Here, Peter Quince.

(I.ii.16ff.)

In both *Pyramus and Thisbe* and the framing play of *A Midsummer Night's Dream*, naming stands as an important, governing idea. The names of Titania's fairies, Peaseblossom, Cobweb, Moth (or Mote), Mustardseed, etc. are, of course, rootedly English. Moreover, Bottom assumes that their names are indissolubly linked:

> I shall desire you of more acquaintance, good Master Cobweb: if I cut my finger, I shall make bold with you. ... Good Master Mustardseed, I know your patience well. That same cowardly giant-like ox-beef hath devoured many a gentleman of your house: I promise you, your kindred hath made my eyes water ere now.
> (III.i.175ff.)

In the case of Oberon's sprite, no single name proves adequate to his nature, so that the essentially English nomenclature expands to include 'Robin Goodfellow', 'Hobgoblin' and 'sweet Puck' (II.i.34ff.) – the merest gestures toward the plethora of names in which such creatures traditionally gloried. Reginald Scot's *The Discoverie of Witchcraft* (1584) records that

> Our mothers' maids have ... so fraied us with bull beggars, spirits, witches, urchins, elves, hags, fairies, satyrs, Pans, fauns, sylens, Kit-with-the-Canstick, Tritons, centaurs, dwarfs, giants, imps, calcars, conjurors, nymphs, changelings, Incubus, Robin Goodfellow, the spoorne, the Mare, the Man in the Oak, the Hell wain, the Firedrake, the Puckle, Tom Thumb, Hobgoblin, Tom Tumbler, Boneless, and other such bugs, that we are afraid of our own shadows. [23]

The sheer number of these names records a commitment to precision and absolute aptness in the matter of nomenclature. Names conceived thus are obviously deeply resistant to change. When Wall announces

> In this same interlude it doth befall
> That I, one Snout by name, present a wall
> (V.i.155)

and the Lion tells us

> Then know that I as Snug the joiner am
> A lion fell, nor else no lion's dam;
> For if I should as lion come in strife
> Into this place, 'twere pity on my life.
> (V.i.218–21)

the amateur actors are reinforcing this important principle. Bottom – despite his transformation – is supposed to remain, at bottom, the fundamental self his name proclaims. Indeed, the process of joining or weaving together carnival role and social role, actor and audience, stage and auditorium could stand as the ultimate 'marriage' that the play aims to celebrate. Perhaps the physical structure of theatres like The Globe seemed, in their 'embracing' of their audiences, to propose and foster such a union. James Burbage, father of the actor Richard Burbage and the first builder of public playhouses, was a joiner by trade.

Yet change will not finally be warded off. All these named, rooted persons nevertheless undergo a kind of metamorphosis into the characters they play in *Pyramus and Thisbe*, and one of them, Bottom, suffers the most fundamental metamorphosis of all. Of course, they also remain the same. If there is any humour in Bottom's translation, it lies in the fact that, to some extent, he remains Bottom in spite of it. Yet their experience of 'or' springs out of their commitment to 'and'. Their names may give their essence, but their essence, paradoxically and inexplicably, somehow seems subject to change.

To return for the moment to the name with which we began: Nedar. At first sight the character seems simply an 'and', a repetition of the function of Egeus. But the fact that Nedar never appears on stage leaves a serious dimension of the matter open. And a Nedar indeterminate, unfixed, a potential 'or', remains a loose cannon careening dangerously across the play's deck. In truth, 'Nedar' engages with and fundamentally challenges the principle that names guarantee some kind of permanence and are resistant to change. If it were an anagram, the name would inevitably manifest an imperative for change (it would even propose a change from English to Greek) whilst at the same time – also as an anagram – it would disconcertingly assert a claim to remain the same. An anagram's fate is to embody the difference that repetition generates, to hint at 'or' beneath the surface of 'and', to live stretched between the tensions of contrary readings. *Nedar*. It is as if it aimed to disfigure 'and' altogether.

WALL

We owe to Brecht the observation that bad acting has considerable value in that it affords insights into the workings of drama itself.[24] That certainly proves to be the case with the performance of

Pyramus and Thisbe. Its capacity for constant penetrative impinge-
ment on the 'main' narrative comes partly from its illuminating
mimicry in miniature of the framing play's characteristic modes
such as, here, in Peter Quince's disastrous performance, its hesitant,
hiccuping circularity.

> If we offend, it is with our good will.
> That you should think, we come not to offend,
> But with good will. To show our simple skill,
> That is the true beginning of our end.
> Consider then, we come but in despite.
>   (V.i.108–12)

Nevertheless, *Pyramus and Thisbe* offers more than a mere cari-
cature or travesty of aspects of *A Midsummer Night's Dream*. In
effect, a wholesale revisionary and revealing re-reading takes place,
in the course of which certain crucial changes of emphasis occur;
and the use to which these are put indicates the extent to which the
'embedded' text aims to 'mean by' the drama which hosts it. Most
clearly, *Pyramus and Thisbe* intensifies the enclosing play's concern
with transgression. Of course, transgression is in any case a clearly
signalled theme of *A Midsummer Night's Dream*. Bottom, a mere
weaver, crosses massive social boundaries to become a version of
the heroic lover. In his role as an ass, at the lower end of creation,
he 'marries' Titania the fairy princess at the higher end. Acting, or
role-playing, has always contained an obvious potential for transgression, particularly in a society regulated by rigid social hierarchies. But *Pyramus and Thisbe's* foregrounding of role-playing
throughout, particularly in the rehearsal scenes, positively trumpets
its concern with the issue, something which the performance
promises to reinforce when we hear it characterised in terms which
themselves cross fundamental boundaries: it is 'hot ice', 'merry and
tragical ... tedious and brief' (V.i.55ff.).

As a kind of monument to transgression, *Pyramus and Thisbe*
seems appropriately enough to be constructed wholly and uniquely
under the aegis of 'or'. From its very first appearance in Ovid, to its
most famous representation in this play, its story is only ever told
after the consideration of alternatives. In the *Metamorphoses* we
hear that one of the daughters of Minyas 'knew a great many
stories, so she considered which of them she ought to tell ... she
hesitated as to whether it should be the tale of Dercetis of Babylon

who ... was changed into a fish ... Finally she chose this last, for it was a little known tale.'[25] In *A Midsummer Night's Dream*, Theseus is invited to choose between 'The Battle with the Centaurs' or 'The riot of the tipsy Bacchanals' or 'The thrice three Muses mourning' before settling on *Pyramus and Thisbe*. Permanently commutable, 'or' haunts even the glimpses we see of the play in rehearsal. Indeed rehearsal, with its testing out of alternatives, is the dramatic mode which 'or' most comfortably inhabits.

Acts of transgression not only cross boundaries, they also reveal them, and *Pyramus and Thisbe's* literal-minded presentation of a fundamental boundary on the stage, and the clear intention of the mechanicals to make meaning from it, constitutes a memorable and telling statement. In the absence of the fathers (or mothers) of the enclosing play, the restrictive devices which keep the lovers apart here find themselves materially represented by a wall (played, curiously, by Snout, who was originally cast to play Pyramus's father) aided and abetted by a moon (played by Starveling, originally cast as Thisbe's mother).

Walls traditionally support, separate and thus preserve by division. A wall both recognises difference and proposes its maintenance: it is a bulwark against change. Since we are here dealing with speaking walls, we might say that a wall, with its commitment to conservation, to more of the same, characteristically says 'and'.

All societies make use of walls, literally or metaphorically deployed, and they obviously supply a major means of generating and reinforcing meaning in any culture. To breach a wall, or to transgress the boundary it marks, risks challenging the structure of differences on which meaning in a society is based. To breach or transgress a wall is to say 'or'.

It follows that the paradox of a wall *intended* for breaching must generate a fundamental contradiction. It will say 'or' as well as 'and'. Yet, of course, such contradictions undoubtedly exist although the aim of any discourse will normally be to occlude them. A good example of the paradox of the wall expressly intended for breaching occurs in respect of female sexuality. Obviously a number of symbolic 'walls' surround the virgin female. Yet these must be breached in order that licensed procreation may take place and the culture persist. Virginity itself, and indeed the physical hymen, appears not infrequently in Elizabethan writing as a 'wall' which the male marriage partner/lover must breach, but in circumstances carefully controlled and approved by law and custom. This generates the contradictions in which the rite of passage marked by loss of virginity is shrouded: 'legitimate' violation, 'cohesive' breaching, an 'authorised' transgression, an act of physical violence undertaken as an ultimate act of gentle responsiveness, the drawing of blood in the name of love.

Pyramus and Thisbe's Wall, which aids and abets its own breaching, clearly foregrounds the issue of boundaries and their transgression, and in so doing serves to highlight particular aspects of the framing play. The contradictions linking violence and affection, from Egeus's threat to 'disfigure' his daughter, to those surrounding sexual defloration, abound. The idea of 'wooing' with a sword, of 'winning love' through 'doing injuries' (I.i.16–17) proliferates from the beginning of *A Midsummer Night's Dream*. 'Wounding' in the name of love is symbolised in Oberon's account of 'Cupid's fiery shaft' which penetrates the 'little western flower,/Before milk-white, now purple with love's wound' (II.i.166–7). That, in turn, becomes the source of the love-juice which sparks the plot. In Montrose's words, 'the imagery of the text insinuates that ... Oberon's maddening love-juice is a displacement of vaginal blood'.[26] The story of *Pyramus and Thisbe* in its turn insists on and reinforces the same motif with its spectacularly symbolic bloody ending (as well as in Pyramus's encounter with Thisbe's bloodstained mantle and, in this production, Bottom's malapropian conclusion that 'lion vile hath here deflower'd my dear' [V.i.281]). Presented to a society as fundamentally conservative as Theseus's Athens, however, even a 'courteous' and obliging Wall involves a challenge to respectability which may risk the penalty of hanging. The problem is that however much the players' anxiety and consequent stratagems try to avoid such a confrontation, it seems built in to the very medium in which they now find themselves involved.

Steven Mullaney's work effectively defines the role of the Elizabethan theatre in terms of walls and its relationship to them.[27] The theatre's place and status were marginal and ambiguous precisely because it was situated outside the City's walls, within the ambivalent area known as the 'licentious Liberties'. The ambiguous role of the players ('double-dealing ambodexters') is confirmed by the contradictory allegiances and functions of the theatres. Neither within nor without the city, irregular and uncertain in their standing, they existed 'where the powers of city, state and church came together but did not coincide'.[28] By 1599 the city was ringed with playhouses, but the flight of the theatres from the city centre to its margins demanded to be seen metaphorically as a flight to liberty, not banishment.

The notion of margin, as Mullaney points out, proposes an appropriate metaphor in that it refers to an indeterminate space used for commentary on a main text, a commentary whose arguments inevitably challenge and threaten to become part of that text and even to submerge it. In social terms, the theatre certainly seemed capable of undermining the imaginary wall dividing 'margin' from 'main text'. Worse, its refusal of that polarity's stability threatened to bring other defining walls and boundaries within the society into crisis. As we have seen, the theatre also breached the wall separating audience from performer. And as *Pyramus and Thisbe* confirms, it persistently encouraged those engaged with it to become participants in a social context that wished them to remain spectators.

What the city feared from the theatre was precisely the political dimension of this impulse towards participation. After all, the theatres were places where unemployed and unemployable 'masterless men' might 'recreate themselves'.[29] The extra-mural status of the theatre, its embodiment of the idea of a limit or 'Liberty' confronting and challenging social restraint, confirms the capacity of this kind of drama to question the structure of commonsense which the city endorses. By definition, the margin is where authority faces its own limits. Characteristically, the very existence of those restricted to a periphery will inevitably bring the fundamental, meaning-making status of the centre into question. The periphery's role is to be the abode of the threatening 'other' by which the centre's 'norm' can be defined.[30] But it is no mere lair. In fact, it offers a unique vantage point from which the process of 'meaning by', as this operates at the centre, can be observed. As a result, possible alternative processes can be plotted and different meanings conceived from there. Its 'otherness' characterises precisely the nature of the challenge it inevitably makes. The periphery, the margin, is the position from which, in the terms I have been using, the theatres might be said to scream 'or' in the face of the city's 'and'.

AUTHOR! AUTHOR!

One could hardly expect Bottom and his troupe to be wholly sensitive to the critical revisionary role in which this seems to cast them.

Yet there is a palpable edge to their humility, an exhilarating sense that their play has the power to disconcert as well as entertain, that a heady potential for 'offence' lies, for once, near to hand. The performance of *Pyramus and Thisbe* is not quite the comfortable and comforting occasion that some readings try to make it.[31] In a similar case, my own words composed for Nedar, claiming to speak in the play's name, might seem to assert, from the margin or the periphery, a malapert equality with the Bard at the centre that is not quite laughable enough. To write the poet's words for him! To leap, at one bound, the wall separating commentary from creativity! For a literary critic, as for a rude mechanical, this is a part to tear a cat in, to make all split! In some eyes, it might also bear an uncomfortable resemblance to the sin against the Holy Ghost.

In mitigation, I will plead that I am only making overt and raising to a slightly higher power a process which, in literary criticism, is usually covert and gently occluded. Foucault cites commentary on texts as a major 'internal' system of cultural exclusion and limitation whereby discourses are established and confirmed, restricted and focused.[32] Most commentary – at least in the Anglo-American academy – certainly ends by building a kind of wall around the texts it deals with, one which aims to define the work by containing it. It performs a policing action whose *modus operandi* almost literally involves a kind of repetition. For criticism's fundamental mode, as perceived at large in Britain and North America, is indeed that of retelling the text's story for it, of rewriting the poet's words on his or her behalf, of re-presenting the work of literature as it supposedly fully, and finally is, with all its contradictions, silences and ambiguities finally teased out, realised, resolved, and cemented into place. Institutions and syllabuses supply moat and fortification. It is a way of saying 'and'.

There are many aspects of *A Midsummer Night's Dream* which lead finally to the topic of literary criticism. Not least is the way in which the obligations and responsibilities of filiation, the problematic relationships between parents and children with which the play begins, are ultimately and emblematically repeated, re-presented and resolved through the agency of larger social relationships, or affiliations, and the concomitant activity I have called 'meaning by'. In other words, in the presentation of *Pyramus and Thisbe*, the filiative bonds and duties agitating Egeus, Hermia, Helena and the rest find themselves recuperated in the transactions of a specific social grouping, that of the 'rude mechanicals'. Whatever its poten-

tial, their comic performance effectively re-reads and redeploys the
narrative, managing to drain the tragedy away without seriously
undermining the practices that caused it. Edward Said cites this
transition from a 'failed idea or possibility of filiation' to a kind of
compensatory social order, or affiliation, as a central feature of our
cultural experience:

> if a filial relationship was held together by natural bonds and natural
> forms of authority – involving obedience, fear, love, respect and in-
> stinctual conflict – the new affiliative relationship changes these
> bonds into what seem to be transpersonal forms – such as guild con-
> sciousness, consensus, collegiality, professional respect, class, and the
> hegemony of a dominant culture.[33]

What the performance of *Pyramus and Thisbe* seems to indicate
is that the affiliations developed in the business of 'making
meaning' in society offer a way, by means of repetition and re-
representation, of dealing with issues that are otherwise apparently
intractable. In short, the efforts of the mechanicals to 'mean by'
Pyramus and Thisbe reformulate and reassemble problems on
behalf of and for the benefit of a community that overtly mocks, yet
covertly gains reassurance from the procedure. This process – it is
one of containment – can be seen as a kind of acculturation, one
which it is often considered to be the business of the academic literary critic to promote and authenticate. On this basis, Said concludes that the relationship between filiation and affiliation can be
said to lie 'located at the heart of critical consciousness'.[34]

Certainly within the academy – that very model of affiliation –
criticism's role is often thought to involve smoothing the journey
from one condition to the other. Indeed, the herding of texts within
the academy's affiliative structures and the branding of them as approved cultural products has often been taken as the major function
of the academic literary critic. It is a process which, in requiring the
text to be appropriately dissected and redeployed, domesticated and
tamed, has seemed to make the academic critic an inveterate pro-
moter of 'and'.

Theseus would certainly approve of that function. His project,
speaking for the audience of *Pyramus and Thisbe*, clearly involves
sifting and realigning the mechanicals' performance in order to discover a preferred meaning in it. Invited by Philostrate to 'find sport
in their intents' (V.i.79) he confirms that, in respect of the mechanicals' text, 'Our sport shall be to take what they mistake' (V.i.90)

and he goes on to elaborate a miniature theory of critical reading whose procedures can effectively police any public text. His examples prefigure exactly what happens in the case of *Pyramus and Thisbe*:

> Where I have come, great clerks have purposed
> To greet me with premeditated welcomes;
> Where I have seen them shiver and look pale,
> Make periods in the midst of sentences,
> Throttle their practis'd accent in their fears,
> And, in conclusion, dumbly have broke off,
> Not paying me a welcome. Trust me, sweet,
> Out of this silence yet I pick'd a welcome,
> And in the modesty of fearful duty
> I read as much as from the rattling tongue
> Of saucy and audacious eloquence.
>
> (V.i.90ff.)

The grounding procedure recommended here is one of picking out, and painfully isolating and reassembling the units of a preferred version of a text. Applied to reading, it presents that activity as a selective, shaping and revising redeployment, a carefully moderated process of 'meaning by' which offers to speak for the text, to 'repeat' what it says, to insist on its behalf that the text does say certain things, to allow that it also says a possible range of other things, but no more. Usually, the interpretation focuses on contradictions, which it smoothes over, ambiguities, which it disentangles and limits, and silences which it confirms, accounts for, or which it makes to speak in accordance with what has been recognised as an overriding point of view. Critical reading thus conceived threads its way between two extremes: on the one hand, that represented by Borges' creation Pierre Menard, whose *Don Quixote* repeats every word of Cervantes' text as these occur on the page but by that very act claims to generate a wholly new text; and on the other hand, a commentary which produces new words that the text does not contain, but which can be said to present and reinforce its essential meaning more rigorously than those supplied by its first author.

My words for Nedar would seem to fall into this latter category. Thus my bringing of this silent character to the point of speech could be said to be not so much impudent or sacrilegious as to involve the implementation of the first principle of one kind of literary criticism: to present a confirming and, since I write as an academic literary critic, an affiliating repetition which aims to function as an act of containment, a beating of intellectual bounds which is also the beating of a tribal drum.

If that is so, then, to redirect one of the arguments outlined above, *Pyramus and Thisbe* can be permitted no 'essential' quality which would guarantee a consistent commitment to 'or'. Theseus's redeploying shadow (no less than my own) falls across all claims as to its function. Read in a particular way, perhaps as Theseus proposes to do, it could just as easily be made to say 'and'. At the very most, Theseus's speech and my words for Nedar could be said to exemplify a principle whereby 'and' is enabled to disguise itself as 'or'. And this is confirmed if all commentary can in any case, by Foucault's limiting definition, only be of the sort that 'allows us to say something other than the text itself, but on condition that it is this text itself which is said, and in a sense completed'.[35]

We might add to that assessment an earlier one made by Hazlitt which is – from one point of view – no less disconcerting on the subject of literary texts. Writing of *Coriolanus*, he points to what he sees as poetry's final complicity with the social forces that it sets out to question. The language of poetry, he claims, 'naturally falls in with the language of power' on the grounds that it springs not from the understanding, 'a distributive faculty which seeks the greatest quantity of ultimate good, by justice and proportion', but from the imagination, 'a monopolising faculty, which seeks the greatest quantity of present excitement by inequality and disproportion'.[36] The American critic Lionel Trilling would certainly agree. Poetry's 'affinity with political power', he writes, makes it 'not a friend of the democratic virtues'.[37] Elizabethan poetic drama's apparent collusion with conservative political positions has often seemed to mark it as inimical to change – something seized on by the eighteenth-century radical John Thelwall when he argued that it was precisely because the Puritans were 'friends of liberty' that they despised the theatre.[38] By this light, everything says 'and', nothing says 'or'. It is cheerless picture.

MR ASQUITH'S SMILE

On 6 February 1914, the figure of Nedar actually trod the English stage. Harley Granville-Barker's 'golden' production of the play brought what he evidently read as Helena's father into the final act where, speechless, he brought symmetry to the grouping around the performance of *Pyramus and Thisbe*.

It was a production which took place at one of the most crucial moments in British cultural history. The First World War was only months away. Industrial unrest was rapidly burgeoning: between January and July 1914 no fewer than 937 strikes took place. A General Strike, based on the Triple Alliance, loomed. A massive rebellion – almost a revolution – seemed on the cards in Northern Ireland. By March, a mutiny among officers at the Curragh garrison there had ushered in what George Dangerfield calls 'a new and terrible England'.[39] And yet there was a further factor which, by the time Parliament opened on 10 February, could be seen to have more revolutionary implications than any of these. Like *A Midsummer Night's Dream*, it focused centrally upon the rights of women.

The Suffragette movement can in many respects be credited with the initiation of modern militant street politics involving organised and violent protest. Its outrageous campaign of bombs, wire-severing, window-smashing, picture-slashing, heckling, hunger-strikes, invasion of political meetings, sit-down protests and the like had been met by remedies that now seem familiar: imprisonment, pulpit denunciation, endless prevarication and, an appalling specific, the use of the dreaded feeding tube.

Yet matters were obviously reaching a climax. Suffragette arson was to set no less than 107 buildings on fire during the first seven months of 1914. Mrs Pankhurst had already endured several hunger strikes, and between 9 March and 18 July of that year was to raise her record of such experiences to ten. By now, says George Dangerfield, 'her appearance was terrifying'.[40] Royalty had become involved. In June of the previous year, Emily Wilding Davison had made the supreme sacrifice for the cause and thrown herself under the hooves of the King's horse at the Derby.

The theatre naturally offered an irresistible arena, particularly if royalty could be involved. In December 1913, at a gala performance at Covent Garden of Raymond Roze's opera *Jeanne d'Arc* given in the presence of the King and Queen, some suffragettes secretly barricaded themselves in a box directly opposite the monarch's, stood up at the close of the first Act and, using a megaphone, addressed their Majesties forcefully. They were at pains to draw parallels between nature and art: between the women's struggle outside the theatre and Joan of Arc's fight for liberty in the face of torture and death within it. When they were ejected, forty or more other women in the audience waited until the performance had begun again before raining suffragist literature down onto the outraged spectators.[41] On another occasion, the King found himself confronted by a woman who had chained herself to a seat in the stalls at a matinée at His Majesty's Theatre, in order to denounce him loudly as 'You Russian Tsar!'[42] By 1914 the public protests were drawing even nearer. At a Drawing Room in that year, May Blomfield fell dramatically to her knees before the royal couple crying 'For God's Sake, Your Majesty, put a stop to this forcible feeding!'[43]

The Royal Presence, as reports had it, 'remained serene' but the theatricality of such protests must, by 1914, have given its advisers pause.[44] Did they, we may wonder, have any qualms over their Majesties' proposed visit to the Granville-Barker production of *A Midsummer Night's Dream*, with its pivotal scene in which Hermia is reminded of the duties a daughter owes to her father?

Granville-Barker's production characteristically sought very firmly to link the present to what he perceived as the realities of a Shakespearean past in which nothing was to be spared. The fairies were given a bizarre and slightly threatening mien that deliberately challenged traditional preconceptions involving small children swathed in tulle. The music of Mendelssohn was firmly banished in favour of traditional English airs set by Cecil Sharp.

Symmetry at many levels was a feature of the production and that is usually seen as the basis for the inclusion in the company of Nedar, as Helena's father. Helena was played by the famous actress Lillah McCarthy, co-producer of the scintillating Savoy Shakespeare productions and at that time also Granville-Barker's wife, although the marriage was by then under some strain. They began to live apart from 1916 onwards and divorced two years later. In an oddly vacuous account of her life, Lillah McCarthy refers to this as 'the most beautiful production of my career' – principally, it appears, because of the golden wig she wore, which apparently made the audience – and the King and Queen when they came – 'love' her. [45]

No doubt they did. A golden wig has immeasurable power. Nevertheless, six years before, on Sunday, 21 June 1908, a possibly less immediately lovable Lillah McCarthy had ridden as one notable amongst others at the very head of a procession organised by The

Women's Social and Political Union to Hyde Park, where 250,000 suffragettes had gathered.[46] The *Daily Express* said of the occasion, 'It is probable that so many people never before stood in one square mass anywhere in England.'[47]

As Lillah McCarthy later put it, 'We were all suffragettes in those days ... I had walked in processions. I had carried banners for Mrs Pankhurst and the Cause.'[48] Indeed, she had done more. Her auto-biography tells of a particular occasion, 'a year or two before the war' when, finding herself briefly alone in the Cabinet Room of Number 10 Downing Street, she boldly wrote 'Votes for Women' in red grease paint across the blotting paper on the Prime Minister's desk. 'When the rehearsal for which I had gone to Downing Street was over, Mr Asquith came to me. We had tea together. He asked: "Why do you think women should have the vote?" By Heaven I told him! I poured out arguments in no unstinted measure. He greeted them with a quizzical smile.'[49]

It is a moment to savour. Mr Asquith's smile, capable of dissolving the theatre's revolutionary potential represented by that intrusive red grease-paint, lingers across the years until it acquires almost symbolic status as a characteristic British way of deflecting social upheaval: silent (and in this case male) reproof. Possibly, it even glimmers faintly within Granville-Barker's production of *A Midsummer Night's Dream*, as if Asquith had suddenly found himself translated into the silent male Nedar, there to curb the potential upheaval that, like an unruly daughter, Lillah McCarthy might so easily have in-jected into the role of Helena. We can be quite precise about the context. In London, in 1914, one toss of that golden wig could have made the character shriek 'Votes for Women'. The slightest vocal inflection might have externalised the production's potential for 'or'. Of course, nothing of the kind took place.

To say that this is what Granville-Barker intended is perhaps to propose a significance for silence that the occasion hardly warrants. Nevertheless, it seems reasonable to suggest that quiescence in such matters was not merely desirable, but as much part of what was 'meant by' the production as the determined 'Englishness' of Cecil Sharp's music (which silenced Mendelssohn) and the menacing fairies (which suppressed grassy banks and tulle). Given the play's and the occasion's potential, as I have tried to sketch these, it was a silence which spoke.

When Lillah McCarthy came to write her account of these years, a similar soundless fatherly male presence continued to supervene.

By the gambit of legally forbidding any mention of his own name in her reminiscences (he is referred to only obliquely, for example, as 'the producer'), Granville-Barker's absence generated a tacit, rebuking presence there too.[50] His mute male Nedar had been eloquent on his behalf in 1914. Under the producer's on-going surveillance, subsequent texts were to remain evidently (albeit paradoxically) unproductive, permitted only to say 'and'.

ROUND OR ROUND THE MULBERRY BUSH

Must all readings, all performances, fail to release the 'or' for which 'and' creates the potential? History suggests that Liberty needs more effective friends than Mr Asquith. And Hazlitt's view is a partial one. It mistakenly separates poetry from the response and analysis that always and everywhere accompany it. It is also a mistake to think of literary criticism as something subsequent to and dependent upon 'creative' writing. There is no writing without criticism, and the distinction between them is surely misleading. There are few 'creative' writers (Hazlitt amongst them) who are not also critics. All writers are critical readers of writing, even if their reading is limited to their own work. In other words, it is vital to resist the simple dismissal of criticism as necessarily parasitic. The presentation of critics as mere lice on the locks of literature saves the face of too many third-rate writers, as Oscar Wilde knew.[51] And the division between 'creative' writer and critic confirms too many ideological contours to be taken at face value.

Also, as I have argued above, no commentary can simply repeat the text in its own terms, or lay claim to the discovery of its once-for-all 'meaning'. No criticism can simply dance around and around the same mulberry bush. All criticism – whether it intends to or not – effectively creates a potential space for 'or': there is no escape from metamorphosis, and the study of the process by which critical analysis systematically converts literature to its own purposes could even become, as I have suggested elsewhere, the basis of a new notion of the subject 'English', and so the means of breaking asunder the affiliation whose conservative mode both Said and Foucault deplore.[52]

A critical stance which self-consciously seeks to raise this process to the highest power, to embrace its implications rather than occlude them, must thus have a high priority. The method of such a

commentary would, of necessity, be to refuse absolutely to encounter the text on its own terms, to refuse the text's own hierarchy
of character and event, and to read and re-read it seeking out what
it suppresses, marginalises and silences as part of its own project.

Marx could be said to have made these stratagems the basis of a
powerful method of historical analysis. Its *locus classicus* occurs in
his *The Eighteenth Brumaire of Louis Bonaparte*, an account of
Louis Napoleon's coup of December 1851, in which a savage 'replaying' of events and a mordantly satirical retelling of a particular
narrative becomes the central concern. Marx begins by citing
Hegel's view that 'all facts and personages of great importance in
world history occur, as it were, twice'. But he points out – interestingly from the point of view of the performance of *Pyramus and
Thisbe* – that Hegel forgot to add that what occurs the first time as
tragedy, takes place the second time as farce. The force of Marx's
formulation lies in its energetic grasp of the power for change this
offers to the reteller of the story. His aim is to depict the 1851 coup
as a farcical repetition of its predecessors in circumstances 'that
made it possible for a grotesque mediocrity to play a hero's part'.[53]
And it is precisely Marx's recapitulation of the events, particularly
from 1848 to 1851, his redescription, and his careful replay of a
complex series of developments and relationships, that demonstrate
his point, produce and justify the polemic, and show 'meaning by'
in the process of taking place. The *Eighteenth Brumaire* is thus, as
Edward Said has argued, an exemplary text for literary critics: its
method 'to repeat in order to produce difference', its mode an 'and'
designed to produce 'or'.[54]

Herein lies whatever significance may be claimed for the words I
have immodestly invented for Nedar: they say 'and' in order to generate 'or'. It is of course vital that they turn the character into a
woman, Helena's mother. That simple step, that repetition which is
also a re-reading and a redeployment of something apparently
'obvious' in the text, makes all the difference. Indeed, it makes
meaningful difference possible, and the issues at stake in 'meaning
by' the play overt and unavoidable. It does so, not because Nedar
necessarily *is* female, but because, in twentieth-century terms, the
suggestion that she could be unseats a number of presuppositions
investing the play and demonstrates an indeterminacy, an undecid-
ability, that is a feature of all texts. Any 'resolution' of that indeterminacy will generate a coherent reading, but it will of course be one
haunted by the alternatives that its own existence has perforce sup-

pressed. It will be a reading aware of, and embodying, its own potential status as an 'or' rather than an 'and'. Given that, Nedar's words may 'repeat' the text, but at the same time, to flatter both myself and them, they also offer to present it for the first time.

Pyramus and Thisbe, the repetition as farce of the near-tragedy of *A Midsummer Night's Dream*, yields a potent symbol of the lovers' transgression: the blood-darkened mulberry tree. Human history has a way of imposing its own metamorphoses even on fictional events – in this case by its domestication of the mulberry tree and the metaphorical draining away of its bloody import, so that the colour of its leaves no longer hints at death or defloration. But oddly enough, the story of the metamorphosis of the mulberry tree finally has a rather precise and reassuringly farcical connection with Shakespeare. Legend has it that when he bought New Place in Stratford-upon-Avon, within a year or so of writing *A Midsummer Night's Dream*, the Bard planted a mulberry tree in its Great Garden. By the eighteenth century, the great increase in his fame had caused seekers after mementoes to pester the then owner of New Place, the Rev. Francis Gastrell, to such a degree that in 1758 he ordered the tree cut down. It was then sold to a Mr Thomas Sharpe, a watchmaker, who proceeded over the next forty years to bring about a rather more mundane, but no less effective metamorphosis by carving the remnants into hundreds of tiny objects – far more, it was said, than a single tree could genuinely yield – and selling them to visitors and tourists at great profit.[55]

Their appeal is understandable. Some sort of organic link with the imagined past continues to be one of the central fantasies of modern society. Shadowy yearnings for an originary, pastoral root from which we can be said to spring, are considerable, formative agencies. They have sparked many a grassy, rabbit-ridden production of *A Midsummer Night's Dream*. An 'original' growth from Shakespeare's Garden! Planted by the Bard's Hand! Like other wooden structures – the Birthplace, Anne Hathaway's Cottage, the Original Globe Theatre – the mulberry tree seems to offer a continually self-renewing 'and', one which nature in this case seems, in the very rotation of the seasons, always to confirm.

In fact, such are the needs of the twentieth century that present-day visitors to Shakespeare's garden find themselves in the presence not of one, but of two mulberry trees. The first and larger specimen lays stress on its filiation by announcing itself to be 'a scion of the tree planted by Shakespeare near his last residence'. The second, smaller tree confirms its filiative status as an 'offspring of the parent tree nearby', but then, proclaiming its planting 'by Dame Peggy Ashcroft, 8th September 1969' moves almost predictably into the sphere of affiliation by recording its commemoration of the two hundredth anniversary of the first Shakespeare Festival organised by David Garrick in 1769. Both trees seem to proclaim 'and', the second even adding an 'and' to the first. The issues addressed by *A Midsummer Night's Dream* could find no better memorial.

But if we needed a subtler emblem for the use of criticism in our society, the industrious Mr Sharpe – unsung final heir to the Pyramus and Thisbe legend – has perhaps genuinely whittled it for us. In producing an endless series of different objects carved from the same source, and indeed outstripping that source's material capacity to supply and sustain them, he is an apt figure for the literary critic, generating 'or's which masquerade as 'and's, flagrantly making and remaking whatever the text might be said once to have meant in order the better to 'mean by' it now. We can only, in the spirit proposed by the mechanicals of *A Midsummer Night's Dream*, urge that such a figure should shamelessly and fully embrace the implications of its function: name his name, in short, and announce boldly that he is Sharpe the Watchmaker. We know that to be no final bulwark against the onslaught of time. But at the very least, as Peter Quince promised, its bearer might escape hanging.

From Terence Hawkes, *Meaning by Shakespeare* (London, 1993), pp. 11–41

NOTES

[Terence Hawkes was one of the first British critics to address Shakespeare in the light of the European critical theory that emerged in the 1950s and 1960s. In particular, his *Shakespeare's Talking Animals* (1974) was one of the first attempts to apply structuralism to Shakespeare. *That Shakespeherian Rag* (1986) marked a clear advance towards poststructuralism and its indeterminacies, the title alluding to T. S. Elliot's *The Waste Land*, where Shakespeare's name and everything it represents is refracted through the psychological and cultural breakdown that coincided with the First World War. *Meaning by Shakespeare*, from which 'Or' is taken, carries all that a stage further. Again, the title of the book is very instructive, this time in being so ambiguous. The phrasing seems to echo the credits on movies: Color by Technicolor, Casting by Stallmaster Associates, Meaning by Shakespeare – as if meaning (sense, purpose, intention) is only one small part of a synthetic process, and something that can be plugged in or pulled out, as required, just as the persons responsible can be hired and fired at whim by the producer. This inevitably calls into question the role of the author in the production or demarcation of meaning: how great or small is it? One of the bedrocks of student response which no teacher of literature ever really escapes is the question: 'How do we know the author meant that?' – as if this is the only final determinant of what a text 'means'. In poststructuralist thinking, the author and his conscious intentions are no determinant whatever of a text's meaning, which can only be established (and then, never definitively) by its reception. Each new reception will generate a new meaning. So another way of construing 'Meaning by Shakespeare' would be suggested by the (slightly unidiomatic) 'What are *we* meaning by Shakespeare': that is, in what sense do we use that totemic name? What expectations and assumptions do we conjure up with it, what cultural freight? 'Or', as the first sustained play-reading in *Meaning by Shakespeare*, examines all these questions at some length. It is a measure of the remarkable open-endedness of *A Midsummer Night's Dream* that it should lend itself so well to such a project. Ed.]

1. See T. Walter Herbert, *Oberon's Mazed World* (Baton Rouge, LA, 1977), p. 16.

2. See Louis Montrose, '"Shaping Fantasies": figurations of gender and power in Elizabethan culture', in Stephen Greenblatt (ed.), *Representing the English Renaissance* (Berkeley, CA, 1988), pp. 31–64. See especially p. 40. [Reprinted in this volume. Ed.]

3. Richard Levin, 'The poetics and politics of Bardicide', *PMLA*, 105:3 (1990), 491–504.

4. Coppélia Kahn, 'The absent mother in *King Lear*', in Margaret Ferguson, Maureen Quilligan and Nancy Vickers (eds), *Rewriting the Renaissance: The Discourses of Sexual Difference in Early Modern Europe* (Chicago, 1986), pp. 33–49.

5. See Montrose, 'Shaping Fantasies', p. 32. Also *A Midsummer Night's Dream*, ed. Harold F. Brooks (Arden edn, London, 1979), pp. liii, lv.

6. See Mary Beth Rose, 'Where are the mothers in Shakespeare? Options for gender representation in the English Renaissance', *Shakespeare Quarterly*, 42:3 (Fall 1991), 291–314.

7. Cf. Montrose, 'Shaping Fantasies', p. 53.

8. See Glynne Wickham, 'From tragedy to tragi-comedy, *King Lear* as prologue', *Shakespeare Survey*, 26 (1973), 33–48.

9. Montrose, 'Shaping Fantasies', p. 46. Cf. Coppélia Kahn's judgement concerning *King Lear*, a play in which 'The only source of love, power and authority is the father – an awesome, demanding presence' (p. 36). Mary Beth Rose's extremely fruitful essay [see note 6] seems to miss

Nedar's potential altogether, announcing that 'in the six most celebrated romantic comedies (*Love's Labour's Lost, The Taming of the
Shrew, A Midsummer Night's Dream, As You Like It, Much Ado
About Nothing*, and *Twelfth Night*) no mothers appear at all', although she does register that a 'ghost' mother, Innogen, appears in the
stage direction in the early printed texts of *Much Ado* (p. 292).
However, her conclusion that, in Elizabethan terms, mothers tend to
be marginalised or erased, that the desirable adult society is deliberately 'construed as motherless', and that the 'best mother is an absent
or a dead mother' is very much to the point here. The article as a
whole is a mine of valuable information. See especially pp. 301–2,
307–12. Nedar's role as a mother who is at once 'erased' and 'asserted'
(see p. 312) certainly enacts a contemporary paradox to which
Professor Rose rightly draws attention, and on that basis I might
perhaps query her statement that 'Shakespeare's drama fails either to
reproduce or to appropriate these representations' (p. 313).

10. See David Young, *Something of Great Constancy: The Art of A
Midsummer Night's Dream* (New Haven, CT, 1966), pp. 70–1.

11. Cited in John Dover Wilson (ed.), *A Midsummer Night's Dream*
(Cambridge, 1924), pp. 141–2.

12. See ibid., p. 142.

13. David Young, *Great Constancy*, p. 71.

14. Dover Wilson (ed.), *Dream*, pp. 80–6.

15. Germaine Greer's *The Change, Women, Ageing and the Menopause*
(London, 1991), gives a full and combative account of the situation.
See especially pp. 213–44.

16. See Eric A. Havelock, *Preface to Plato* (New York, 1967; first pub.
Cambridge, MA, 1963), p. x.

17. Matie Molinaro, Corinne McLuhan and William Toye (eds), *Letters of
Marshall McLuhan* (Oxford, 1987), pp. 416–19.

18. McLuhan, ibid., pp. 510, 525.

19. A 'forme' is a term associated with printing, and refers to a body of
type secured in a chase and ready for use.

20. I am drawing heavily here on Edward W. Said's authoritative discussion of the complexities which characterise relationships of filiation
and affiliation. See his *The World, The Text, and The Critic* (London,
1984), pp. 16–25, 174–7, and *passim*. The essay 'On repetition' (ibid.,
pp. 11–25) is particularly relevant.

21 Ovid, *Metamorphoses*, 1, 1–176, XV, 879. I am using the translation
by Mary M. Innes (Harmondsworth, 1955). See pp. 29–33 and 357.

22. Harry Levin, 'Shakespeare's nomenclature', in Gerald W. Chapman (ed.), *Essays on Shakespeare* (Princeton, NJ, 1965), pp. 59–90. See p. 76. Cf. William C. Carroll, *The Metamorphoses of Shakespearean Comedy* (Princeton, NJ, 1985), pp. 32ff.

23. Cited in Herbert, *Mazed World,* p. 31.

24. Bertolt Brecht, 'On experimental theatre', in *Brecht on Theatre*, trans. and ed. John Willett (London, 1964), p. 132.

25. Ovid, *Metamorphoses*, IV, 28–63, p. 95.

26. Montrose, 'Shaping Fantasies', pp. 51–2, 63n.

27. Steven Mullaney, *The Place of the Stage: Licence, Play and Power in the Renaissance England* (Chicago and London, 1988), *passim*.

28. Ibid., pp. 8, 20–1.

29. Ibid., p. 51.

30. Ibid., p. 40.

31. Cf. Annabel Patterson's provocative reading of *A Midsummer Night's Dream* against the background of contemporary riots: *Shakespeare and the Popular Voice* (Oxford, 1989), pp. 52–70. [Reprinted in this volume. Ed.]

32. See Michel Foucault, 'The order of discourse', in Robert Young (ed.), *Untying the Text* (London, 1981), pp. 48–78. See especially pp. 56–7.

33. Said, *The World*, p. 20.

34. Ibid., p. 16.

35. Foucault, 'Discourse', p. 58.

36. See Jonathan Bate's excellent account of Hazlitt's criticism, from which these and the following quotations derive, *Shakespearean Constitutions: Politics, Theatre, Criticism 1730–1830* (Oxford, 1989), p. 165.

37. Cited in Bate, ibid., p. 166.

38. Ibid., p. 177.

39. See George Dangerfield, *The Strange Death of Liberal England, 1909–1914* (New York, 1961, first pub. 1935), p. 395.

40. Ibid., p. 368.

41. Emmeline Pankhurst, *My Own Story* (London, 1914), pp. 335–6.

42. Ibid., p. 554.

43. Dangerfield, *Strange Death*, p. 377.

44. Ibid.

45. Lillah McCarthy (Lady Keeble), *Myself and My Friends* (London, 1933), p. 174.

46. E. Sylvia Pankhurst, *The Suffragette Movement* (London, 1931), p. 284.

47. Emmeline Pankhurst, *Own Story*, p. 114.

48. McCarthy, *Myself*, pp. 148–9.

49. Ibid., p. 149.

50. Ibid., p. 161.

51. See Oscar Wilde, 'The critic as artist,' in *The Artist as Critic: Critical Writings of Oscar Wilde*, ed. Richard Ellmann (London, 1970), pp. 340–408.

52. See Terence Hawkes, *That Shakespherian Rag* (London, 1986), pp. 122–4.

53. See David McLellan, *The Thought of Karl Marx* (London, 1971), pp. 60–4.

54. Said, *The World*, p. 124. Said's whole account of *The Eighteenth Brumaire* (pp. 121–5) is extremely valuable and I have made extensive use of it here. The distinction drawn between this and Kierkegaard's *Repetition* is also helpful and provocative: see pp. 120–1.

55. See E. K. Chambers, *William Shakespeare, A Study of Facts and Problems*, vol. II (Oxford, 1930), p. 198; and Schoenbaum, *Shakespeare's Lives* (Oxford, 1970), pp. 159, 190.

Further Reading

There is a very thorough *Annotated Bibliography* of *A Midsummer Night's Dream*, compiled by D. Allen Carroll and Gary Jay Williams (New York: Garland, 1984), which describes all substantive criticism and significant editions up to the early 1980s. The *Annual Bibliography of English Language and Literature* (Cambridge: Bowes & Bowes) lists more recent work, though without commentary; the annual reviews of work on Shakespeare in *Shakespeare Survey* (Cambridge: Cambridge University Press) and *The Year's Work in English Studies* (London: John Murray for the English Association) may help you find the most relevant items among the ever-increasing output. On-line or CD-ROM computerised database bibliographies, such as the *Modern Language Association of America (MLA) Bibliography* and that of the *British Humanities Index*, offer very rapid and convenient access to a great deal of information, much of it very recent, but you need to use them patiently and with discretion if you are not to be overwhelmed.

SOURCES AND INFLUENCES

Unusually, for a Shakespeare play, there is no direct narrative source for *A Midsummer Night's Dream*. It is clear however, that Shakespeare was influenced by a variety of precedents, including Ovid's *Metamorphoses* with its pervasive theme of transformation and the introduction of the Pyramus and Thisbe story, which Shakespeare probably knew both in the original and in Arthur Golding's 1567 translation. Theseus and Hippolyta both figure in Plutarch's *Lives of the Noble Greeks and Romans*, translated by Sir Thomas North in 1579, and in Chaucer's 'The Knight's Tale', but also more widely in classical and medieval mythology. Bottom's transformation clearly owes something to the tale of Lucius in *The Golden Ass* of Apuleius. These are all reviewed by Harold F. Brooks in his Arden Edition of *A Midsummer Night's Dream* (London: Methuen, 1979), pp. lviii–lxxxviii; 129–53.

Recent discussions of these, and other possible influences, include: Jonathan Bate, *Shakespeare and Ovid* (Oxford and New York: Oxford University Press, 1993); Hanne Carlsen, '"What Fools These Mortals Be!": Ovid in *A Midsummer Night's Dream*', in Graham D. Caie and Holge Norgaard (eds), *A Literary Miscellany Presented to Eric Jacobson* (Copenhagen: University of Copenhagen, 1988), pp. 94–107; James R. Andreas, 'Remythologising "The Knight's Tale": *A Midsummer Night's Dream* and *The Two Noble Kinsmen*', *Shakespeare Yearbook*, 2 (1991), 49–67; John S. Mebane, 'Structure, Source, and Meaning in *A Midsummer Night's Dream*', *Texas Studies in Literature and Language*, 24 (1982), 255–70; Larry Langford, 'The Story Shall be Changed: The Senecan Sources of *A Midsummer Night's Dream*', *Cahiers Elisabethains*, 25 (1984), 37–51; J. J. M. Tobin, *Shakespeare's Favourite Novel: A Study of 'The Golden Asse' as Prime Source* (Lanham, MD: University Press of America, 1984); James P. Bednarz, 'Imitations of Spenser in *A Midsummer*

Night's Dream', *Renaissance Drama*, 14 (1983), 79–102. See also Montrose, 'Shaping Fantasies', essay 5 in this volume, note 19 (pp. 135–6). Specifically on Shakespeare's Theseus, see D' Orsay W. Pearson, '"Unkinde Theseus": A Study of Renaissance Mythography', *English Literary Renaissance*, 4 (1974), 276–98, which emphasises some of Theseus's less attractive associations; M. E. Lamb, '*A Midsummer Night's Dream*: the myth of Theseus and the Minotaur', *Texas Studies in Literature and Language*, 21 (1979), 478–91, which finds more positive things to say; and Barbara A. Mowat, '"A local habitation and a name"': Shakespeare's text as construct', *Style*, 23 (1989), 335–51, which examines the complexities of translating the source models into the Shakespearean text and character.

TEXTS AND CONTEXTS

There have been two major critical editions of *A Midsummer Night's Dream* in recent years, those by Harold F. Brooks in the Arden Shakespeare series (London: Methuen, 1979) and by Reginald A. Foakes in the New Cambridge Shakespeare series (Cambridge: Cambridge University Press, 1984). Both follow the almost universal precedent of taking the 1600 first quarto version of the play as their copy text. It should be noticed, however, that Stanley Wells and Gary Taylor, the general editors of *William Shakespeare: The Complete Works* (Oxford: Clarendon Press; New York: Oxford University Press, 1986) opted to base their version of the play on the 1623 folio text, justifying their decision in *William Shakespeare: A Textual Companion* (same publishers, 1987): 'we have found no reason to doubt that the bulk of the Folio directions represent the play as originally and authoritatively staged. Those directions which clearly envisage a different staging from that implied in the Quarto seem to us to be dramatic improvements for which Shakespeare was probably responsible' (p. 280). This remains contentious. One small editorial detail which none of these picked up, but which could have significant implications for our understanding of what actually happens between Bottom and Titania, is explored by Homer Swander in 'Editors vs a text: the scripted geography of *A Midsummer Night's Dream*', *Studies in Philology*, 87 (1990), 83–108.

Brooks and Foakes differ on another matter. The former inclines positively to the view that the play was written for an aristocratic wedding, quite possibly one graced by Queen Elizabeth; the latter remains sceptical. For other discussions of this matter, see Steven W. May, '*A Midsummer Night's Dream* and the Carey–Berkeley Wedding', *Renaissance Papers* (1983), 43–52; William B. Hunter, 'The First Performance of *A Midsummer Night's Dream*', *Notes and Queries*, 230 (1985), 45–7; and Marion Colthorpe, 'Queen Elizabeth and *A Midsummer Night's Dream*', *Notes and Queries*, 232 (1987), 205–7 – which conclusively establishes that the queen was *not* present at the Carey–Berkeley wedding, perhaps the likeliest context in which the play might have been written to order (though Ernst Honigmann has championed an association with the Earl of Southampton's family, in *Shakespeare: the Lost Years* [Manchester:

Manchester University Press, 1985], pp. 150–3). David Wiles looks at the play as a test case for the whole notion of 'occasionalist' plays in Elizabethan England; his focus on the era's obsession with astrology is intriguing but inevitably rather speculative: *Shakespeare's Almanac: 'A Midsummer Night's Dream'*, *Marriage and the Elizabethan Calendar* (Woodbridge, Suffolk: D. S. Brewer, 1993).

'DREAM'

Although dream, as theme or motif, readily lends itself to certain kinds of psychoanalytic and poststructuralist modes of reading, it is so central to *A Midsummer Night's Dream* that it has provided a starting point for a number of important readings of the play that do not fit very conveniently under other labels. These include David P. Young, *Something of Great Constancy: The Art of 'A Midsummer Night's Dream'* (New Haven, CT: Yale University Press, 1966); James L. Calderwood, *Shakespearean Metadrama* (Minneapolis: University of Minnesota Press, 1971); Marjorie B. Garber, *Dream in Shakespeare: from Metaphor to Metamorphosis* (New Haven, CT: Yale University Press, 1974); William C. Carroll, *The Metamorphoses of Shakespearean Comedy* (Princeton, NJ: Princeton University Press, 1985). Recently, James L. Calderwood has returned to the play with a monograph, *A Midsummer Night's Dream* (New York: Twayne Publishers, 1992), the most original sections of which link dream with the Renaissance practice of anamorphism (the distortion of objects so that they can only be seen properly from one perspective).

HISTORICIST READINGS

There are many inflections, and varying ideological implications, to the reading of Shakespeare in the context of his time. Among the most influential discussions of these matters have been Robert Weimann, *Shakespeare and the Popular Tradition in the Theater* (Baltimore, MD: Johns Hopkins University Press, 1978), a sophisticated Marxist approach; Stephen Greenblatt, *Shakespearean Negotiations: The Social Circulation of Social Energy in Renaissance England* (Berkeley, CA: University of California Press, 1988), a new historicist collection of essays; Leah Marcus, *Puzzling Shakespeare: Local Reading and its Discontents* (Berkeley, CA: University of California Press, 1988), which explores the texts in relation to the micro-politics and history of their day; Steven Mullaney, *The Place of the Stage: License, Play and Power in Renaissance England* (Chicago: University of Chicago Press, 1988), which argues that the physical location of the theatres in the liminal zone beyond the control of the city authorities coloured the nature of the material they staged; Annabel Patterson, *Shakespeare and the Popular Voice* (Oxford: Basil Blackwell, 1989), which emphasises the populist and quasi-democratic strain in Shakespeare; Richard Wilson, *Will Power: Essays on Shakespearean Authority* (Hemel Hempstead: Harvester Wheatsheaf, 1993), a post-Marxist exploration of Shakespeare's deferential accommodation with the power structures of his day; and Jean E. Howard, *The Stage and Social Struggle in Early Modern*

England (London and New York: Routledge, 1994), which examines the phenomenon of theatricality itself within the culture of Shakespearean England. Jean Howard, with Marion O'Connor, also edited a very useful anthology of essays, *Shakespeare Reproduced: The Text in History and Ideology* (London: Methuen, 1987) which brings together a variety of viewpoints on these matters.

Much has been written specifically on New Historicism and Cultural Materialism as approaches that have centrally informed the historicist reading of Shakespeare. There are helpful discussions of the issues in Jonathan Dollimore's introduction to J. Dollimore and A. Sinfield (eds), *Political Shakespeare: Essays in Cultural Materialism* (Manchester: Manchester University Press, 1985); Stephen Greenblatt's *Shakespearean Negotiations*, cited above; Lynn Hunt (ed.), *The New Cultural History* (Berkeley, CA: University of California Press, 1989); H. Aram Veeser (ed.), *The New Historicism* (New York: Routledge, 1989); R. Wilson and R. Dutton (eds), *New Historicism and Renaissance Drama* (London: Longman, 1992); Louis Montrose, 'New Historicisms' in S. Greenblatt and G. Gunn (eds), *Redrawing the Boundaries: The Transformation of English and American Studies* (New York: Modern Language Association of America, 1992), pp. 393–418.

Two essays which address the historical/political location of *A Midsummer Night's Dream* itself are: Theodore B. Leinwand, '"I Believe We Must Leave the Killing Out": Deference and Accommodation in *A Midsummer Night's Dream*', *Renaissance Papers* (1986), 11–30; and Paul Yachnin, 'The Politics of Theatrical Mirth: *A Midsummer Night's Dream, A Mad World, My Masters*, and *Measure for Measure*', *Shakespeare Quarterly*, 43 (1992), 51–66.

PSYCHOLOGICAL AND PSYCHOANALYTIC CRITICISM

There are a number of useful collections of essays exclusively devoted to Shakespeare, in this complex and burgeoning field, including Murray M. Schwartz and Coppélia Kahn (eds), *Representing Shakespeare: New Psychoanalytic Essays* (Baltimore, MD: Johns Hopkins University Press, 1980); Norman N. Holland, Sidney Homan and Bernard J. Paris (eds), *Shakespeare's Personality* (Berkeley, CA: University of California Press, 1990), and B. J. Sokol (ed.), *The Undiscover'd Country: New Essays on Psychoanalysis and Shakespeare* (London: Free Association Press, 1993). The latter contains a helpful 'Bibliography of Psychological and Psychoanalytic Shakespeare Criticism 1979–1989' by Christine Levey, pp. 217–48.

The most distinguished recent monographs in this field include the following (their titles indicate their scope and orientation with unusual felicity): Coppélia Kahn, *Man's Estate: Masculine Identity in Shakespeare* (Berkeley, CA: University of California Press, 1981); Joseph P. Westlund, *Shakespeare's Reparative Comedies: A Psycholanalytic View of the Middle Plays* (Chicago, University of Chicago Press, 1984); W. Thomas MacCary, *Friends and Lovers: The Phenomenology of Desire in Shakespearean Comedy* (New York: Columbia University Press, 1985); C. L. Barber and

Richard P. Wheeler, *The Whole Journey: Shakespeare's Power of Development* (Berkeley, CA: University of California Press, 1986); Barbara Freedman, *Staging the Gaze: Psychoanalysis, Post-modernism and Shakespearean Comedy* (Ithaca, NY: Cornell University Press, 1990), a Lacanian study; Janet Adelman, *Suffocating Mothers: Fantasies of Maternal Origins in Shakespeare's Plays, 'Hamlet' to 'The Tempest'* (New York and London: Routledge, 1992).

There are also a striking number of individual essays on *A Midsummer Night's Dream* with psychological motifs or in psychoanalytic mode: Melvin D. Faber, 'Hermia's Dream: Royal Road to *A Midsummer Night's Dream', Literature and Psychology*, 22 (1972), 179–90; Mordecai Marcus, '*A Midsummer Night's Dream*: The Dialectic of Eros-Thanatos', *American Imago: A Psychoanalytic Journal for Culture, Science and the Arts*, 38 (1981), 269–78; Vicki S. Hartman, '*A Midsummer Night's Dream*: A Gentle Concord to the Oedipal Problem", *American Imago*, 40 (1983), 355–69; Barry Weller, 'Identity Dis-Figured: *A Midsummer Night's Dream', The Kenyon Review*, n.s. 7 (1985), 66–78; Allen Dunn, 'The Indian Boy's Dream Wherein Every Mother's Son Rehearses His Part: Shakespeare's *A Midsummer Night's Dream', Shakespeare Studies*, 20 (1986), 15–32; Maurice Hunt, 'Individuation in *A Midsummer Night's Dream', South Central Review*, 3 (1986), 1–13; Jan Lawson Hinely, 'Expounding the Dream: Shaping Fantasies in *A Midsummer Night's Dream*' in Maurice Charney and Joseph Reppen (eds), *Psychoanalytic Approaches to Literature and Film* (Rutherford, NJ: Fairleigh Dickinson University Press, 1987), pp. 120–38; Helen Golding, '"The Story of The Night Told Over": D. W. Winnicott's Theory of Play and *A Midsummer Night's Dream*', first published 1988, reprinted in Gary F. Waller (ed.), *Shakespeare's Comedies* (London, Longman, 1991) pp. 92–105.

PERFORMANCE CRITICISM

Much current performance criticism of Shakespeare is indebted to two major studies by Michael Goldman: *Shakespeare and the Energies of Drama* (Princeton, NJ: Princeton University Press, 1972) and *Acting and Action on Shakespeare* (Princeton, NJ: Princeton University Press, 1985). There is a central debate in this field over whether a performance, so to speak, reproduces or releases meanings already latent in a text, or whether each new performance produces meanings of its own: see W. B. Worthen, 'Deeper Meanings and Theatrical Technique', *Shakespeare Quarterly*, 40 (1989), 441–55; James Kavanagh, 'Shakespeare in Ideology' in John Drakakis (ed.), *Alternative Shakespeares* (London: Methuen, 1985), pp. 144–65.

Shakespeare Bulletin (Norwood, NJ: New York Shakespeare Society) is a journal dedicated exclusively to performance criticism. There are also regular reviews of major North American Shakespeare productions in *Shakespeare Quarterly* (Washington, DC: Folger Shakespeare Library) and British ones in *Shakespeare Survey*. Ronald Watkins and Jeremy Lemmon have attempted to describe how *A Midsummer Night's Dream* might have been performed in Shakespeare's own day in '*A Midsummer Night's*

Dream' In Shakespeare's Lifetime (Totowa, NJ: Rowan & Littlefield, 1974), while David Selbourne confirmed the continuing status of the Peter Brook Royal Shakespeare Company production of the play as the most fascinating one of modern times in his exhaustive *The Making of 'A Midsummer Night's Dream'* (London: Methuen, 1982).

Performance must increasingly include work on film and video as well as in the theatre; there are currently at least three productions of *A Midsummer Night's Dream* available on video: the Peter Hall Royal Shakespeare Company version (originally released 1968; re-released by Warner Home Video, 1988); the BBC Shakespeare version (BBC/Time Life, 1982); and the ABC Video version (1988) of the 1982 Joseph Papp New York Shakespeare Festival production. And the classic 1933 Hollywood version, once much derided for – among other things – James Cagney as Puck, also repays more attention than was once supposed. On these matters see Jack J. Jorgens, *Shakespeare on Film* (Bloomington, IN: Indiana University Press, 1977); J. C. Bulman and H. R. Coursen (eds), *Shakespeare on Television* (Hanover, PA: University Press of New England); Gary F. Waller, 'Decentring the Bard: the Dissemination of the Shakespearean Text', in G. Douglas Atkins and David Bergeron (eds), *Shakespeare and Deconstruction* (New York: Peter Lang, 1988) pp. 21–46. Incidentally, *Shakespeare Bulletin* absorbed the formerly separate *Shakespeare on Film Newsletter* in 1992. Unfortunately, there is as yet no *A Midsummer Night's Dream* in Manchester University Press's very useful *Shakespeare in Performance* series.

FEMINIST AND GENDER CRITICISM

There is a very thorough overview of the whole question of Shakespeare and feminist criticism in Philip C. Kolin, *Shakespeare and Feminist Criticism: An Annotated Bibliography and Commentary* (New York: Garland, 1991), and a more narrowly focused one in Jvotsna Singh, 'The Influence of Feminist Criticism/Theory on Shakespeare Studies, 1976–1986' in Mario Di Cesare (ed.), *Reconsidering the Renaissance* (Binghampton, NY: Medieval and Renaissance Studies, 93, 1992), pp. 381–93. There are also two valuable collections of essays: C. Lenz, R. Swift, G. Greene and C. T. Neely (eds), *The Woman's Part: Feminist Criticism of Shakespeare* (Urbana, IL: University of Illinois Press, 1980) and Valerie Wayne (ed.), *The Matter of Difference: Materialist Feminist Criticism of Shakespeare* (Ithaca, NY: Cornell University Press, 1991). Not confined to Shakespeare, but a landmark collection in relation to feminism and Renaissance literature as a whole, is M. Ferguson, M. Quilligan and N. Vickers (eds), *Rewriting the Renaissance: The Discourses of Sexual Difference in Early Modern Europe* (Chicago: University of Chicago Press, 1986).

Among the most influential recent feminist monographs on Shakespeare have been Peter Erikson, *Patriarchal Structures in Shakespeare's Drama* (Berkeley, CA: University of California Press, 1985); Lisa Jardine, *Still Harping on Daughters: Women and Drama in the Age of Shakespeare* (2nd edn, Hemel Hempstead: Harvester, 1989); Carol Thomas Neely, *Broken Nuptials in Shakespeare's Plays* (New Haven, CT: Yale University Press,

1985); and Marianne Novy, *Love's Argument: Gender Relations in Shakespeare* (Chapel Hill, NC: University of North Carolina Press, 1984). Most of these have something to say about *A Midsummer Night's Dream* though (apart from the Garner and Montrose items reprinted here), there have been few separate feminist treatments of the play; Judith Lutge Coullie, '"Jack Shall Have Jill"': The Ideology of Love in *A Midsummer Night's Dream*', *Shakespeare in Southern Africa*, 5 (1992), 59–66, is an exception, while D'Orsay W. Pearson's 'Male Sovereignty, Harmony and Irony in *A Midsummer Night's Dream*', *The Upstart Crow*, 7 (1987), 24–35, explores the issue of patriarchal power in the play from a somewhat different perspective.

The following items say little or nothing about *A Midsummer Night's Dream*, but all address important topics in relation to the gender debate around the play: Jean Howard, 'Cross-Dressing, the Theatre, and Gender Struggle in Early Modern England', *Shakespeare Quarterly*, 39 (1988), 418–41 – the sexual politics of the fact that female roles were played by boy actors on the Elizabethan stage has given rise to considerable controversy, especially where such female characters also cross-dress in male costume, which is not the case with *A Midsummer Night's Dream* (see also the Jardine book, *Still Harping* cited above; Phyllis Rackin, 'Androgyny, Mimesis and the Marriage of the Boy Heroine on the English Stage', *PMLA*, 102 [1987], 29–41; and Stephen Orgel, 'Nobody's Perfect: Or Why Did the English Stage Take Boys for Women?', *The South Atlantic Quarterly*, 88 [1989], 7–29); Claire McEachern, 'Fathering Herself: A Source Study of Shakespeare's Feminism', *Shakespeare Quarterly*, 39 (1988), 269–91; Carol Thomas Neely, 'Constructing the Subject: Feminist Practice and the New Renaissance Discourses', *English Literary Renaissance*, 18 (1988), 5–18; Linda Boose, 'Scolding Brides and Bridling Scolds: Taming the Woman's Unruly Member', *Shakespeare Quarterly*, 42 (1991), 179–213.

FESTIVE CRITICISM

The earliest, and still very influential, text in this field is C. L. Barber, *Shakespeare's Festive Comedy: A Study of Dramatic Form and Its Relation to Social Custom* (Princeton, NJ: Princeton University Press, 1959), which sees the comedies' echoing of traditional festive practices as essentially normative, re-enacting rites of passage by which the community accommodates itself to the passing year. This has something in common with Northrop Frye's anthropologically-based criticism, most fully applied to Shakespeare's comedies in *A Natural Perspective: The Development of Shakespearean Comedy and Romance* (New York: Columbia University Press, 1965). François Laroque's *Shakespeare's Festive World: Elizabethan Seasonal Entertainment and the Professional Stage* (Cambridge: Cambridge University Press, 1991) expands on Barber by exploring much more minutely actual festive and ritual practices of Shakespeare's day, but does not theorise or historicise the dramatists' representation of such practices.

Pressure to both theorise and historicise festive elements in the drama really begins with belated publication in the West of Mikhail Bakhtin's

Rabelais and his World, trans. Helene Islowsky (Cambridge, MA: MIT Press, 1968; reprinted Bloomington, IN: University of Indiana Press, 1984), which celebrated carnival as a genuine expression of popular feeling and culture (and so, potentially, political will) that was normally repressed by those in authority and the 'high' culture they patronised. This approach was enthusiastically applied to Renaissance drama by Michael Bristol in *Carnival and Theatre: Plebeian Culture and the Structure of Authority in Early Modern England* (London: Methuen, 1985).

But it has been widely objected that Bakhtin underestimated the extent to which carnival was allowed, controlled, even encouraged by those in authority, and so ultimately a form of containment rather than a vehicle of radical change. The anthropologist Victor Turner published a number of studies that explored such tensions and contradictions, including *The Ritual Process: Structure and Antistructure* (Chicago: Aldine, 1969; reprinted Ithaca, NY: Cornell University Press, 1977), *Dramas, Fields and Metaphors: Symbolic Actions in Human Society* (Ithaca, NY: Cornell University Press, 1974) and *From Ritual to Theatre* (New York: Performing Arts Journal Publications, 1982). Peter Stallybrass and Allon White explored this 'problematised' view of carnival in relation to Renaissance drama in *The Politics and Poetics of Transgression* (London: Methuen, 1987). These matters have also been widely commented upon by historicist critics, including Marcus, Patterson and Wilson, cited above.

Notes on Contributors

David Bevington is a Phyllis Fay Horton Professor of Humanities at the University of Chicago, where he has worked since 1967. His books include *From 'Mankind' to Marlowe* (1962), *Tudor Drama and Politics* (1968), and *Action is Eloquence: Shakespeare's Language of Gesture* (1984). He has edited two separate editions of the *Complete Works of Shakespeare* (individual plays, 1988; single-volume, 1992) and of *Medieval Drama* (1975) as well as *The Macro Plays* (1972). He is currently editing Lyly's *Endymion* and co-editing *Dr Faustus*, both for The Revels Plays, of which he is one of the senior editors.

Shirley Nelson Garner is Professor of English at the University of Minnesota, Twin Cities. She co-edited (with Clare Kahane and Madelon Sprengnether) *The (M)other Tongue: Essays in Feminist Psychoanalytic Interpretation* (Cornell University Press, 1985) and (with the Personal Narratives Group) *Interpreting Women's Lives: Feminist Theory and Personal Narratives* (Indiana University Press, 1989). She has published articles on Shakespeare and women writers and is currently editing (with Madelon Sprengnether) a collection of essays on *Shakespearean Tragedy and Gender*, which is forthcoming from Indiana University Press. She is a founder of *Hurricane Alice: A Feminist Quarterly* and currently directs The Center for Advanced Feminist Studies at the University of Minnesota.

Terence Hawkes is currently Professor of English at the University of Wales, Cardiff. He has lectured in a number of countries for the British Council. His books include: *Shakespeare and the Reason* (1964), *Metaphor* (1972; rev. edn 1977), *Shakespeare's Talking Animals: Language and Drama in Society* (1973), *Structuralism and Semiotics* (1977; rev, edn 1983), and *That Shakespeherian Rag* (1986); *Meaning by Shakespeare* is his most recent book. He is also general editor of the New Accents series of books, and was until recently editor of the journal *Textual Practice*.

Barbara Hodgdon is Ellis and Nelle Levitt Professor of English at Drake University. She is the author of *The End Crowns All: Closure and Contradiction in Shakespeare's History* (Princeton, 1991) and *Henry IV, Part Two* in the Shakespeare in Performance Series (Manchester, 1993). She is presently at work on a book entitled *Restaging Shakespeare's Cultural Capital* which focuses on performed Shakespeare.

Norman Holland is Marston–Milbauer Eminent Scholar at the University of Florida. A reader-response and psychoanalytic critic, his best known books are *The Dynamics of Literary Response* (1968, 1975, 1989); *The I* (1985); and *Holland's Guide to Psychoanalytic Psychology and Literature-and-Psychology* (1990). His most recent book is *The Critical I* (1992).

Elliot Krieger left academic life shortly after *A Marxist Study of Shakespeare's Comedies* was published, and took up a career in newspapers, largely with the *Providence (RI) Journal-Bulletin*. He is currently editor of its Sunday magazine, *The Rhode Islander Magazine*.

Philip C. McGuire, Professor of English at Michigan State University, is the author of *Speechless Dialect: Shakespeare's Open Silences* (1985) and *Shakespeare: The Jacobean Plays* (1994). He is also co-editor of *Shakespeare: The Theatrical Dimension* (1979) and is writing a book on *Measure for Measure* for the Shakespeare in Performance series.

Louis Adrian Montrose is Professor of English Literature and Chairman of the Department of Literature at the University of California, San Diego. He has published widely on Elizabethan literary culture and on the theory and practice of historical criticism. He is currently completing studies on the cultural politics of the Elizabethan theatre and on the Elizabethan discourse of discovery.

Annabel Patterson is Professor of English at Yale University. In addition to *Shakespeare and the Popular Voice*, she has written or edited books on Marvell, on Milton, on Virgilian pastoral, the Aesopian fable, and the history of censorship. Her most recent books are *Reading Between the Lines*, a collection of essays that address such issues as canonisation, revisionist history, and feminist criticism; and *Reading Holinshed's Chronicles* (Chicago, 1994), which rediscovers the *Chronicles* as a rich archive for cultural historians.

Richard Wilson is a Reader in English at Lancaster University. He has published essays on Shakespeare and early modern popular politics, and on Marlowe, and is author of a volume on *Julius Caesar* (1992) and *Will Power: Essays on Shakespearean Authority* (1993). He co-edited (with Richard Dutton) *New Historicism and Renaissance Drama* (1992) and is currently completing a study of Marlowe and merchant venture capitalism.

Index